POLITICAL TRADITIONS IN FOREIGN POLICY SERIES
Kenneth W. Thompson, Editor

AMERICA AT THE BRINK

Rusk, Kissinger, and the Vietnam War

OF EMPIRE

LAWRENCE W. SEREWICZ

LOUISIANA STATE UNIVERSITY PRESS

BATON ROUGE

Published by Louisiana State University Press
Copyright © 2007 by Louisiana State University Press
All rights reserved
Manufactured in the United States of America
First printing

Designer: Barbara Neely Bourgoyne
Typeface: Adobe Jenson Pro
Printer and binder: Edwards Brothers, Inc.

Library of Congress Cataloging-in-Publication Data
Serewicz, Lawrence W.
America at the brink of empire : Rusk, Kissinger, and the Vietnam War /
Lawrence W. Serewicz.
p. cm. — (Political traditions in foreign policy series)
Includes bibliographical references and index.
ISBN-13: 978-0-8071-3179-4 (cloth : alk. paper)
ISBN-10: 0-8071-3179-2 (cloth : alk. paper)
1. United States—Foreign relations—1961–1963. 2. United States—Foreign
relations—1963–1969. 3. United States—Foreign relations—1969–1974.
4. Rusk, Dean, 1909–1994—Political and social views. 5. Kissinger, Henry, 1923—
Political and social views. 6. Vietnamese Conflict, 1961–1975—Diplomatic history.
7. United States—Foreign relations—Vietnam. 8. Vietnam—Foreign relations—
United States. 9. Imperialism—History—20th century. 10. Intervention
(International law)—Case studies. I. Title. II. Series.
E840.S396 2006
327.73009'045—dc22

2006008948

To my parents, my first teachers

CONTENTS

ACKNOWLEDGMENTS

Several groups of people and institutions have helped me finish this book. The first group includes friends and colleagues from my time at Claremont Graduate School, where the idea for this book began when Bill Rood, Keck Professor of International Relations emeritus, suggested that a critical examination of Rusk and Kissinger was in order. Without his help at the beginning and at all the critical stages along the way, the book would not have been completed. My debt to him is one that all students owe to their best teachers. Colin Bartel, Steve Dominguez, and Pam Zeiser, friends and colleagues from my first days of graduate school, have been supportive from the beginning. Gordon Babst, Ted Bonzon, Pat Coaty, and Andy Hira helped strengthen my grasp of political philosophy and the American regime. Finally, a number of professors and colleagues at Claremont Graduate School, home then to a large number of Straussians, tried their best to help me understand the work of Leo Strauss, so that I could apply it to the study of foreign policy. I also want to acknowledge Professor Kenneth W. Thompson, who supported the manuscript from the first stages; John Easterly, who picked it up at a critical juncture and carried it forward; and Elizabeth Gratch, for her editing skill in improving the manuscript and saving me from countless errors. Still, any errors that remain are my own.

Friends and colleagues from the University of Hull helped me shape my ideas further. Colin S. Gray, chairman of International Politics there, was generous with his time and his knowledge concerning the strategic culture in the Nixon era. He helped me better understand the geopolitical challenges facing the American regime, and without his timely help this work would remain unfinished. My friends Adam Baddeley, Tom Kane, and Dale Walton heard more about the Machiavellian Moment and Dean Rusk than anyone else. Their own work was invaluable in deepening my understanding of the strategic issues at play within the Vietnam War. Our late-night discussions concerning the Vietnam War, the American regime, and geopolitics were immensely useful in helping me shape my arguments. Without their generosity this would be a poorer book.

Finally, I need to acknowledge the help and assistance of the archivists at the Lyndon B. Johnson Library in Austin, Texas, who helped me to come to grips with using the National Security File system and showed me the pleasures of archival work. The archivists at the Richard B. Russell Library for Political Research and Studies at the University of Georgia Libraries, in Athens, Georgia, also deserve my thanks for their help in making sense of the Rusk Papers.

I would like to acknowledge the generous financial support of the Earhart Foundation, which made it possible for me to research and write this book.

My parents and my brothers and sisters all helped in a number of important ways, and I want to acknowledge their support. Over the years they have provided resources, from a spare room to a spare battery, and encouraged me at all the important stages to complete this book.

Finally, and most important, I would like to acknowledge my wife, Damaris, who was there when the book was finished, when it mattered most. Our son, Zachary, spent hours trying to help me type the final revisions. Without his wonderful help the book would have been done a little sooner.

AMERICA AT THE BRINK OF EMPIRE

INTRODUCTION:
REPUBLIC OR EMPIRE?

The Vietnam War created a foreign policy crisis for the United States by forcing the nation to confront the limits of its identity within the international system. What was America's role within the system? Was it simply to support the world order embodied within the principles of the United Nations Charter, which had been drafted in 1945? Or did America have a greater responsibility than other countries because the charter expressed principles similar to America's founding principles? Secretary of State Dean Rusk, who served from 1961 to 1969 under presidents Kennedy and Johnson, argued that the United States had a commitment to defend the so-called decent world order expressed by the UN Charter.[1] Vietnam created a foreign policy crisis because America saw the conflict as a challenge to the security of the world order. Aside from the material or practical problem of defending South Vietnam and the principles of that world order, the crisis embodied a philosophical problem: Could a republic, a limited government, sustain an apparently unlimited commitment to defending such principles on a global basis?

The foreign policy crisis can be seen in the change in foreign policy philosophy from Rusk to Henry Kissinger, who served under Richard M. Nixon. Rusk was secretary of state when the United States expanded its involvement in Vietnam in 1965. Among administration officials it was he, in particular, who justified America's commitment by arguing that the United States, through its exceptionalism, had a special responsibility to uphold a decent world order. Kissinger, who became secretary of state as the United States was ending its involvement in the Vietnam War, justified disengagement by arguing that as an "ordinary" country the United States had limited power to reform the world. Rather than reforming the international system, the task for the nation was to stabilize and manage it.

This book explores how and why the underlying philosophy of U.S. foreign policy changed from one based upon liberal internationalism, represented by Rusk, to one based upon a more pragmatic policy, exemplified by Kissinger. The change represented more than a shift in foreign policy emphasis between political administrations; it reflected an underlying shift in how America viewed itself, the world, and its role in the world.[2] According to the conventional view, the main cause for this change was that President Lyndon Johnson's decision to commit American ground troops to South Vietnam was flawed. Here I develop that argument to suggest that the United States failed because Johnson's methods for undertaking an undeclared war in pursuit of a decent world order, in short his abilities as a statesman, threatened a crisis within the American political regime. The nation's attempt to defend a decent world order created instability within the existing foreign policy philosophy of liberal internationalism.[3]

The philosophical question at the heart of the foreign policy crisis created by the Vietnam War was "Should the United States be a republic or an empire?"[4] The choice describes the alternatives for American foreign policy within the international system. Simply put, a republic, reflecting its limited domestic structure, takes on a proscribed role in maintaining the world order. It supports the world order but does not identify itself with it. An empire, by contrast, because its survival depends on the security of the global order, takes responsibility for defining, defending, and promoting that world order.[5] "An imperial state, by definition, must have as its purpose the creation and maintenance of order."[6] A republic acts within the international system, whereas an imperial power seeks to act above it by imposing order upon it.

The foreign policy crisis stemming from the nation's involvement in the Vietnam War raised questions for the American republic. Could a republic sustain such an outward-looking, "imperial" role in the international system without endangering its "republican" domestic structure?[7] In other words, could a republic undertake a world-ordering role without becoming an empire? In particular, could the United States continue to defend a decent world order without succumbing to the temptations for tyranny and other abuses of power that result from pursuing an imperialistic foreign policy?[8] The nation's foreign policy crisis sparked an identity crisis for the American regime:

Could the United States reconcile its domestic identity with the obligations inherent in its international commitments?[9]

The foreign policy crisis that emerged during the course of the Vietnam War existed on two levels. First was the military problem of defending South Vietnam, which epitomized the problem of the U.S. role in the world order. At the second level the crisis emerged from the tensions created by the interrelationship of domestic and foreign policies. Reconciling the two realms, while at the same time adjusting to its immediate role within the international system through its actions in Vietnam, required an effective use of statesmanship.[10]

A nation's foreign policy always reflects its domestic regime, but foreign policy has a reciprocal impact on the domestic political structure. America's decision to defend South Vietnam, which was in effect an unlimited foreign policy commitment to defend a decent world order, challenged the notion of limited domestic government. Johnson's approach to the Vietnam War, his inability to resolve the competing demands and choices between domestic policy and foreign policy, created a potentially dangerous imbalance between the executive and the legislative branches of the government. A half-century later the tension between these branches continues to influence U.S. foreign policy and reflects the ongoing tension in the U.S. government's relationship to the international system. When, under Johnson, the United States linked its security with the interests of the larger global system by committing to defend the principle of a decent world order, the foreign policy crisis it was facing became evident. But in seeking a middle path between limited domestic government and the unbounded demands of a foreign policy commitment halfway around the world, Johnson's attempts to balance the two realms only made the crisis worse.

Robert Tucker explored this question in 1968 in his monograph *Nation or Empire?*[11] He argued that the United States' foreign policy of defending the world order in South Vietnam exposed a dangerous tension between the American regime and the international system. "In any case, the insistence of imperial powers on identifying themselves with a universal—or potentially universal—community is almost invariable. It is neither accidental nor mysterious, then, that imperial states almost invariably refuse to distinguish between the security of the imperial state and the security of the greater community."[12] Tucker argues that the tension did not stem from the decision to defend South Vietnam but, rather, began back in 1947 with the Truman Doctrine, which promised aid to countries deemed by the United States to be threatened by the expansion of the Soviet Union.

According to Tucker, the Truman Doctrine set the stage for the Vietnam War by identifying the United States' purpose as defending freedom around the world wherever it is challenged: "In its essential form the rationale of American foreign policy has remained unchanged since World War II. This rationale is based on a vision of world order—a vision that embodies the American purpose—the principal elements of which were set forth in the Truman Doctrine."[13] Thus, in committing the nation to greater involvement in South Vietnam in order to defend a country at risk of losing its sovereignty to a communistic government, Dean Rusk was acting to fulfill the doctrine's principles, but by doing so, he was also expanding the range of the Truman Doctrine to include a place as far away, geographically and culturally, as Southeast Asia.[14] The United States undertook a universalistic—or, as Tucker would argue, an imperialistic—foreign policy by identifying its national security with that of South Vietnam and thereby with the integrity of the decent world order.[15] If one place in the world order was challenged, all were challenged—or, in more imperialistic terms, if one outpost falls, the others are endangered.[16]

Tucker examined alternative approaches within American foreign policy and what they mean for the domestic regime, but he did not explore the philosophical consequences for America, a republic from its inception, of having an expansive foreign policy. Although he looked at the domestic problems, Tucker did not examine the part that Johnson's statesmanship played in exacerbating domestic problems. Furthermore, and as Rusk would point out, the roots of America's commitment to a decent world order can be found in the UN Charter.[17] The commitment to the charter, not the Truman Doctrine, marks the point at which there was a fundamental shift in U.S. foreign policy. Undoubtedly, invoking the Truman Doctrine, and extending its reach to Southeast Asia, radicalized the nation's existing commitment to global security embodied in the UN Charter.

Tucker points out that antecedents to America's support for the world order can be found within the documents that led to the nation's founding as a republic: "There is nothing new in this insistence upon identifying America's security with her purpose. That insistence is apparent in the Truman Doctrine, which, in turn, reflects a tradition that goes back to the very origins of American diplomacy."[18] By placing the foreign policy crisis sparked by America's involvement in the Vietnam War within a larger political-philosophical context, I argue that its roots go back even before the nation's founding and that it in fact represents a challenge shared by all republics. Like them, in the words of historian J.G.A. Pocock, the United States faced a "Machiavellian Moment."[19]

The Machiavellian Moment represents a time when a republic's identity as a limited government is challenged. The challenge can come from two separate although potentially interconnected sources, one internal and the other external. Internally, the republic risks disintegration because the political virtue necessary for self-government has been corrupted. This corruption of the political system destroys the balance within the government and leads to the centralization of power, which in turn precludes an independent sphere of political action wherein, for example, a citizen can practice civic involvement. Too much centralization can lead to rule by a single individual, or several, and in any case is antithetical to the notion of a republic. Externally, the republic might face threats from rival states, which in turn affects the nation's internal system because to meet these challenges the government must expand its control over the domestic realm. Resisting external threats puts pressure on the domestic sphere because resistance, especially when the challenge involves military force, requires a more centralized government.[20] If a republic moves from citizen self-government to the rule of one person, it has become a corrupted system. Although my focus here is on foreign policy, the United States' attempt to uphold a world order in South Vietnam created instability and threatened a crisis within the American regime. Could the United States reconcile its domestic structure, based upon limited government, with the expansive and unbounded task of maintaining a world order?

In the sixteenth century Machiavelli had warned in the *Discourses* that a republic invariably faces the choice between expanding or sustaining itself. If it attempts the former, it will overstep its bounds and collapse.[21] If it attempts the latter, it will collapse from internal corruption (bk. 1, chap. 6). Although later theorists have argued that a republic's choice between expansion or breakdown can in fact be resolved by focusing expansion into a different realm or promoting belief in an extended republic, as the American founders accomplished through *The Federalist Papers*, for the United States in the 1960s the challenges to the nation's stability were compounded by the pressure to choose between maintaining or expanding the U.S. role within a decent world order. A full discussion of the domestic political consequences of the government's commitment to defending South Vietnam is beyond this book's scope. Here I will argue, instead, that during the Vietnam War the United States faced a "near" Machiavellian Moment: it was experiencing a foreign policy crisis but not a complete breakdown of the American regime. Simply put, the foreign policy crisis, while severe and divisive, did not lead to the republic's demise. By changing its foreign policy, the United States resolved the immediate tension between its political regime and international responsibilities without compromising its identity as a republic. But because the fundamental problem remains, the ongoing foreign policy crisis facing the United States, whose roots lie in the turbulent period of the Vietnam War, has never truly been resolved.

THE MACHIAVELLIAN MOMENT

Pocock argued in his influential 1975 work, *The Machiavellian Moment: Florentine Political Thought and the Atlantic Republican Tradition*, that a republic's political principles are universal but bounded. They are circumscribed by the functions and responsibilities of citizenship, which give a republic its strength, and keep the principles that underpin the system from disrupting the fragile balance between the universal character of a republic and the political system's physical limits. A republic exists in a delicate and dynamic balance in which internal pressures, ultimately the threat of corruption to the system, can undermine the political virtue needed to sustain it and external pressures, such as threats from other states, can destabilize it and cause its destruction. To fend off external pressures, a republic might embark on political and physical expansion to widen the boundaries of its universal principles. Therefore, a republic must work continually to keep the internal structure stable and balanced against combined external and internal pressures. To put it differently, in order to protect its integrity, *a republic must maintain the clear distinction between foreign and domestic realms*. If the domestic realm begins to blur into the foreign policy, or external, realm, then the fragile balance can begin to dissolve. When at war, for example, a republic may seek to centralize power in order to succeed. Such a process occurred in ancient Rome when the republic would turn to a dictator during national emergencies. The danger is that a republic will begin to rely upon the more centralized system, first to expand and then to sustain its power in the external realm. In the case of Rome the consolidation of power in one man undermined the republican political structures, based on citizen rule, that had flourished in a decentralized system.

Pocock describes the problem for republics: "The Machiavellian Moment denotes the problem itself. It is a name for the moment in conceptualized time in which the republic was seen as confronting its own temporal finitude, as attempting to remain morally and political stable in a stream of irrational events conceived as essentially destructive of all systems of secular stability."[22] Again, when a republic confronts its political limits in the temporal world, it faces the choice between expanding or disintegrating. The danger, however, does not arise from a single decision but results from a gradual transformation that occurs in response to internal and external challenges. The task for republican statesmen is to bind the universal principles within a limited political space and thereby keep its external responsibilities and its domestic realm in balance. A republic, according to Pocock, "was at once universal in the sense that it existed to realize for its citizens all the values which men were capable of realizing in this life, and particular, in the sense that it was finite and located in space and time. It had had a beginning and would consequently have an end; and this rendered crucial both the problem of showing how it had come into being and might maintain its existence, and that of reconciling its end of realizing universal values with the instability and circumstantial disorder of its temporal life."[23]

The republic faces two difficulties. Inside there is pressure from the universal values bound up within the republic—to expand the sphere of citizenship. The drive to energize this "realm of virtue" gives the republic tremendous vitality. External challenges, on the other hand, the stream of irrational events, force the republic to maintain its domestic character. If the republic accedes to external pressures, it destroys the limits that make it a republic. Thus, at the political-philosophical level of its founding principles, a republic is aware of its limits in power, space, and time.

An empire, in contrast to a republic, never faces a Machiavellian Moment. An empire is not a bounded intellectual entity. It possesses an ideal that is already universal, and the question of expansion has already been decided. The only limits to an empire are physical, not philosophical. The empire's efforts at expansion are only hampered when it is confronted by limits to its resources or by the power of other states. To maintain its stability, an empire expands its power, supporting the universality of its system. Although it may face adjustments within its structure, these are changes in degree, not of kind. To place the practical political question in political-philosophical terms, when an empire expands territorially, it does not need to reassess its founding principles.

An empire perceives itself as immortal because its universal idea knows no limit to its political sphere. In this context immortality means that an empire is not founded with an understanding of its potential demise or its inherent fragility. An empire by definition is always extending outward—even a pause in its expansion does not invalidate its universal idea. Whereas a republic recognizes territorial limits and the potential of the temporal limits, an empire does not. An empire does not try to maintain itself within a limited particularity and does not face the same necessity of relying upon political self-restraint. Although an empire faces the danger of collapse, it does not face the threat of being transformed from a universality into a particularity. Empires do not become republics without first collapsing and disintegrating.

Was the United States, in the 1960s, willing to undertake an imperial role within the international system to defend the so-called decent world order? The question highlights a Machiavellian Moment in U.S. foreign policy, a key turning point when the limits to America's role in the international realm challenged the identity of the American regime. Was the United States willing to act within the world order it had helped to found, remaining a republic? Or would it act outside that order, taking on an imperial role, to defend South Vietnam? The challenge to the decent world order required an unlimited effort. Secretary of State Rusk accepted America's responsibility to defend the decent world order but argued that it could be pursued with limited means. He believed that the choice between remaining a republic and becoming an empire could be avoided. Defending South Vietnam was a special case, not the first step toward becoming an empire. The United States would stay in South Vietnam, acting within the international system, until the situation improved, rather than trying to expand the decent world order through force. When it appeared that victory would require a more robust effort, one that would transform the United States and the international system, the United States scaled back its effort to promote a decent world order and left South Vietnam to its fate.

Neither victory in South Vietnam nor the defense of the decent world order could be achieved by half-measures. Either goal would have required U.S. domestic policy to be reordered, which meant that the ambitious domestic political reforms that President Johnson was attempting would have to be scaled back or stopped. The military problem in Vietnam—defeating North Vietnam's aggression—revealed the larger philosophical problem of reconciling the American regime to an open-ended commitment such as defending the decent world order. Even though the United States did not pursue "victory" in the sense of conquering North Vietnam or waging war for Eurasia, nevertheless it did pursue a policy that put the American regime under great strain. Johnson knew that a declared war, or even an exclusive focus on the Vietnam War, would undermine his domestic reforms. Instead, he wanted to fight and win without resorting to full-scale war. In other words, the goal was not to conquer or defeat North Vietnam, as suggested by Clausewitz's theory of war.[24] Unlike during World War II, in which the domestic realm had to be reorganized for "total" war, Johnson sought to avoid upsetting the domestic political situation by trying to fight the war on a peacetime budget.[25] Johnson was trying to win the war by keeping the Communists from succeeding, which would require less effort than a total war for victory. Even though the conflict was to be kept limited in terms of ends and means, the war did not stay within those limits. The Communist forces kept escalating their effort to reach their final goal of all-out victory. By keeping down the costs of war and defining success as "not losing," Johnson had put himself in a strategic situation in which his opponent, who was willing to pay a higher price, had the advantage. Moreover, Johnson had limited his ability to raise the ante at the strategic level because he wanted to keep the United States from being distracted from the Cold War's main battleground—Europe and the strategic conflict with the Soviet Union.

Johnson had to keep the war limited in Vietnam to avoid disturbing the international system and to avoid destabilizing the domestic arena. The task was to keep the war's financial, political, and military costs from dividing the domestic sphere. If he focused on the war, the domestic structure would become captive to the war effort and the Great Society programs he sought to put in place would suffer, just as Franklin Roosevelt's and Harry Truman's reforms had been stymied by war. Despite his best efforts to avoid this outcome, in 1968 it finally happened. Johnson went from expanding the Great Society to defending it.[26]

The Machiavellian Moment is a useful analytical device for understanding how the Vietnam War transformed American foreign policy and threatened the American regime. Dean Rusk can be seen as a pre–Machiavellian Moment figure in that his foreign policy philosophy identified the United States with the world order. His view embodied a belief in America's exceptionalism whereby the nation's principles could be expanded into the external realm in an effort to reshape the world. Johnson can be seen as a Machiavellian Moment figure who sought to extend the power of the U.S. government simultaneously in the domestic and external realms to keep them in balance. The decision to fight an undeclared war and to enact broad and ambitious domestic reforms reveals his flawed statesmanship. Instead of balancing the two realms, his decisions threatened to bring the foreign policy crisis into the domestic realm. Johnson could not reconcile the conflicting pressures in each realm. Henry Kissinger represents a post–Machiavellian Moment figure because his foreign policy philosophy represents an attempt to reform the republic's foreign policy. The external realm would be brought into balance with the domestic realm through an approach focused on the limits to America's power and the need for the nation to act as an ordinary country.

Dean Rusk's foreign policy philosophy of liberal internationalism shaped the decision in 1965 to commit troops to a limited war. He believed that the United States' security was bound up with the security of the UN world order: the decent world order, which in this case had to be defended in South Vietnam. By expanding the range of America's exceptionalism to the whole world and equating the domestic regime's security with the stability of the international system, Rusk, through the decision to pursue an undeclared limited war, raised that important political-philosophical question of whether the United States would remain a republic or would become an empire.[27] The decision to commit resources and troops to fighting communism in Vietnam represents a "near Machiavellian Moment" in U.S. foreign policy—"near" because the American regime did not face immediate disintegration as a result of this decision. But clearly the United States had reached a point where it had to choose a path that would in time determine its future relationship to the international system and thereby its identity. The decision by Rusk, and Johnson in turn, to defend the decent world order revealed the lingering problem of reconciling the American regime to the international system.

Can the United States be exceptional in both realms, or must it make a choice? Johnson tried to avoid making a choice between the domestic realm and the external realm, but that decision compounded the problem. Nixon and Kissinger's response to the emerging imbalance between the domestic political regime and the nation's international responsibilities was to pursue a limited international role in Vietnam. They rejected the universalism within the foreign policy philosophy of liberal internationalism because their policy reflected a changed view of the United States. Kissinger's foreign policy philosophy reflects a post–Machiavellian Moment approach by emphasizing the constraints on America's power to shape the world and therein expressed a bounded view of the United States. Kissinger acted *as if* America had suffered a Machiavellian Moment when it had lost its exceptionalism and ability to reform the international system because the United States had to act as a "normal" country. He would reform America's commitment to the world to avoid an absolute decline in the nation's international position. Kissinger is not a true post–Machiavellian Moment figure, however, because the United

States was not facing a permanent or terminal decline. Kissinger and Nixon offered a limited but nevertheless flawed reconciliation between America and the international system.

Rusk and Kissinger will be compared and contrasted through three major questions. What was their vision of the world? What was their understanding of the United States' role in the world? And what was their vision of the United States? The questions correspond to the three areas of change in foreign policy philosophy from Rusk's liberal internationalism to Kissinger's realpolitik-influenced policy. The first question addresses the changed geopolitical outlook in the United States' foreign policy. In the Kennedy and Johnson period the geopolitical framework was a bipolar world, whereas Nixon and Kissinger viewed the international system as made up of multiple centers of power. The second question takes account of the changes in foreign policy philosophy. The administration's identification with the world order called into question the United States' identity, as a republic, within the international system. The third question addresses how each man's view of America influenced his view of the nation's role in the world. In sum, Rusk and Kissinger represented the different foreign policy philosophies that guided the United States into and out of Vietnam.

The changes in American foreign policy cannot be understood without looking at Lyndon Johnson's statesmanship. Johnson pursued an undeclared limited war in July 1965, to avoid the perceived policy choice between all-out escalation (war) and withdrawal (peace). He believed he could protect his domestic programs and at the same time meet his foreign policy commitments only by pursuing a limited war.[28] Johnson hoped to maintain balance among both realms by following a middle path policy. Ideally, the middle path would give him the flexibility to deflect criticism of either policy choice. While the approach had worked well for domestic policy, in the international sphere it only delayed but did not resolve the philosophical dilemma for American foreign policy.[29]

The limited war revealed the tension between the domestic and foreign policy realms because foreign policy responsibilities threatened changes within the domestic realm. During the Johnson presidency the balance of power between the president and the Congress appeared to shift dramatically toward the president. Justified by foreign policy demands, presidential power increased, with domestic political consequences.[30] Even though the legislative branch agreed to these changes, its consent was based in large part on arguments that the war in Vietnam was intrinsically tied to the Cold War crisis and the technical requirements for providing an efficient nuclear deterrent.[31] Johnson's foreign policy decision to pursue an undeclared limited war created an imbalance between the executive and legislative branches as the president relied upon his foreign policy prerogative to justify his actions. As the Federalist Papers warned, foreign policy commitments can affect the domestic balance between the executive and the legislative branches of government.[32] The growing friction between branches of government produced a Machiavellian Moment for the United States because, as it turned out, Lyndon Johnson's statesmanship was not capable of reconciling the American regime to the international system. Yet Johnson's flawed handling of the crisis cannot be understood without looking at the foreign policy philosophy leading up to it and following it.

Dean Rusk represents a starting point for understanding the U.S. foreign policy crisis of the 1960s and the changes taking place in foreign policy philosophy. His vision of the world order, liberal internationalism, found its initial and most emphatic expression in the Truman Doctrine. Contained within the Truman Doctrine's philosophy, however, was the dangerous temptation of universalism, which sought to make a set of governing principles apply to all nations. Universalism, combined with anticommunism in the form of a policy of global "containment," helped lay the foundation for the United States' involvement in Vietnam. Rusk's speeches as secretary of state invoke the theme of universalism, and he spoke often and eloquently of the universality of America's revolution of freedom.[33] Rusk's foreign policy philosophy expressed a deep belief in progress and in America's ability to improve the world.[34]

Rusk and Johnson believed that America was leading the world to a better future and that its main challenger in the world, communism, imperiled freedom in general and the potential to reap freedom's benefits.[35] At the heart of this foreign policy outlook was the argument that economic development and theories of modernization were vital to defeating the Communist wars of national liberation.[36] President Kennedy, who accepted the Communist challenge, supported the anti-insurgency policies of economic theorist W. W. Rostow, who would later serve as Johnson's special assistant for national security affairs from 1966 to 1969; these policies embodied Rostow's view of Third World economic development.[37] To fight communism's vision of progress, America had to promote its own such vision. After Kennedy's death, Johnson expanded its scope.

Johnson and Rusk shared similar backgrounds, which shaped their views of America. They had both grown up in poverty; Rusk would later remark that his childhood was spent in conditions close to those in less-developed countries.[38] Each man had been able to transcend his humble beginnings and reach the pinnacle of political power. Their shared outlook rested upon a vision of progress, and their individual success was a testament to the American dream and its belief in a better future. Johnson, as a Rooseveltian New Dealer, had witnessed the government's power to make life better for people. Thus, his administration carried with it a vision of American progress not only at home, as the Great Society, but also abroad. The beliefs guiding the administration's domestic policy carried over into foreign policy. By accepting the legitimacy of the United Nations and committing to its principles, American foreign policy after World War II embodied a belief that the United States, by its actions, could make the world a better place.

At a less theoretical level Rusk played an important role within the Kennedy and Johnson administrations. He represented a connection to the innovative period of American foreign policy that had emerged after World War II. Rusk held several posts within the State Department during the nation's turn toward globalism. He had helped shape the Truman Doctrine, negotiate the United States' involvement in the United Nations, and develop the influential National Security Document no. 68 (NSC-68).[39] During his tenure as secretary of state, he repeatedly turned to the ideas expounded in these documents. Perhaps most significantly for the question of what role the United States should play in Vietnam, he served as assistant secretary of state for the Far East during the Korean War and the McCarthy hearings.[40] As the historian H. W. Brands has pointed out, it was during these years that Rusk learned several lessons that would resonate in the issue of Vietnam. The first lesson was about the dangers of incurring a domestic political backlash for even appearing to be soft on communism. Rusk had experienced this backlash firsthand when he testified at the loyalty hearings of several friends.[41] A second lesson was the danger of underestimating China. Rusk had served in the Chinese-Burma-India (CBI) theater during World War II and was aware of China's problems. He was the only one in both Kennedy's or Johnson's administration to experience the logistical, political, and military demands of waging war in Asia. His experiences in China shaped his thinking on the Vietnam War. For example, his participation in the major international event from this period, the Korean War, colored his view of the Chinese Communists.[42] The war demonstrated to Rusk the need to stand up to aggression and the potential danger of underestimating China's concern for the security of its borders. This was a lesson that Rusk perhaps overemphasized regarding Vietnam.[43] A third lesson, though more nuanced than the others, was the need for a secretary of state to demonstrate loyalty to the president's positions. Rusk's tutelage under George C. Marshall and Dean Acheson solidified his views about loyalty. Rusk's steadfastness and his refusal to appear at odds with the president endeared him to Johnson, who was acutely conscious of the potential problems that could come from his having inherited Kennedy's advisors and feared that they might not view him with the same degree of attachment as they had for his predecessor.

A further point to remember is that at the time Rusk's strong belief in international law put him at odds with others in the State Department, such as historian George F. Kennan, who, while serving in various diplomatic posts, emphasized power politics as a basis of foreign policy and was in fact instrumental in developing the nation's Cold War policies. Rusk's belief in the rule of law informed his vision of world order and underpinned his anticommunism. If, as Rusk saw it, the Communists, in fomenting political change through military force, did not play by the legal rules, then they had to be opposed.[44]

LYNDON JOHNSON:
THE FAILED FOREIGN POLICY PRINCE

As 1965 commenced, the military situation in South Vietnam began to deteriorate further. At the start of this fateful year, President Johnson escalated the air war against North Vietnam in order to impede its support of the Communist insurgency in South Vietnam. When the air campaigns failed to stem the tide, South Vietnam appeared to be near to collapsing militarily. Johnson, fearing the political and strategic consequences should South Vietnam be defeated, committed United States troops to the ground war. In doing so, the president committed the United States' prestige and, perhaps most important, the American public directly to the war and its outcome.[45] The success or failure of the war would have not only international consequences—most significantly the continued freedom of South Vietnam— but it would also have domestic political, economic, and philosophical consequences. A crisis of confidence developed at home out of the public's perception that it was impossible to reconcile the nation's ideals with its performance in the war.[46]

Johnson decided to maintain a middle path between difficult choices of domestic and foreign policy. He did not want to widen the war, and he did not want to pull out altogether, so he chose an incremental strategy that would, he believed, allow him to reconcile both choices. This strategy was based upon a belief that the administration's aims in Vietnam were limited— keeping the South safe from North Vietnam's aggression—and could be kept from interfering with goals and activities affecting the domestic realm. Secretary of State Rusk argued that the United States would withdraw if North Vietnam would leave its neighbor alone.[47] To avoid losing the war, the United States ratcheted up the pressure on North Vietnam.[48] However simple the goal, Johnson's refusal to escalate the conflict by taking the ground war directly to North Vietnam complicated the effort. The president worried that invading North Vietnam would prompt China's intervention, which would create a military problem similar to the one that caused China's intervention in the Korean War. The Chinese had already warned the United States indirectly that they would intercede if the United States went into North Vietnam.[49] All Johnson felt he could do was to order the troops to dig in and wait out the North Vietnamese. Clearly, Johnson's choice of strategy was shaped by his concerns about the international and domestic consequences.

The Cold War milieu created three major interrelated problems for Johnson and his ability to act. The first was the belief shared by members of the administration that the loss of Vietnam to the Communists would lead to further losses around the globe, the so-called domino theory. The second problem, while related to the first, focused on domestic politics. Johnson wanted to honor John F. Kennedy's commitments at home because of their intrinsic importance and because they offered him political cover,[50] and he feared that "losing" Vietnam, in the sense that China had been lost in 1949, would create a domestic political backlash and would hamper his ability to undertake domestic reforms. Finally, Johnson was haunted by President Kennedy's Inaugural Address proclamation that America would "pay any price and bear any burden."[51] Johnson did not want to face a conservative backlash for having failed to secure South Vietnam or a liberal one for having betrayed Kennedy's commitments. Johnson and his policies were hindered by the problem of dealing with Vietnam; he was caught in a stalemate, with no choice but to persevere.[52]

The domestic and international constraints facing LBJ highlight his difficult choices as a statesman as well as significant dilemma inherent in the Machiavellian Moment. Machiavelli had pointed out the potential for a clash between what he called "virtue," attention to the needs of the citizens, and "*virtu*," military skill, within a republic.[53] In pursuing virtue, Johnson hoped to reform American society so that all citizens could participate in the

American dream. In pursuing *virtu*, he hoped to demonstrate the nation's resolve and ability to combat Communist aggression. Johnson was committed to changing the nation's domestic front, which constricted his war effort. He wanted to achieve his Great Society, but at the same time he did not want to lose Vietnam.

Military victory in Vietnam, according to the principles stated by Rusk, would have required tough policy choices, and the pursuit of "victory" through either alternative would have domestic and international consequences. The first choice was to hold on until North Vietnam gave up. This meant that the United States might have to fight twenty years of a quasi-colonial war. As military historian Lloyd Gardner has pointed out, Special Assistant to the President Douglas Cater, in a memo to his colleague McGeorge Bundy, had expressed this concern: "On the same day, July 28, that Johnson announced the troop buildup, Doug Cater . . . invited McGeorge Bundy to a meeting to discuss the government's information program, 'primarily as it pertains to the domestic audience.' The 'home front' was a real front line in this war, said Cater, and he attached an outline of what was to be discussed. The basic assumption they would work from, he wrote, was that 'we are going to have a 10 to 20 year period of "twilight war."' That situation required a 'sophisticated consensus of the American people' to avoid the dangers of 'polarization and extremism.'"[54] The geopolitical consequences of an American victory would have been far-reaching for China and the Soviet Union. As the historian and political scientist Hans Morgenthau pointed out, the stakes were especially high because victory by the United States and South Vietnamese would have created a democratic outpost on the Eurasian landmass.[55]

The second policy choice was to change the strategy, and the war, by invading North Vietnam. This would entail fighting China, if necessary, in order to defend South Vietnam. But fighting China over North Vietnam could lead to World War III. Such international challenges would have required a massive domestic political effort to sustain them and carry them forward. America's domestic political structures would have had to undergo radical changes to achieve these international goals.

The imbalance between the Johnson administration's domestic structure and its foreign policy can be seen in the tension created between the executive and legislative branches by the Vietnam War. Until Vietnam the trend toward greater presidential power in deciding foreign policy had not presented a significant domestic political problem. But when Johnson intervened in Vietnam, the tension became a crisis. The war, in particular, worsened the tension between the executive and legislative branches. The legislative branch, feeling pushed to the limits of its political identity, reacted to the increased power of the executive in foreign policy by actively restraining the executive both in the external realm and the domestic realm. Congress sought to curtail Johnson's foreign policy excesses by passing the War Powers legislation in 1973. The following year, in response to what it viewed as domestic political excesses by the executive, Congress moved to impeach Nixon, which reflected the legislative branch's concern to bridle an out-of-control executive. The domestic crisis reflected the potential onset of the corruption of the political virtue that upholds a republic that Machiavelli had warned about. The central government's expanded role in the everyday life of citizens threatened to undermine their capacity for self-government. The vast federal government, strengthened by Johnson's need to carry out the reforms and to conduct the war, threatened the idea of a limited republican government.

The United States' failure in Vietnam challenged the underlying assumptions and philosophy of its foreign policy. The Vietnam War created a crisis of confidence within the United States, which helped Richard Nixon win the 1968 presidential election.[56] Nixon and his advisor and later the secretary of state, Henry Kissinger, knew that they had to extract the United States from Vietnam by readjusting foreign policy. To accomplish that goal, the two men reversed Johnson's decision to commit troops. Their foreign policy philosophy attempted to bring the ends and means back into balance.[57] As the historian Peter Dickson has pointed out, Kissinger's statesmanship exemplified a post–Machiavellian Moment outlook.[58] Kissinger's approach to statesmanship is not based upon notions of hope and progress, as was Rusk's pursuit of a decent world order, but rests on the perception of what the nation has lost and what must be done to hold back further decline. Dickson argues that, as a post–Machiavellian Moment figure, Kissinger was acutely aware of the limits of power.[59] The international system had changed, and the foreign policy philosophy that had led to U.S. involvement in Vietnam was insufficient. His geopolitical vision, while not shirking global responsibilities, was predicated upon a sophisticated calculation of power relations. Thus, Nixon and Kissinger changed the underlying geopolitical vision from universalistic globalism, which was sanctioned by the vision of a decent world order, to a more pragmatic policy based on limited U.S. power and the emerging triangular diplomacy.

Understanding Kissinger and Nixon helps us to see the immediate consequences of the near Machiavellian Moment. The war had divided the public and hampered the economy, which contributed to the United States' weakened international position. Kissinger believed that in this period of turmoil creative statesmanship was necessary to keep the nation from falling irretrievably into a state of political chaos. Nixon and Kissinger were particularly aware of the limits to America's power in the sphere of economics, with rampant inflation and the high costs of war wreaking havoc on the U.S. economy and creating a crisis within the international system that precipitated the closing of the "gold window."[60] The American dollar would no longer be backed by gold, and the United States had to devalue its currency to help finance the costs of the war. Economist Jacob Viner has argued that the United States had financed its war effort, in part, by the gold reserves it held, which led to balance-of-payments problems.[61] An assertive Soviet Union and China's increased importance led Nixon and Kissinger to design a foreign policy, a structure of peace, that would include them. Unlike Rusk, Kissinger did not base their admission into the structure of peace on the normative basis of the UN Charter but upon the realpolitik demands of the triangular diplomatic structure that was put in place to manage the changed international system.

Nixon and Kissinger responded to the crises in foreign policy and in the global system by reordering United States' foreign policy. They returned a measure of balance to the United States' foreign policy and to the international system. Their moderate goal, however, required extraordinary means, and they stressed the need for the United States to achieve freedom to act within the structure of peace. The United States would be understood as one actor within the system, helping to manage the international system rather than trying to reform it.

In reacting to the foreign policy crisis, Kissinger sought to reconcile the United States to the international system by accepting that its power to change the system was limited. In this new age of constraints the United States would not seek to reform it but would contribute to maintaining its stability. The challenge for Kissinger was to dispel the public belief that the United States, by giving up its universalistic foreign policy mission, had invalidated the domestic political principles that sustained it. Stressing the limits of power within foreign policy, however, had a spillover effect on domestic opinion. The domestic realm faced a crisis of confidence. Did an unexceptional foreign policy mean an unexceptional domestic regime? Unlike Rusk, Kissinger was unable to balance the nation's domestic principles with its foreign policy.

The Vietnam War changed the foreign policy philosophy guiding the United States. In the war in Vietnam the United States confronted the philosophical question of what kind of nation it should be, a republic or an empire. The question, signaling a Machiavellian Moment, arose because the Johnson administration was unable to reconcile the demands of the external realm and the domestic regime. Johnson, guided by Rusk, started out with the goal of defending a decent world order, whose principles, embodied in the UN Charter, were under threat in South Vietnam. Over time, however, the views of the United States and the United Nations began to diverge. America's mission in South Vietnam had been justified as supportive of the UN system's principles, but by 1965 that mission had alienated America from the other members of the international system. The imbalance within the external realm was mirrored by the emerging imbalance, over the issue of war powers, between the U.S. executive and legislative branches. The administration argued that war and domestic reforms required a strong president, but this came at the expense of the legislative branch. The president's prerogative in foreign policy threatened to undermine Congress's ability to counterbalance the growing executive power in either the domestic or the external realm.

The changes in foreign policy philosophy from Rusk to Kissinger can be seen in the different ways each man viewed the United States, the world, and the U.S. role in the world. As a pre–Machiavellian Moment figure, Rusk's foreign policy embodied a belief in America's exceptionalism. For Rusk the United States, by spreading its political principles, would bring freedom to the world. The United States' role was to support the revolution of freedom— the wellspring of the United Nations—against the forces of coercion, but the Vietnam War clouded that utopian vision. The war and its outcome fundamentally changed the United States. The domestic realm, expressing growing disillusionment about the war and reeling from the demands of financing both the escalating war and a host of domestic reforms, rebelled. The American public grew increasingly anxious and restless. Was the United States unraveling? Had it reached the limits of its ability to distribute prosperity and security? Could the United States continue to support its foreign policy commitments and still take care of its citizens?

In the post–Machiavellian Moment Kissinger presented a foreign policy of limits, seeking to reconcile America to changes within the international system and in the country itself. Kissinger appealed to the American public to regard the United States as an ordinary country and not one that could reform the world. Kissinger could not satisfy the American public concerned with its exceptionalism at home. How was the United States to fit its enduring universalistic, if limited, domestic political principles to a world made up of sovereign nations? Even though his foreign policy philosophy of realpolitik gave structure to a foreign policy based upon the limits of power, Kissinger's foreign policy could not address the question of what to do to sustain the universal principles bound up within the American regime. In other words, he reformed American foreign policy but was not able to reconcile that to the domestic realm. If the United States could not export its promise to the world, as suggested by Kissinger's reformed foreign policy, did that invalidate the universal value and validity of its founding principles in the domestic realm?

Rusk's and Kissinger's foreign policy philosophies reveal an ongoing foreign policy dilemma for the United States. Neither man was able to reconcile the United States with the international system, whose members do not necessarily support the same principles and values. Whereas Rusk, to a great extent, identified the United States' interests as bound up with the UN system, Kissinger downplayed that identification. As a result, he could not fit the nation's universalistic political principles to a more limited international role. The dilemma, then and now, is more than a question of power, or its limits; it is a question of national identity.

The United States might have identified its interests with the international system, but the international system did not necessarily identify with the United States. The Vietnam War forced the United States to face the limits of its power to shape the international order. Before the Vietnam War these questions had been muted, though their traces could be seen in former policies such as the Truman Doctrine. The underlying tension between the United States and the international system had never been directly confronted. The United States' view that the UN system and the international system were coterminous had not been considered a problem. Even though the Cold War rivalry with the Soviet Union hampered the system's functioning, it did not imply to the American public that the U.S. political regime was flawed. As the most powerful of the founding members of the UN system, the United States faced important questions about its activities in Vietnam: Was there a limit to how far the country would go to defend the international system? Was it willing to transcend the UN system, if required, in order to defend it? Would the United States transform itself to sustain a decent world order?

Underlying these questions is a tradition of uncertainty about the United States' role in the international system. How would the United States relate to the UN system if the two administrations disagreed about what constituted a threat?[62] Rusk believed that the United States could sustain its role as a protector of the world order because, in simple terms, the domestic regime was in balance with the nation's international role. He had not envisioned that such a role might create an imbalance between the domestic regime and the nation's foreign policy or between U.S. foreign policy and the principles of the international system. The effort to reform the international system, to create a decent world order, was in fact beyond the United States' power and its political system. Kissinger's worldview provided for complexity, and as a result, as Nixon's secretary of state, he helped shape what has been described as a more realistic role for the United States in world affairs. Despite their different philosophies and policy approaches, Rusk and Kissinger represent different points along the same continuum, both of them seeking to define the proper relationship of the United States and the world but neither one fully achieving his goal. A key question that remains to be answered a half-century later is whether the United States can find its place within the world system while working from within that system, or must one or the other entities be transformed?

I

DEAN RUSK:
PACTA SUNT SERVANDA

When John F. Kennedy proclaimed in his Inaugural Address that the United States would "bear any burden, pay any price in the defense of liberty," his words electrified the nation. His bold vision touched upon a strain of idealism deep within the American spirit to suggest that the nation would not only renew itself but would also renew the world.[1] America would fulfill its mission to create, through its foreign policy, a decent world order. The man to carry out that task was Dean Rusk. Although Rusk was pragmatic in pursuing the task, it touched upon his idealistic belief in America's mission. In pursuit of noble ideals, the decent world order sketched out in Kennedy's Inaugural Address would deepen America's involvement in the Vietnam War.

After Kennedy's death Lyndon Johnson sought to uphold his predecessor's legacy. In his own inimitable style Johnson embraced Kennedy's commitment to South Vietnam and intensified it by waging an undeclared war. The undeclared war and the commitment to South Vietnam were issues that would dominate his presidency. Even compelling domestic measures such as the Civil Rights legislation were often handled with an eye toward the Vietnam War. As Robert Dallek has pointed out, Johnson feared that anti–Vietnam War protests would merge with the Civil Rights movement to destroy his Great Society program.[2] Initially, Johnson accepted Kennedy's legacy as a way to fulfill and expand a domestic agenda that JFK had proposed but had been unable to complete. Johnson's desire to fulfill the promises at home and abroad, however, created irreconcilable goals that weakened his presidency and strained America's political and social fabric. Johnson believed that he could not shirk his commitment to protecting Kennedy's legacy. In his first major speech after Kennedy's death, in fact, Johnson stressed his intentions during his presidency to continue the work of the past administration.[3] Just as he would carry out Kennedy's plans in the domestic sphere, Johnson committed himself to perpetuating JFK's foreign policy agenda. He did not think he could repudiate Kennedy's commitment of U.S. force in South Vietnam without damaging his domestic reforms.

In South Vietnam Johnson sought a middle path between what he perceived as two extreme policy alternatives, declaring war or withdrawing, both potentially damaging to him politically. Yet to win in Vietnam would require a broader war, and to avoid committing the nation to a losing cause, Johnson would have to withdraw. Either option, he realized, would be fatal to his domestic reforms.[4] Johnson solved this problem by adopting a middle path between the policy alternatives—undertaking an undeclared limited war.[5] To create a foreign policy that would maintain that middle path, Johnson turned to his secretary of state, Dean Rusk.

Rusk, as Johnson's chief deputy in world affairs, had to consider the options: to withdraw was to endanger the decent world order, but to declare war was to take an unnecessary risk and might even precipitate World War III.[6] Rusk faced a complicated task. The challenge was not simply expounding the vision or the promise of a decent world order but to find a pragmatic way to convince others that it was important to defend that promise in South Vietnam yet to be cautious and strategic in order to avoid a broader escalation by other nations and potentially World War III. The task was made more difficult by Johnson's pursuit of an ambitious domestic policy. The effort and focus required for either task would be daunting, but to do them nearly simultaneously bordered on the impossible. Could any president, even one as dynamic as Lyndon Johnson, devote enough attention and energy to such divergent demands? The tasks divided the president's attention and his political capital, as they divided the public's attention and nearly divided the country.

One way to unify the public behind the foreign policy would be to declare war, but neither Rusk nor Johnson wanted to do so. Rusk feared that this might start a war fever that would be hard to control and thus could destroy the world order, and Johnson did not want to destroy his domestic reforms by inviting a divisive debate over his foreign policy.[7] Another way to unify the public's attention was to withdraw, but Rusk and Johnson feared that withdrawal from South Vietnam would undermine the credibility of the United States' other foreign policy commitments.[8] Moreover, Johnson feared that withdrawal would cause a political backlash that would wreck his domestic programs. Rusk's foreign policy philosophy was guided by a belief that America had a commitment to defend a decent world order, which required America to defend South Vietnam until the situation there improved.[9] America would defend a decent world order, but that defense would not be a crusade to impose its notions of order on the world. A limited goal required a limited war, yet the constraints of domestic reforms meant it would have to be an undeclared war, in that neither the government nor the public would be put on a wartime footing. Johnson would defend South Vietnam, fulfilling a commitment, but an undeclared war would avoid a public debate, which would have distracted attention and resources from the domestic agenda.

In defending liberty and supporting containment, Rusk's foreign policy philosophy reflected the globalist themes within the United States' post-1945 foreign policy. Two seminal documents from the Truman era, the Truman Doctrine and National Security Council document of 1950 entitled "United States Objectives and Programs for National Security" (NSC-68), stood as guides to his foreign policy. What set him apart from that earlier tradition, however, was his attempt to connect policy and rhetoric. As Hans Morgenthau pointed out, the Kennedy and Johnson administrations were trying, unlike previous administrations, to match their policies to their rhetoric.[10] Rusk saw the Vietnam conflict as embodying the central challenge to the international system. Could the United States promote and defend a decent world order based upon the rule of law as outlined by the United Nations Charter?[11] In South Vietnam competing visions of the political good—how South Vietnam should be organized—were at war, and the same struggle was occurring throughout the international system.[12] According to Rusk, on the one side, the Soviet Union and the People's Republic of China (PRC) advocated a world revolution and political change by force. On the other, the United States represented a revolution of freedom, which advocated political change by the rule of law. The rule of law is central to the UN Charter and the American regime. It is no accident that the UN world order emerged simultaneously with the United States' rise to globalism.[13] Rusk's faith in these principles was first displayed in that fertile period after World War II when American foreign policy undertook what it saw as its global responsibilities.

Before he became deputy undersecretary of state in the Truman administration, Rusk served as assistant secretary of state for United Nations Affairs. The post reflected, and strengthened, his interest in international law. He was involved in developing both the Truman Doctrine and NSC-68, and these documents in turn helped shape his response to the Communist world revolution. During the Korean War Rusk had served as assistant secretary of state for the Far East, an experience that had influenced his views on the region.[14] The lessons Rusk learned in these years reappeared during his tenure as secretary of state. For example, he knew the dangers of domestic political backlash for even the appearance of being soft on communism and had experienced this backlash firsthand when he testified at the loyalty hearings of several friends during the McCarthy era.[15] He also recognized the danger of underestimating China, a lesson learned from the Korean War. Even before that, Rusk had served in the Chinese-Burma-India (CBI) theater during World War II, where he worked with the Chinese and developed an awareness of the country's problems and potential. China's response in the Korean War demonstrated to Rusk the risk of underestimating China's concern for its territorial security—a lesson that Rusk, and others, perhaps learned too well regarding Vietnam. Another lesson Rusk had learned, though less obvious than the others, was the need for the secretary of state to demonstrate loyalty to the president's positions and to maintain unity with the secretary of defense.[16] Rusk's loyalty and refusal to appear at odds with the president suited Johnson's political style.[17] Rusk had also come to believe that Indochina was the most strategically important area of Southeast Asia.[18] He applied these lessons, which shaped and reflected his foreign policy philosophy, as U.S. secretary of state.

In that role Rusk pursued a foreign policy based in liberal internationalism.[19] He sought to sustain a decent world order based upon the liberal principles bound up within the UN Charter and the American regime.[20] His goal reflected the promise of a liberal world order implicit in America's post–World War II foreign policy framework and the UN Charter. Rusk, with Johnson, created a crisis in American foreign policy because his attempt to apply the Truman Doctrine to South Vietnam revealed a dangerous gap between the country's desire to maintain a limited domestic regime and its ambitious efforts to create world order. The crisis was more serious than a mismatch between commitments and immediate resources; after all, America had the material resources to fight a long war in South Vietnam. It created an imbalance between the principles of the American regime and its foreign policy responsibilities that could force the nation to have to change fundamentally.

To understand Rusk's foreign policy philosophy, which set the context for the crisis, we rely upon three general questions: What was Rusk's view of the world? What was Rusk's view of the United States? And what was Rusk's view of the United States' role in the world? These questions are not an attempt to deconstruct Dean Rusk's operational code but are meant to create an overview of his foreign policy philosophy.[21]

DEAN RUSK'S WORLDVIEW
Rusk's Understanding of the International Arena

Rusk's worldview was shaped by what he perceived as the central crisis of the post–World War II period. The crisis was larger than the struggle between the Soviet Union and the United States or the ideological struggle between communism and liberal democracy. The crisis was between two conflicting world orders: one based on coercion versus one based on freedom.[22] The former followed the law of the jungle, "might makes right," while the latter stood for political change by the rule of law. This struggle was made urgent by the immense political, economic, and social changes occurring around the world.

The old political, economic, and social international orders were rapidly being replaced as colonialism dissolved in the late 1950s and early 1960s. Although change occurs in varying degrees at all times, Rusk saw the 1960s as a period of dramatic and historic change.[23] The newly independent states were the new battleground in the contest between coercion and freedom.[24] If these states succumbed to the Communists' wars of national liberation, the world of freedom would be diminished. This struggle dominated Rusk's geopolitical outlook.

Rusk's geopolitical vision, his expansion of the Truman Doctrine to the Pacific Rim, was critical to his worldview. He saw the world as a bipolar ideological struggle between the forces of coercion and freedom, but he did not equate coercion solely with the Soviet Union and the Communist states. The ideological struggle between liberal democracy and communism perhaps shaped the international arena, but it did not define it because, as Rusk believed, all men sought freedom. Therefore, one could not identify the Soviet Union completely with the forces of coercion, which left room for diplomatic negotiations. Rusk was willing to engage in diplomatic negotiations if they sought constructive goals such as maintaining the general peace.[25] His belief that there was a global struggle for freedom led him to apply the Truman Doctrine to South Vietnam and expand America's geopolitical concerns and responsibilities from Europe to the Pacific Rim.[26]

The goals of the decent world order were based upon the principles outlined in the preamble to the United Nations Charter. Although Rusk understood that his primary task was to defend the United States, he believed that a world order based on the rule of law, as suggested by the charter, would create the mechanisms necessary to deal with military aggression and make the world more peaceful. A decent world order would achieve three primary goals. First, it would maintain the peace by creating mechanisms to avoid World War III.[27] Second, it would encourage political change through peaceful means rather than by resorting to the use of arms. Rusk did not deny political change, but he did oppose any change that was carried out through violence without the consent of the people. Third, a decent world order would foster economic development. The newly independent states were free but poor. Poverty and want of basic human necessities were often the cause of political turmoil and war. Rusk worked to alleviate poverty not simply as a pragmatic response to the threat of Communist revolution, however, but because to him, who was fundamentally an idealistic thinker, it undermined the dignity of humanity. In sum, a world order based on the rule of law would channel conflict into a legal mechanism rather than recourse to arms and would thereby offer a better chance for economic development.

Rusk's world order was designed to achieve and maintain peace. The world had just emerged from twenty years of war, and it was now time to strengthen the sinews of peace. Peace would allow states to pursue their political and economic development unimpeded. If states were free from outside aggression or coercion, then they could develop economically, which would reduce scarcity and want, primary causes of war. It was up to the United States and other defenders of the decent world order to intervene to stop military aggression and to offer aid and support for economic development. In order to achieve development, however, the newly decolonized states would have to undergo a program of modernization. The question aside from the question of coercion or freedom was whether these states would follow a Western-style development or a Communist model. Thus, the 1960s, a period of rapid modernization for the underdeveloped states, were also a period of political unrest because of the deep ideological conflict that beset the world. If the problems from modernization could be worked out without the threat of Communist revolution, Rusk believed a decent world order could be developed. As Rusk well understood, the United States was founded by a revolution for freedom and was an example for the world of how such a revolution could be achieved when guided by the rule of law.[28] If America could help to channel political change into peaceful measures, then other benefits such as economic development could occur.

To attack poverty and underdevelopment Rusk sought to bolster economic development in the newly independent states. The United States could help in several ways. First, it could offer an alternative economic development model from that offered by communism. The larger political struggle encompassed a struggle over economic systems.[29] The economic success of the American system in overcoming poverty was apparent to Rusk. Economic and political development could change a society for the better, and with America's help and guidance other countries could experience the same benefits as the United States.

Beyond offering a developmental model and stopping military aggression, a third way America could help other states and maintain global peace was by providing foreign aid. As Rusk put it in an official statement in 1964: "Foreign aid remains, as it has been throughout the post-war period, an indispensable instrument of our foreign policy . . . But the Communist threat makes our aid imperative if freedom is to survive and ripen in vast areas of the world. And surely it is better to save freedom by helping new nations get on their feet than to wait until it can be saved only by committing America's youth to combat."[30] Foreign aid was an important part of the United States' post–World War II foreign policy and was a potent force in the Cold War.[31] Yet aid was not designed solely to further America's interests against communism. The Marshall Plan was the most successful of the foreign aid projects because it had been designed to combat several enemies: poverty, malnourishment, and poor living conditions.[32] America could help economic development additionally by improving world trade. More trade would raise worldwide prosperity and would reinforce the economic, and therefore political, ties between nations. Peace was the foundation for economic and political development, which were important goals in their own right, but they also represented the basis for a decent world order.

Rusk understood that neither the world order nor the United Nations was an American creation; rather, America was the United Nations' most ardent supporter and defender because it embodied the best hope for avoiding war and defending freedom for all nations. The American regime, expressed in the principles of the Declaration of Independence and the Constitution, represented the world's greatest experiment in liberty within a nation. Following these principles, America had helped establish the United Nations. In the international system the United Nations offered a framework for states to exist without the threat of war and established their basic freedom and equality. Just as Rusk felt the American regime offered the best hope as a model for any nation, the United Nations offered the best system for creating world order.[33]

Although Rusk's vision for a world order of freedom may appear idealistic in the face of the Communist challenge, his positive strategy and his world outlook were not based upon naive idealism.[34] Rusk knew that the rule of law was difficult to achieve because one had to meet military aggression directly, firmly, and with military force. Words would not stop bullets. For that reason he repeatedly stressed that the United States and its allies had to be strong militarily. His idealism did not overlook that such beliefs had to be backed up by action, military force if necessary, if they were to succeed. Although he had idealistic goals, Rusk was pragmatic in their pursuit. Such ideals were not an excuse for a crusade; rather, they were the code by which one lived and acted within the international system. The conflict in South Vietnam demonstrated this duality between idealism and pragmatism within Rusk's foreign policy philosophy. Rusk saw it as a challenge not only for the rule of law and a world order based on freedom but also to the United States' credibility in maintaining its commitments. On this basis, it is easier to understand why Rusk could have equated the United States' commitment to South Vietnam with the commitment to Berlin.[35] If the UN world order was to succeed and America's commitments were to be met, America had to fight whenever those commitments were challenged, and wherever. The consequences of neglecting such commitments had been demonstrated in Europe in the 1930s.

Rusk had witnessed how, before World War II, the League of Nations and liberal democracies had failed to stand up to Japanese and German aggression. Tyrants such as Hitler, Mussolini, and Tojo had simply ignored the demands of the League of Nations when it condemned their actions. The Western democracies had failed to stop these tyrants because they had failed to back up their commitments. Their failure to counter the initial aggression meant that they were later forced to wage a more costly war and one with higher stakes. Rusk learned from his experiences in Munich that unchecked aggression could quickly lead to a general war.[36] He believed that freedom and peace were indivisible because a challenge to freedom in a particular state meant a challenge to freedom everywhere. If America was not willing to fight in South Vietnam when its commitment to the principle of upholding freedom was being challenged, where would it fight, and what would it fight for? Could allies be certain the United States would defend the same principles if they were again challenged, for example, in Berlin? Under Rusk's foreign policy program America's commitment would not be found wanting. When challenged in South Vietnam, Rusk acted to defend his ideals.

Rusk believed that a world order could be maintained only if the United States were vigilant in upholding it. America was ideally suited to this task because of its dedication to liberty and its abundant material resources. There were four mechanisms by which America could maintain and promote a decent world order, all of them built upon the foundation of commitment. If nations were unwilling to commit to that type of world order and to support it when challenged, then it could not be maintained. Here I will set aside the first and most obvious mechanism, the United States' unilateral military action, for two reasons. First, the United States has never undertaken extensive military action outside the Caribbean without an ally. Second, if the United States must defend its borders without allies, then there is not much of a world order left.

The second mechanism for upholding and achieving a world order was collective security as embodied in the UN Charter and seen in the security alliances such as the North American Treaty Organization (NATO). The third mechanism, regional military alliances, fit between collective security and diplomacy in its effectiveness for responding to global threats. Regional military organizations such as NATO and the South East Asian Treaty Organization (SEATO) strengthened the United States' foreign policy, and its membership therein demonstrated its commitment to the region's security. A fourth mechanism was diplomacy. Diplomacy develops and strengthens the small ties that connect nations, and the same ties in turn help to maintain the world order. These various mechanisms are designed to sustain the world order and resist political change through military aggression.

Rusk had learned these lessons firsthand. In Germany in 1933 Rusk had witnessed the Nazis' rise to power. He also followed the events surrounding Japan's invasion of China.[37] These events taught Rusk about the need to be vigilant to defend order against those who would undermine it:

> When I was a student in Germany many years ago, I lived in Neue Babels-
> berg, and I had a canoe, and I used that canoe as often as possible in the
> lakes that surrounded Neue Babelsberg, near Potsdam. One day I pulled the
> canoe up on the bank and went into a restaurant for lunch. When I came
> back the canoe was gone. I reported it to the water police, and they with
> their boats scouted around a while. And then after a while they came back
> with the canoe and said, "We have found your canoe and have caught the

thief, and he will be punished, but you yourself will be fined five marks for tempting thieves." My German friends with legal background have vociferously denied that there has been a crime in Neue Babelsberg called "tempting thieves" and that I perhaps was the victim of an ambitious police officer.

But nevertheless the lesson has been worth many times more than the five marks to me, because I believe that we in our democracies are confronted with the fundamental problem of how we avoid tempting thieves. Our problem is how to pursue the human, the long term, the civilized purposes of democratic societies and yet maintain the resolution and the strength to make it clear that thieves shall not have their way.[38]

Although the story may have been apocryphal, it contains an insight into how Rusk understood the need to fulfill one's commitment either to an ally or to a decent world order. Early in Rusk's tenure as secretary of state, the United States faced an immediate and grave challenge over its commitment to Berlin's freedom. How the United States responded to the challenge in Berlin, Rusk and Kennedy understood, would have major consequences for their other commitments. Their principled commitment to collective security meant that the security of Vietnam was as important as the security of Western Europe. Although Western Europeans might disagree with that logic, Rusk believed it. In Vietnam Rusk would not tempt thieves; he would act.

In Vietnam Rusk believed the principle of collective security was at stake. If America did not come to the aid of South Vietnam when it faced outside aggression, Rusk feared, it would undermine America's other commitments, especially the commitment to collective security.[39] The United Nations was a collective security structure, exemplified through Article 51, but it required members to recognize and act together against threats. In Vietnam that threat was never fully articulated to the world or to the American public, which made it difficult to present a convincing and coherent argument for collective action.[40] Even without a collective security response, Rusk argued that the United States had a historical commitment, beginning with Eisenhower, to South Vietnam and its continued independence. Neither Rusk nor Kennedy nor Johnson was going to back down. As Lyndon Johnson declared, "We did not choose to become the guardians of the gate, but there is no one else."[41] Neither collective security nor the regional defense structure, SEATO, worked effectively in Vietnam. Even though states in the region, such as South Korea, recognized that their security was tied, at least indirectly, to the United States' effort, a regional collective response did not develop because states did not view the threat in the same manner. Whereas the United States saw it as a threat to the world order, other states, not concerned with that issue, did not feel their physical security was being challenged.

A further problem was that the American public was skeptical that South Vietnam's defense was a question of American security, much less of collective security. The public was skeptical because the administration was often vague or unclear about the true nature of the threat. Was it a civil war, or was it the first step in a war of worldwide aggression? What was the threat to America from this faraway country? Even though Rusk continually stressed that North Vietnam's aggression presented an urgent and fundamental problem, the American public was never fully convinced. His outlook having been shaped by his Munich experience, Rusk stressed that this initial aggression represented the larger trend of Communist aggression in the region. Thus, by defending South Vietnam's liberty, America was ultimately defending its own liberty.

Aside from the issue of collective security, Rusk also focused on military alliances such as NATO and SEATO as mechanisms to defend the decent world order. Unlike collective security, the commitment to these alliances could be invoked relatively easily. In Vietnam, Rusk argued, the SEATO treaty justified America's commitment. Although these military alliances were developed to meet overt direct military aggression, they also helped to stem indirect aggression or subversion. These arrangements made it possible for an ally to give support to the country under threat and share the security burden.

A final mechanism, perhaps the most direct but least powerful, was diplomacy. Diplomacy would foster the small ties that help states to understand each other's policies and to defuse or avoid crises that could lead to war. Diplomacy and diplomatic process were essential to Rusk's world order because they were based upon international law and reinforced the rule of law. For example, we can see Rusk's pragmatic side in his efforts to pursue a negotiated settlement to the Vietnam conflict.[42] Yet, for all its importance, diplomacy and even collective security were fundamentally unstable measures. They relied upon the power and persistence of one's commitment, which, in a democracy, could shift relatively quickly, especially if the threat were not clear.

Rusk's Handling of Threats to the World Order

Rusk's world order faced a variety of threats. The dominant threat came from aggression, directly or indirectly, by states intent upon political change through military force. While Rusk was aware that the Communist states did not always act in concert, he accepted that the Communists were working toward a world revolution.[43] Soviet premier Nikita Khrushchev and Chinese Communist leader Mao Tse-tung expressed the threat in terms of the wars of national liberation with South Vietnam as a test case for communism's commitment to thwarting American "imperialism." The danger in South Vietnam was not direct military aggression but, rather, the threat from indirect aggression, such as responding to wars of national liberation. When Rusk was in the State Department in 1947, the danger of overt aggression leading to a general war was the administration's main concern. Even though North Korea's invasion of South Korea was a stark reminder of that possibility, the most pressing threat in the post–World War II era was indirect aggression. American foreign policy and collective security were unable to deal effectively with this threat, which points to a central problem for Rusk's decent world order.[44] Indirect aggression tended to blend with the more extreme and violent forms of political opposition. It challenged the policy of containment by revealing that the level of aggression made it difficult to differentiate between central and peripheral threats. Overt aggression such as that which sparked the Korean War could be identified for what it was, but indirect aggression was harder to identify as a threat worthy of a collective security response. The key question was how or when to determine if such a threat required a response from the international community.

Communist wars of national liberation thrived in societies already weakened by the economic, political, and social problems and opportunities created by decolonization. These states were vulnerable to Communist efforts to demonstrate that the world revolution was an inevitable historical success. As Henry Kissinger pointed out, Marxism succeeded in the underdeveloped world because it could best explain where political authority should reside.[45] Rusk sought to counter this threat by implementing a positive strategy that encouraged economic and political development and offered a different understanding of where power should reside. His boss, John F. Kennedy, for example, created the Peace Corps as a way to counter underdevelopment.[46] The Peace Corps and programs such as the Alliance for Progress were part of the United States' positive foreign policy strategy to counter communism in developing countries.[47] W. W. Rostow, a key architect for this policy and later Johnson's national security advisor, argued that modernization was a cornerstone to the United States' anti-Communist strategy.[48]

In one form or another South Vietnam encapsulated the threats to Rusk's world order. North Vietnam had waged indirect aggression against

South Vietnam. Tied into North Vietnam's aggression was the ever-present threat of the regional conflict spiraling into a devastating larger war. The Soviet Union and China feared that the United States might invade North Vietnam, which would trigger a nuclear war. Policy makers in Washington also feared that the war could escalate into a nuclear exchange.[49] Rusk was quite careful to reiterate that the United States did not want a wider war that would require the United States to invade North Vietnam. As he stated in later years, he was convinced that such an invasion would bring China into the conflict.[50] Moreover, South Vietnam suffered from political and economic underdevelopment. It needed economic growth and political stability nearly as much as it needed to be defended against the Communist insurgency. The conflict in South Vietnam represented the threat to America's attempt to create a decent world order. By equating South Vietnam's security with America's, Rusk raised the question for American citizens: How far were they willing to support abroad the principles that they lived by at home?

RUSK'S VIEW OF THE UNITED STATES

Rusk's view of the United States was influenced, in large part, by his background and his deeply held belief in the nation's institutions and ideals. He saw America as an exceptional country with a duty to defend a decent world order. To Rusk a country demonstrates the principles of its regime by the goals of its foreign policy.[51] On this issue we can see a great difference between Rusk and Kissinger. Rusk believed in America's exceptionalism and its mission in the world. Kissinger, by contrast, believed that the United States should act as a normal country and was circumspect about the role of exceptionalism in foreign policy. While Kissinger did not dismiss the notion entirely, he found that it constrained the foreign policy that he wished to pursue. Rusk saw exceptionalism as a key element within his foreign policy because his own experience as a U.S. citizen embodied the success of the American dream.

Born in Georgia in 1909, he saw how Roosevelt's New Deal legislation had accelerated America's political and economic development. Growing up in extreme poverty, his humble beginnings deeply influenced his view of America. As Warren Cohen has observed, "The poverty of Rusk's antecedents and the story of his rise are the stuff of which the American Dream is made."[52] Rusk, grateful for the blessings that the United States had conferred on him, sought to return the favor by exporting the American dream to the world. Cohen has called Rusk's view of the United States "liberal exception-alism."[53] According to this theory, the United States was a chosen country exempt from the Old World's corruption because of its founding in liberty. Its exceptionalism was tempered by liberalism that guided it to use its advantages for the betterment of humanity. Although the United States owed much to the British political traditions, America was the best example to the world because its institutions—limited government and the rule of law—offered the best hope of freedom. In sum, America's successful revolution suggested that freedom was achievable for all men, not just Americans.

Rusk believed that the United States' foreign policy goals reflected its political principles. Within his foreign policy addresses, a central theme was that men and women around the world could achieve the American dream. The American model of economic development offered the possibility for improving the world. The American dream was supported by a strong belief in progress, the general belief that human beings can better their situations by their own efforts and that the future holds improvements over the past.[54] Rusk's faith in progress can be seen in his belief that America was the great experiment in freedom.[55] America's unique status informed the idea of liberal exceptionalism, but it also expressed Rusk's deep faith in, and respect for, the American founding. His faith in the American founding and the principles of the American regime demonstrated a strong streak of idealism. America's founding represented the revolutionary power of ideas and institutions to shape human potential. This is not to say, however, that Rusk was a utopian dreamer, but clearly it suggests the extent to which his idealism and his belief in America's exceptionalism shaped his foreign policy philosophy.

Rusk believed in the American dream because, as Cohen has pointed out, he had achieved it. Rusk would often stress the changes that the United States had undergone in his lifetime. He grew up in a society that was "prescientific, pretechnical, premedical, prepublic health, preeducation—by present day standards."[56] The American dream represented a possible developmental model for other states and a potent weapon in the ideological war with communism.

The Kennedy and Johnson administrations, especially Johnson's, were going to expand the American dream not only to all Americans but also to the world. To fulfill the promise domestically, Johnson embarked upon a massive legislative program that would reshape the face of the United States. From Civil Rights to Medicaid, the government was attempting to reform America. To fulfill that dream in foreign policy, Johnson would wage war in South Vietnam to defend freedom. The two missions reflected the dual, and ultimately conflicting, nature of his statesmanship. The Vietnam policy vacillated between winning hearts and minds, economic development, and an attrition strategy, waging war. What connected these strands was a faith in the American dream and the possibility that government could improve the average citizen's life.

Robert Nisbet wrote: "The idea of progress holds that mankind has advanced in the past[57]—from some aboriginal condition of primitiveness, barbarism, or even nullity—is now advancing, and will continue to advance through the foreseeable future."[58] Progress suggests that man, by a thorough control of nature, could, in the future, achieve a quantifiably and qualitatively improved society. Political and economic reforms would make the future better than the past. As Christopher Lasch has pointed out, the idea of progress is a strong theme within American politics stretching back to the Puritans.[59] One of the best political examples of the government's power to improve the life of the average citizen was Franklin D. Roosevelt's New Deal legislation. The legislation carried a strong strand of progressivism by stressing the role that government could play in improving the life of the average American.

Lyndon Johnson, elected to Congress on Roosevelt's New Deal platform, had witnessed the government's power to make life better for people. Following Roosevelt's lead, his Great Society legislation expanded the role government would play in improving the material life of the citizen. As president, he expanded the government's role in the life of the average citizen. This effort spilled over into his foreign policy because the benefits of the Great Society were not limited to the Untied States but could encompass the whole world. America's success could be shared with the rest of the world.[60]

Rusk's foreign policy philosophy reflected his belief in progress.[61] In terms of economic development, he stressed the American model as an alternative to the Communist development model because, he was convinced, economic progress and freedom went together: "We believe that freedom and progress are historic partners and that the alleged choice between rapid progress and free institutions is false."[62] Freedom produced economic progress, and economic progress strengthened freedom.

The United States represented a great experiment in liberty because its founding expressed the idea that the government derived its just powers from the consent of the governed. This idea was innovative and revolutionary and held nearly universal appeal. Rusk saw his mission as secretary of state to perpetuate that success and expand liberty's boundaries. America embodied the success of the idea that a government that derived its just powers from the consent of the people was the best guarantor of freedom.[63] Consent and liberty went together, and Rusk accepted the challenge within John F. Kennedy's inaugural address to defend liberty. America would "pay any price, bear any burden, meet any hardship, support any friend, oppose any foe to assure the survival and success of liberty." America's founding principles were based upon the universal ideas that all men had "the right to life, liberty and the pursuit of happiness," and so long as regimes guided by them continued to exist, those universal ideas would stay alive. Rusk repeatedly pointed out that the universal principles guiding the American regime were similar to those in the UN Charter. Therefore, as America represented what was best in a particular regime, so the United Nations represented what was best in a world order.

Rusk stressed that the United States presented the world with hope for stability and widespread improvements because its regime embodied the rule of law and the success of freedom. If the world could achieve the rule of law through the United Nations, all nations could live in peace.[64] The United States founding was exceptional because it was dedicated to the ideas of liberty, equality before the law, and that the government derived its just powers from the consent of the governed. The United Nations' founding was exceptional because it attempted to codify juridical equality for all states and offered a mechanism for resolving disputes by recourse to the law rather than force of arms. Just as equality before the law helped bring peace to a domestic setting, the United Nations extended such a possibility to the international arena.

Rusk knew that the United States was founded upon an idea that free citizens could come together and rule without force or fraud. America's promise developed from the belief that one's ambitions could be achieved through persistence and determination. This idealism reflected America's exceptional founding. The American experience fostered the expectation that the future would be better, and, though European leaders often viewed such idealism as naive, according to Rusk it had been vindicated in the founding, and from that initial success the United States derived great strength.[65]

Even as he drew upon that idealism, Rusk tempered it with a pragmatic understanding of limits and the stark realization that force was needed to defend freedom. His idealism contained an element of realism, but it was sturdy and not cynical; rather, it was realism driven by his strategic pursuit of a decent world order. The United Nations would not solve all the problems in the world; he knew there might be cases in which the United States would have to go it alone. That necessity made it all the more important that

America possess military and economic strength and that its alliances and allies be strong as well. Thus, Rusk's foreign policy philosophy, imbued with the idealism of the American regime and the UN Charter, was generously tempered by a strong pragmatic streak.

RUSK'S VIEW OF THE UNITED STATES' ROLE IN THE WORLD

America's exceptionalism suggested that it had a destiny or mission in the world.[66] The first and overriding goal of its foreign policy was to defend the United States. Beyond that goal America would work to maintain the general peace and create a decent world order. America had the special responsibility to defend freedom.[67]

According to Rusk, America's responsibility for creating a decent world order was based upon the defense of freedom. America was secure only when the world was secure and free only when others were free.[68] A further task was to promote and defend the rule of law because where the rule of law extends, so too does freedom.[69] Freedom and the rule of law could only succeed if America's allies were free and able to defend themselves. Therefore, a third task was to help allies defend themselves. Finally, as the world's largest economy, America had a role to play in helping its allies and the newly independent states develop economically.

Rusk believed that the integrity of the United States' commitment, a main pillar of world peace, was being challenged in South Vietnam. Speaking on a television news program, Rusk emphasized the importance of the commitment when he was asked whether the United States' prestige and honor were at stake in Vietnam:

> President Johnson has indicated that our honor is at stake here . . . Wrapped up in this word "honor" is a matter of the deepest concern to the life and death of our nation—because it is very important, when the President of the United States makes a commitment and when he says something to those to whom we're opposed, that what he says is believed.
>
> Now, we have a commitment to South Viet-Nam. We also have 42 allies. The integrity of that commitment is literally the principal pillar of peace in this present world situation. And if the other side should discover or think that they discover that the commitment of the United States is not worth very much, then the structure of peace begins to dissolve rapidly and we shall be faced with dangers we've never dreamed of.[70]

If America's commitment to Vietnam were found to be hollow, it would damage America's credibility with allies and enemies: allies might worry about America's commitment and enemies would be more likely to confront America.

Rusk believed the United States would be able to meet the Communist challenges to America's political, economic, and military strength, which came from the American people and American ideals.[71] The American regime's ideals gave it political strength, which inspired its foreign policy. Rusk's foreign policy philosophy, however, especially his view of America's role in the world, created a gap between the principles of the American regime and its commitment to the world order. America would not falter because of economic or military weakness but because of the growing rift between the principles of the domestic realm and the nation's international responsibilities.

The rift represented more than simply an example of imperial overreaching, in which commitments are greater than resources can provide for, because the gap reflected a philosophical change as well as a geopolitical shift in American foreign policy. Rusk expressed the expanded American commitment to defending liberty at the 1961 SEATO conference in Bangkok. There he explained and justified the expanded defense of freedom as having been derived from the Truman Doctrine. In sum, America had global responsibilities to defend free people resisting aggression, and Rusk would apply the Truman Doctrine to all people in all areas of the world. Communist wars of national liberation and subversion were no longer limited to Western Europe but were now global. America's foreign policy had to have a global reach in order to meet this expanded challenge.

This sense of responsibility to secure world order had no geographical barriers. "Our attention here is focused on Southeast Asia. The people of this treaty area, no less than elsewhere, have an inherent right to create peaceful, independent states and to live out their lives in ways of their own choosing. Loss of freedom means a tragedy whether that misfortune overtakes a people on any continent or any island in the seven seas."[72] Rusk's argument transformed the Truman Doctrine's implied regionalism into a universalistic imperative.[73] In a word, America's limited domestic principles were now unlimited and applied to the world. America would intervene in Southeast Asia, in particular in South Vietnam, to defend freedom and the decent world order. The changed geopolitical framework created greater responsibilities, and the foreign policy philosophy justified their defense, which set the context for a foreign policy crisis. America's security was now identified with the freedom and security of the world order, and South Vietnam was the test.

The expanded foreign policy commitment had domestic consequences as critics rejected Rusk's collective security arguments that justified South Vietnam's defense. They argued that the conflict was in fact a civil war affecting one nation and not the first step in a Communist world revolution. Rusk could understand why the American people would be skeptical about collective security.[74] Yet the fundamental question remained of how to avoid a general war without having some system of collective security.[75] In the context of the foreign policy crisis, Rusk asked how the American public would justify its commitment to a decent world order, which reflected the principles of the American regime, without defending against challenges.

With U.S. involvement in Vietnam the geopolitical scope of America's responsibilities had expanded from the Atlantic region to the Pacific Rim. With relative stability in the Atlantic region, particularly in Europe, the Cold War struggle had shifted to other regions such as Southeast Asia. The geopolitical focus of American foreign policy changed under Kennedy and Johnson and became meeting the Communist threat in the developing world. If America did not respond, it could lose the worldwide struggle against communism in this new area. Moreover, with the Pacific Rim becoming an increasingly important trade center, the stakes in the struggle in Southeast Asia were significant.[76] Following the Soviet Union's test of its first atomic weapon in 1948, China's loss to Communist powers in 1949 and the outbreak of the Korean War in 1950, the region was heating up as a point of competition between the two dominant ideological systems operating in the world at that time. The Korean War had changed America's strategic focus in the region.[77] Geoffrey Sloan has argued that America's response to the Korean War began the geopolitical policy of "indiscriminate" globalism.[78] After China's loss to the Communists, the United States undertook steps to contain Communist China and the threat it posed on the Eurasian landmass, and it sought to aid those countries in the region that were resisting communism.[79] According to Sloan, the geopolitical strategic focus changed from a point strategy to a line, or perimeter, strategy.[80] Thus, when Rusk saw South Vietnam challenged, he believed it to be part of a process that had begun with the fall of China and appeared to be gathering momentum. What he saw was more than the domino theory: Rusk saw clear signs of a world revolution.[81] Yet the global struggle between the liberal democracies and communism was expanding. America had become committed to indiscriminate globalism out of apparent necessity.[82]

In the mid-1960s the superpower competition appeared to have shifted to the Pacific Rim, although the threat of nuclear or conventional war by the Soviet Union against Western Europe remained. Nikita Khrushchev's threat of wars of national liberation focused on the developing world. As Peter Rodman has argued, the stalemate in the European theater and in the race for weapon superiority left only the developing world as a possible flank to attack the West.[83] In Asia the situation carried a particular level of urgency because of China's power and proximity and the fact that, according to Rusk, it was promoting the worldwide Communist revolution. In the Communist camp Mao criticized the Soviet Union for failing to carry forward the world revolution.[84] A litmus test for its commitment to revolution was through support for North Vietnam against American "imperialism."[85]

Whereas the Communists argued that they were merely resisting American imperialism, Rusk identified America's behavior with the defense of liberty within the world order. This expanded the geopolitical responsibility of American foreign policy, creating the foundation for a potential Machiavellian Moment in foreign policy.[86] Rusk's commitment to Vietnam created a shift in the United States' foreign policy philosophy. Rusk fulfilled the language of the Truman Doctrine by extending it beyond Europe to South Vietnam. That, however, only tells the geopolitical story. The foreign policy philosophy began to change as Rusk matched policy to rhetoric in an attempt to create a decent world order. In doing so, Rusk and Johnson departed from the prudent calculations made in the Truman and Eisenhower years by expanding America's responsibilities. Under Rusk the belief in a decent world order, implied in the commitment to the UN Charter, became an explicit policy objective. The United States could not shrink from the global struggle, for, in the language Kennedy and Rusk had used, to fail to support freedom was in effect to oppose it. Unfortunately, the task, while in the best spirit of the American regime, was beyond its capabilities as a republic. The defense of a decent world order in South Vietnam damaged American foreign policy, it damaged the idea that America had a special role to play in the international system, and, finally, it caused Americans to question America's exceptionalism.

The United States was exceptional to the degree that it represented a founding in freedom in the New World. America's idealism had not yet encountered the apparent cynicism and realpolitik that had descended on Europe.[87] After Vietnam that belief started to be questioned. Rusk saw the pursuit of liberty as offering the world the possibility of redemption. Yet he was not on a crusade, even though he believed that the tide of history was turning toward those who promoted freedom.[88] America had inaugurated a world revolution that was slowly gathering strength, and soon the whole world might enjoy freedom. As Rusk would say, the winds of freedom are blowing through the world.[89] Thus, if liberty and progress were to succeed, the New World would have to redeem the Old World.

While Rusk never spoke directly in the language of the Machiavellian Moment, he did acknowledge that America was the guardian and promoter of liberty for the world. He believed that America's exceptionalism had been demonstrated in that role by how it handled its power. To him it was hardly insignificant:

> It is not of small significance—indeed it is of greatest historical importance—that the most powerful nation the world has known has not been seeking aggrandizement, that it has committed itself to protecting and promoting freedom for the human race as a whole. And this dedication may be the most significant single factor of the 20th century. Lord Acton once said, "power corrupts." If our friends from other countries would forgive a presumptuous remark, I believe the record since 1945 would indicate that Lord Acton needs some revision. Because the power in the hands of the American people, beginning in 1945, has not corrupted them in their basic purposes and commitments toward a decent world order.[90]

Rusk's belief in America's commitment to liberty introduces two points that are important for understanding the Machiavellian Moment and the U.S. crisis in foreign policy. The war in Vietnam reveals a tension between America's founding principles and its commitment to those principles within its defense of the decent world order. The idea that America is a redeemer nation and thus there are two worlds—the new, exceptional one and the old, mundane one—can be seen in Rusk's vision of the decent world order.[91] As he saw it, America's fight for liberty would create one world of freedom, and America would redeem the world.

2

LYNDON JOHNSON'S FLAWED STATESMANSHIP
AND THE NEAR MACHIAVELLIAN MOMENT
IN AMERICAN FOREIGN POLICY

On 28 July 1965 Lyndon Johnson committed the United States to an un-declared limited war in South Vietnam. That commitment would change the nation and its foreign policy. The war would damage the U.S. economy, tarnish its international prestige, divide the public, and force Johnson's with-drawal from the 1968 presidential campaign. The choice for an undeclared, limited war marked a turning point for Johnson's presidency, U.S. foreign policy, and the American regime. At first glance the choice appeared to fulfill America's commitment to liberal internationalism. According to Johnson's secretary of state, Dean Rusk, America would defend the decent world order because in doing so it was also defending itself. Yet, as the war and the decent world order continued to demand increasingly more attention and more re-sources, the commitment appeared to be incompatible with the needs of the country's domestic structure. Broadly understood, the foreign policy task, as defined by Johnson and Rusk, appeared to be open-ended, and the domestic realm, which is based upon limits enforced through constitutional checks and balances, could not sustain it. Foreign policy demands were threatening the constitutional balance between the branches of government.[1]

This chapter examines the Vietnam War from a political-philosophical perspective and argues that the undeclared war created a foreign policy crisis that nearly pushed the United States to the breaking point, a "Machiavellian Moment," in the words of J.G.A. Pocock.[2] This moment refers to a crisis within a republic when it faces challenges to its identity as a limited govern-ment. The moment occurs when a republic confronts its mortality and has to choose between being transformed into an empire or being dissolved by external pressures or internal corruption. When a republic confronts its political limits in the temporal world, it must reform itself or disintegrate. "The Machiavellian Moment . . . is a name for the moment in conceptualized time in which the republic was seen as confronting its own temporal finitude, as attempting to remain morally and political stable in a stream of irrational events conceived as essentially destructive of all systems of secular stability."[3]

A republic, according to Pocock, faces two difficulties. The internal danger is that the republic can disintegrate because the political virtue necessary for self-government has been corrupted. The external dangers come from other states or from a government's own attempt to expand the domestic realm—to externalize its domestic principles in an attempt to maintain internal stability. Eventually, the republic will attempt to transform the bounded universal principles at work within the regime into a universal system. Such a change is indicated by the increased centralization of authority within the government whereby the republic begins to turn from self-government into the rule of one person.[4] The focus here, however, is on the foreign policy aspects of the transformative moment because in the case of the United States it was the external effort to support the world order that created instability within the American regime. The challenge for a republic attempting to uphold a world order is to reconcile its domestic structure, based upon a limited government, with the expansive and unlimited task of maintaining a world order.

The Machiavellian Moment refers to a transitional point faced by all republics at some point in their existence. According to Pocock, a republic's political principles are universal but are bound up within the sphere of citizenship. A republic must keep its external responsibilities and its domestic realm in balance: "It was at once universal in the sense that it existed to realize for its citizens all the values which men were capable of realizing in this life, and particular, in the sense that it was finite and located in space and time . . . [T]he problem of showing how it had come into being and might maintain its existence, and that of reconciling its end of realizing universal values with the instability and circumstantial disorder of its temporal life."[5]

The limits on these principles, which reside in a bounded political realm, keep them from spilling out and disrupting the fragile balance between their universal character and the physical limits within the political system. A republic must continually work to keep the internal structure stable against combined external and internal pressures. The fragile balance within the regime has to be sustained against the instability that might cause collapse and the external pressure that might crush it or create the desire to expand in order to resist an outside threat. To put it simply, the republic must maintain the clear distinction between foreign and domestic realms. If the domestic sphere begins to blur into the external one, the fragile balance begins to dissolve because either the external realm will intrude and transform the internal realm or the internal realm will be expanded to meet the external challenge. A republic's domestic realm is characterized by balance, the rule of law, moderation, and harmony, but immoderation, power, and war mark the external realm.

Pocock's concept is useful in examining U.S. foreign policy, although one can argue that in the war in Vietnam the United States in fact faced a "near" Machiavellian Moment; the crisis it faced was more a matter of foreign policy than of danger to the American regime. In other words, the United States did not face the immediate danger of disintegration, nor was it about to become an empire. Nevertheless, in the context of the Vietnam War the United States was forced to confront the limits of its identity and in this sense faced a crisis over its identity as a republic within the international system. By changing its foreign policy, the United States resolved the tension between its domestic political regime and its international responsibilities without compromising its identity as a republic.

In a war a republic's normally decentralized political structure must change to meet the external threat. To extract necessary resources to be used in the war and to direct strategy, authority tends to become more centralized. In ancient Rome, for example, a dictator would be appointed for the duration of the national emergency, according to an explicit granting of power based upon an awareness by the citizenry that the republic's principles were being threatened. What caused a problem for Rome was its overreliance on centralized power, which weakened the republican political structures that depended upon decentralized authority. More recently, in response to the Great Depression and World War II, the U.S. federal government grew significantly, with support for this greater centralization of power granted by the American people and the legislature. Again at the time of the Vietnam War President Johnson attempted to centralize more authority—specifically, war powers—at Congress's expense without clear support from the people or Congress. Johnson's immoderate statesmanship ultimately threatened the constitutional balance because the undeclared war demanded more from the domestic realm than it could sustain.

By misapplying Machiavelli's advice in chapter 18 of *The Prince*, Johnson failed as a foreign policy "prince."[6] Machiavelli wrote that a prince must be at times a lion and a fox and know when to be one or the other according to the situation. Johnson demonstrated great political skill in the domestic realm, acting as a lion or a fox as needed, but was unsuccessful when he tried to apply these methods to the external realm. What was required, given the tasks of waging war abroad and reforming society at home, was to act as a Platonic statesman. According to Plato's argument within *The Statesman*, a success-ful leader will weave together divergent factions, the aggressive and passive elements within a polity, to create a unified foreign policy for defense against external threats.[7] In Johnson's case he had to weave together support for the war, and therefore an expansive foreign policy, with support for the Great Society, which itself represented an expansive domestic policy. Johnson tried to carry out foreign affairs, the realm of Platonic statesmanship, with the tools and strategies of a domestic politician, Machiavelli's Prince, and thus failed to establish a lasting consensus.

Two broad aspects of Johnson's political character reveal his success as a domestic prince but his failure as a statesman, his foreign policy inexperience and his attempt to erase the distinction between foreign and domestic poli-cies. When combined with an incremental decision-making style, these po-litical characteristics reveal Johnson's flawed statesmanship. At the root of his statesmanship is a propensity for immoderation, an impatience, best charac-terized by his ambitious attempt to carry out an extensive domestic policy and an expansive foreign policy. Johnson's failure reflected a larger crisis within the regime. The American regime, representing a limited and balanced govern-ment, was being asked to sustain an unlimited, open-ended commitment through undeclared war. This approach to war created tension between the needs of the limited domestic regime and those of its external commitments.

The foreign policy crisis brought on by Lyndon Johnson's ineffective statecraft threatened the American regime's constitutional balance. The near Machiavellian Moment that arose for the republic because the undeclared, limited war in Vietnam disrupted the balance between the domestic and external realms reverberated in the subsequent struggle between the U.S. executive and legislative branches. Johnson's failures as a Platonic statesman triggered the constitutional struggle and the regime's crisis.[8] In his study of modern statecraft Wendell Coats states that in its modern usage the term *statesmanship* can be understood as "an activity directed toward securing the conditions for politics to occur, as the basis for agreement about general courses of action, and for moderate reconciliation of differences among fellow citizens."[9] For Johnson the minimal consensus he was able to achieve covered over, rather than resolved, the differences between his administration's domestic and foreign policies. Johnson's attempt to pursue domestic reforms and an undeclared war, as well as his desire to avoid mobilizing public support for the war, divided the country, setting passive and aggressive elements against each other.[10] When it came to managing the situation in Vietnam alongside coping with demands at home, Johnson's foreign policy commitment to the decent world order, advocated faithfully by his secretary of state, conflicted with his domestic policies.

The near Machiavellian Moment that threatened the American republican regime developed from the question of whether America could sustain an expansive role within the international system by continuing to identify its security with the security of the world order yet remain a republic. The nation faced two alternatives. First, it could continue the expansive policy, thereby accepting an imperial role, but this would require it to adjust its domestic political structure and would mean accepting the executive's primacy at the expense of the legislative branch. Alternatively, the nation could accept a reduced role within the international system by disassociating its security from that of the decent world order, and the executive and legislative branches could cooperate more fully on foreign policy.[11] With this approach the domestic realm would be privileged over, or treated equally to, the external realm. Under Johnson's leadership the United States rejected the expansive path by refusing to adjust the domestic realm for the imperial task of defending a world order.

The foreign policy crisis can be understood, from a constitutional perspective, as the result of an imbalance between domestic policy and foreign policy created by the undeclared war. The foreign policy crisis meant that the executive branch had to centralize more power in order to sustain both expansive policies, which meant that it was usurping Congress's constitutional war powers. The constitutional imbalance was exacerbated by Johnson's belief that the line between the domestic and external realms had been erased. The practical consequence was that the legislative branch's concern that the executive branch was usurping its constitutional war powers. At the philosophical level—the central concern for the Machiavellian Moment—the crisis can be understood as follows: Could the American regime, a limited, balanced republican regime, carry out an apparently boundless, imperial commitment intended to uphold a decent world order without being transformed?

The undeclared war, which expressed an expansive and immoderate foreign policy, revealed the larger problem of the attempt to reconcile the American regime to the international system. Johnson's immoderation brought the foreign policy crisis's effects into the domestic sphere. In essence, Johnson's political immoderation threatened to disrupt the necessary political moderation at the heart of the republic. The American regime relies upon an executive branch that is balanced and checked within the domestic sphere by the legislative and judicial branches, yet within "the vast external realm" the executive branch acts with wide latitude.[12] The realms function in harmony so long as they are kept distinct and balanced and so long as there is cooperation between the legislative and executive branches of government. When Congress's role is blurred with that of the executive by an active president, the roles can become confused. Moreover, Congress historically shies away from making direct foreign policy commitments, because it lacks a unitary will and the expertise to counter the president's authority and expertise in this area. Therefore, it took relatively little effort for Johnson, an active leader, to use his foreign policy prerogative to dominate an unassertive Congress.

One could argue that, by failing to realize the limits of U.S. power, Johnson failed as a statesman, behaving as though the country were strong enough, rich enough, and committed enough to succeed in any enterprise he cared to undertake in the domestic and international realms.[13] Furthermore, by failing to accept the notion that the alternatives he faced, withdrawing and letting South Vietnam be defeated by North Vietnam or declaring war and invading North Vietnam, would have unacceptable domestic and international political consequences, he showed a lack of vision.[14] Finally, he pursued an undeclared, limited war as a middle path between these unacceptable tactical choices.

He ultimately decided to try charting a middle path between the nation's foreign policy commitments and his administration's domestic promises, wherein he believed that he could give the American public what they wanted in each sphere.[15] But the undeclared war linked Johnson's domestic and foreign policies in unforeseen ways. Just as he had done so often in domestic politics, Johnson wanted to find a solution to satisfy critics on both sides of the issue.[16] Instead of achieving the flexibility needed to try balancing the two realms, Johnson's statesmanship trapped him between them. He was unable to fulfill his promises in either domain, and his efforts to succeed in one realm only hindered his efforts in the other. The techniques that had succeeded so well domestically proved insufficient for the military strategy being carried out in the external realm.

When he came into office, Lyndon Johnson had relatively little foreign affairs inexperience, and his attempts to treat foreign policy like domestic policy and his belief that the boundary between the two realms could be removed reflect this fact. In a republic the line between the internal and external realm is marked by its constitution, which maps out the domestic political space, but Johnson's approach to foreign affairs seemed to disregard this fundamental point of the Constitution by blurring the lines between the two realms. Johnson's foreign policy relied upon a strong executive branch that threatened to overshadow the legislative branch. The blurred boundaries separating the executive and legislative branches served Johnson's purposes by centralizing power within the executive branch and in effect usurping Congress's constitutional powers to make decisions about war. Congress, nearly co-opted by the executive because of the close relationship between the two that had developed over domestic reforms, had difficulty restraining Johnson's expansive foreign policy in Vietnam.

By focusing on Johnson's political character, my goal is to shed more light on his approach to statesmanship exemplified by his approach to politics and his decision-making process. Johnson was not fated to intervene in Vietnam, and ultimately he was the one who made that choice. Johnson agonized over the decision, constantly trying to find a way to avoid it or solve it.[17] Johnson had choices, but for a variety of reasons having to do with both domestic politics and the external environment he chose poorly.

The same qualities that made Johnson successful as a domestic "prince" failed when he tried to use them in crafting a foreign policy. In chapter 18 of *The Prince* Machiavelli suggests that a prince must know how, when, and to what extent to use different forms of fighting that are needed to succeed: "You therefore must know there are two kinds of fighting, the one with laws, the other with force: the first is proper to man, the second to beasts: but because many times the first does not suffice, it is expedient to recur to the second. Therefore, it is necessary for a prince to know well how to use the beast and the man."[18]

The choice is further complicated because the prince must choose the type of beast needed—either the fox or the lion—for to rely upon one exclusively, according to Machiavelli, leads to ruin. The prince must choose according to the particular needs of the situation. Franklin Delano Roosevelt exemplifies a leader who was successful at the art of statecraft. He understood that he had to move from domestic reforms (behaving like a fox) to foreign affairs (taking on the role of the lion) when faced with the demands of World War II. To be fair, the situations the two leaders faced were very different, and Johnson did not have an event like Pearl Harbor to solidify his consensus. But Roosevelt, unlike Johnson, did not try to avoid making tough choices between the policies.

Franklin Roosevelt understood the need to balance domestic and foreign policy realms, but he also understood that necessity might force him to concentrate on one realm and downplay the other. With the onset of World War II, for example, Roosevelt had to move from domestic reforms as the forward-looking architect of society's New Deal to performing skillfully in foreign affairs. Yet he was able to demonstrate superior Platonic statesmanship by weaving together a lasting domestic consensus. He did this in part because the attack on Pearl Harbor created a spontaneous and sturdy consensus among branches of government as well as among American citizens, but he also succeeded as a statesman by maintaining the distinction between foreign and domestic policies. Unlike Roosevelt, Johnson attempted to continue domestic reforms and fight a war. Johnson, who wanted to surpass Roosevelt as a president, failed to understand how Roosevelt moved from balancing the two policy realms to building a consensus to support foreign policy.[19] Johnson, by contrast, tried to keep the two realms separate in the public's mind so that he could keep a free hand in each realm, though he worked as if they were connected. The problem was that he could not weave them together as equally ambitious policies; instead, he subordinated one policy to the other. Rather than expending the political and material costs of building consensus to sustain his foreign policy, Johnson chose to pursue a limited war based upon a minimal consensus. But such a minimal consensus could not bridge the gap between the two policy domains.

Johnson failed because the middle path he chose, though it appeared to be a compromise and therefore moderate, was in fact extreme; it left him in an inflexible position. As the economy overheated and the situation in South Vietnam failed to go the way the administration hoped, Johnson became trapped by an ambiguous policy that relied too heavily on his political leadership and was unable to reconcile activities in the domestic and external realms. A man of less ambition or greater moderation might have chosen to pursue reforms or war. Johnson failed not because he attempted great goals—an archer hits far targets only if he aims beyond them—but because he could not choose between his goals.[20] His policies followed diverging paths. The only way he could afford to undertake them, politically and economically, was by balancing them or not allowing either to dominate the political landscape. Practically speaking, he needed the domestic economy to grow fast enough so that he could afford both.[21] If the economy had been able to sustain a degree of prosperity so that his reforms at home would have satisfied the citizens and not alarmed or concerned them regarding the costs of his foreign policy, then he might have succeeded. Instead, during his tenure the war dominated the political landscape, the domestic economy became unstable, and the domestic political system became torn by civil unrest, all of which discredited Johnson's middle-path policy. In the language of the Machiavellian Moment his efforts to direct the country were thwarted by a stream of irrational events in the external realm. The delicate balance between the realms was disrupted.

Johnson's political style relied upon finding a middle path of a minimal consensus between policy alternatives. On domestic issues he could find a common ground, however limited, between two positions that would allow him to reconcile the policies and create a minimal consensus. Without a common good, such as in the international arena, Johnson's attempt to weave together conflicting policy choices into a mutually acceptable position was unlikely to succeed. Although states may have common interests on certain issues, agreeing completely on a common good similar to those pursued by the various states in the domestic realm is unlikely because issues are not easily, if at all, divisible. In domestic politics Johnson often achieved a consensus by relying upon the technique of "political judo"; he would use an opponent's position to achieve his own end in order to gain a short-term advantage.[22] For example, he mollified the military, without alarming those who criticized intervention in Southeast Asia, by accepting some of its demands.[23] If a key group gained an advantage from any of his policies, they were more likely to support the consensus position. Johnson attempted to placate the domestic realm with the Great Society reforms while fulfilling his external commitment. Soon, however, struggles over war and reforms began to divide the domestic realm.

With Americans and their legislative leaders divided between reforms and an expansive foreign policy, the undeclared war could not gain full support. Instead of building a substantial consensus created by public debate and full congressional consent, Johnson made do with minimal support expressed through congressional authorization that was obtained after only a brief debate in a crisis atmosphere. By avoiding true consensus, Johnson's margin of error in either realm was reduced, but it also meant he had failed to indicate clearly what would be demanded of the country.[24]

By treating foreign policy as an outgrowth of his domestic policy, Johnson failed to see that, unlike in the domestic realm, he could not maneuver and use pragmatism to adjust his policies to take advantage of his opponents' circumstances in the external realm. In the domestic sphere the goal is often to initiate policy. Once legislation is passed, it can be adjusted in terms of funding, scope, and legislative acceptance over a number of years. The external realm, however, is different. One does not start a war, for example, hoping that strategy, logistics, and goals can be hashed out along the way. If a statesman has not determined his or her goals, settled upon a strategy, prepared the logistical base, and obtained public support before undertaking a war, he will fail. By believing he could develop and define public support for the war as needed, he was treating the war in Vietnam more like a traditional domestic issue.

Although he was fairly knowledgeable about foreign policy through his experience as Senate majority leader in devising and passing legislation to deal with international issues, Johnson lacked actual experience with foreign affairs. He prided himself on being a domestic politician, and his fondness for this work colored his approach to world affairs. Johnson's relative inexperience did not make him a captive of his advisors, however, and he was able to apply his extraordinary political analytical skills to foreign policy decisions. Inexperience in foreign affairs nevertheless affected Johnson's political judgment in a number of ways. In order to balance foreign policy and domestic policy, he had to demonstrate success in each realm. In the domestic realm Johnson focused on passing a housing bill, designed to meet and resolve immediate social needs, rather than encouraging a national debate about the housing issue or designing a long-term housing strategy. His focus on passing legislation left funding, implementation, or policy coherence concerns as secondary issues.[25] Doris Kearns described Johnson's approach as the "politics of haste."[26] But short-term success can create long-term problems, especially in foreign affairs.

Johnson's inexperience in foreign affairs led him to stress continuity with Kennedy's policies, yet his ambition drove him to want to make his mark as president. He wanted to show success on his terms, and his ambitious foreign policy reflected this desire. Johnson's concern for continuity together with his personal ambition, likely contributed to his middle-path policy in South Vietnam. He wanted to continue his predecessor's policies, and thereby protect himself from those who would accuse him of abandoning Kennedy's legacy, but at the same time he wanted to make achievements of his own.[27]

By defending South Vietnam, Johnson believed he was simply fulfilling the commitments created and continued by previous presidents,[28] yet Johnson went far beyond them. Guided by a worldview shaped by the failures of Munich and reinforced by his secretary of state's commitment to liberal internationalism, expressed in collective security, Johnson accepted the duty, as he saw it, to defend the free world.[29] Unlike previous presidents, Johnson attempted to uphold this external commitment while radically expanding domestic political commitments to the American people. Aware that "the bill had come due," Johnson vowed to pay it.[30] The problem was that the bill had come due in both realms, but, given the frail consensus, only one bill could be paid.

Johnson's enthusiasm and insecurity led him to fulfill and expand upon what he perceived as Kennedy's policies. On 26 November 1963, the day after John F. Kennedy's funeral, Johnson met with Ambassador Henry Cabot Lodge, who had arrived from South Vietnam. At that meeting Johnson said, "He did not become President just to see South Vietnam go the way of China."[31] Johnson feared, as had Kennedy, that the loss of South Vietnam would create a political backlash similar to or greater than the one that had followed the "loss" of China.[32] This does not mean that domestic concerns drove his policy, but Johnson's statement shows a desire for continuity as well as his belief in the Cold War assumptions behind the policy, which contributed to his decision to maintain and then expand the U.S. military commitment to South Vietnam. Newspaper columnist Tom Wicker observed how Johnson's approach differed from Kennedy's, arguing that Kennedy and Johnson probably would have made different choices at the meeting with Ambassador Lodge because of their personalities, the context for the decisions, and their respective approaches to the problem.[33] Kennedy kept the question of Vietnam at a distance by keeping his full intentions ambiguous.[34] Johnson connected them, in his own mind, because he believed one policy succeeded or failed based upon the success or failure of the other. As historian Lloyd Gardner has pointed out, Johnson believed his Great Society lived or died by Vietnam.[35] Kenneth Thompson has explored the problematic shift in approach from Kennedy to Johnson in political science terms, arguing that Kennedy seemed unable to reconcile the activist and the pragmatic elements in his foreign policy, which left Johnson to reconcile them.[36]

After Kennedy's death, Johnson sought to reassure the country and its allies by demonstrating continuity within the American government and its policies. On the surface he accepted Kennedy's broad policy goal to defend South Vietnam yet without accepting its assumptions or implications.

Kennedy had kept his position unclear in order to maintain flexibility, but Johnson embraced the commitment unambiguously. Johnson feared that failure in South Vietnam would undermine U.S. foreign policy commitments. Johnson would try to maintain his political flexibility by calibrating domestic and foreign policy. In contrast to Kennedy, who kept his rhetoric and intentions uncertain, Johnson kept his policy execution ambiguous. Johnson tried to keep the war's costs hidden from the domestic realm even as he claimed that the resources to support his foreign policy were unlimited.[37] Johnson had foreign policy flexibility so long as the domestic realm did not react to the costs associated with the nation's foreign policy commitments.

Johnson was now in a situation in which to avoid losing he had to avoid the appearance of escalating the war yet be able to send in more troops in order to "win." Fredrik Logevall makes a similar argument when he discusses what Kennedy, had he lived, might have done in Vietnam. He argues that Kennedy, too, by following a middle path between involvement and withdrawal, was trying to achieve incompatible goals.[38] But by linking the war with his domestic agenda, Johnson radicalized that middle path and, unlike Kennedy, consciously connected the war with the reforms.[39]

Lyndon Johnson undertook an undeclared war to uphold the commitment to a decent world order, which was under threat in South Vietnam, and avoid damage to his domestic reforms. At the root of this strategy was Johnson's belief that he could manage the political and economic consequences of an undeclared, limited war.[40] Tragically, he underestimated the effort required to execute an ambitious foreign policy at the same time that was undertaking extensive domestic reforms. Johnson tried to balance the two realms but failed because he was caught between a foreign policy commitment that drew the country outward and a domestic, political commitment, the creation of the Great Society, which pulled the country inward. The undeclared war was designed to bridge the gap between the two. But, rather than clarifying the relationship between his domestic and foreign policies, thereby creating the basis for weaving them together, the undeclared war kept the relationship ambiguous.

To maintain the two realms, Johnson needed to avoid defeat in South Vietnam but not at the cost of undermining his domestic policies. The undeclared, limited war appeared to be the best middle path between domestic and foreign policies. His limited war strategy presupposed, however, that North Vietnam would not be able to escalate the conflict to the point that the United States would be forced to make an even greater commitment. If the war reached a transition point from a limited war to one that required massive resources, which it did, the United States would have to make a choice between pursuing its domestic policy or its foreign policy. Johnson had sent the country down that path because he believed he had no other option and because he believed his political skills could balance the two countervailing demands. With the Tet offensive of 1968, that moment of choice arrived; by then it was clear that following a strategy of undeclared limited war had failed. Johnson chose not to escalate the conflict and initiated a de facto de-escalatory policy. According to Robert Collins, Johnson chose to draw down, in part, because he could not obtain public support from either Congress or the American people, nor could the economy sustain the extraordinary demands of the nation's foreign and domestic policies. Johnson undertook de-escalation in Vietnam in the belief that it would lead to a negotiated settlement that would salvage his foreign policy and shield his domestic policy.

He feared the political consequences that would come from any failure in either policy-making realm. His fear of failure reflected his approach to domestic politics, in which he had been successful by being a cautious politician. He tried to have the situation in hand before committing to a policy. His caution helped him to avoid being manipulated by other actors. Philip Geyelin wrote that one of Johnson's laws was: "The prime time for decision making is when everybody else has shown his hand."[41] Despite such caution, Johnson would take enormous political risks on certain issues when guided by his extraordinary political instincts. The Civil Rights legislation entailed great risks, but his political instincts told him that the country needed and wanted the legislation. As Joseph Califano and Doris Kearns [Goodwin] have each pointed out in their examinations of the Johnson presidency, LBJ trusted his own political judgment on domestic issues to the extent that he often overruled his domestic political advisors.[42] His sense of timing and his feel for the political moment, which was a key political trait, told him when it was time to take the lead on domestic issues.

Johnson's domestic political success came, in part, because his stated goals and aspirations were in harmony with what the electorate wanted. His Great Society legislation would not have succeeded if it had not resonated with the national will. "As the full scope of Johnson's ambitions gradually became apparent," according to Kearns, "public reaction seemed to demonstrate that he had accurately perceived the national will ... His landslide election in 1964 appeared to constitute popular approval and a mandate to proceed ... During 1964 and 1965, however, Johnson's virtuoso performance obscured the fact that all his achievements depended upon the essential harmony between his acts and popular desires; that without that all his skills and energies would have been futile."[43]

Johnson's early legislative success appeared to vindicate his political instincts, but paradoxically it also helped convince him that he had more to lose from a foreign policy failure. Moreover, his early legislative success and public support meant that, instead of conducting a full debate over the war's aims and cost, he achieved support for his policy through a minimal consensus. He took his popularity and early legislative success for granted and did not prepare the nation for a drawn-out conflict. He proceeded as though the public would simply accept his leadership and goals in such matters.

Johnson believed that because his foreign and domestic policies were interconnected they were capable of being reconciled. He had linked the two areas because he did not think he could keep them separate.[44] If he could balance the two, he could maintain his political flexibility. The goal was not simply to play one off against the other but to achieve a delicate but continuous balancing act. In his 1966 State of the Union Address Johnson argued that there was no longer a dividing line between foreign and domestic policy. He failed to acknowledge that each realm must move at its own pace and logic. In the domestic arena, for instance, issues can usually find reasonable compromises, or an action can be taken to pursue aspects of a given issue (e.g., housing policy, which strives to apply to all Americans, despite apparent structural flaws). Issues of importance in the realm of foreign affairs are not always as easy to resolve; sovereignty, for example, is not something a nation will easily relinquish. In matters of foreign policy, in which opponents rarely seek a common good, there is an inherent inflexibility. Life between countries is not the same as life within countries, where individuals consent to giving up some of their sovereign rights in exchange for certain political benefits.[45]

Lyndon Johnson had an extraordinary understanding of power's nuances within the domestic realm, but it has a different character in the international setting. David Bruce, the American ambassador to Britain, observed after meeting with Johnson on 10 February 1965 that the president was "quite adept at the use of power in domestic politics, [and] has been considering carefully how to exercise it in international affairs."[46] Johnson was acutely aware of his shortcomings in foreign affairs.[47] He often felt unsure in this area, and he often appeared out of his depth. As Kearns pointed out, Johnson did not have the experience to grasp an international situation as he could with domestic policy.[48] In international politics military power is the trump card, but

Johnson often appeared uncertain or uncomfortable about using it. In an evocative and colorful passage Philip Geyelin compared Johnson to a riverboat captain unsure of the open seas of the international arena: "[Johnson was] possessed of an extraordinary feel for power, he had devoted a lifetime to its political application. But he always seemed uncomfortable in its military use. His first inclination was to avoid it, the second to overdo it, not because he relished the dispatch of Marines . . . but in part because he wanted to give those troops he did dispatch the best possible odds in their favor."[49]

In the domestic arena persuasion is rarely replaced by armed coercion because there are rarely issues in which one has to defeat an opponent completely. Instead, one can apply pressures or inducements because the issue can be broken down into parts and an opponent has a minimum point that he will accept, if only to avoid losing completely. Johnson's ability to coerce others to follow his lead, as he did in the domestic realm, was limited in the international arena. His opponents were not bound by the same constraints as Johnson's domestic opponents, nor did they seek the same or even similar goals. The president clearly did not share common ground with Ho Chi Minh concerning South Vietnam.

By connecting his domestic and foreign policies, Johnson forced himself into a corner, caught between the competing demands of each realm. He failed to convince the public and Congress that there was no longer a question of a tradeoff between domestic and foreign policy.[50] Johnson believed that he could succeed in both realms by overcoming the opposition of the "hawks," who wanted war but not reforms, and the "doves" who wanted reforms but not the war.[51] Yet neither realm responded effectively to his control. Johnson's choice of an undeclared, limited war was as ambitious as it was imprudent. Johnson lacked the necessary self-restraint, the necessary virtue, to succeed. His ambitious dreams for the United States were not tempered by prudence. Leo Strauss, commenting on Machiavelli's teachings, explained that a successful prince must possess true virtue. "True Virtue," he wrote, "'the true way,' consists not in the extirpation of ambition but in ambition guided by prudence."[52]

Lyndon Johnson's Approach to Decision Making

Johnson's decision-making style allowed him to emphasize the appearance of continuity by taking incremental steps toward a given goal. The manner in which Johnson pursued decisions was connected to his desire to maintain political flexibility, and flexibility was needed in order to maintain the tenuous consensus. Johnson's incremental, or gradual, approach to the Vietnam policy allowed him to avoid any one decision that marked a major change in policy. Even the announcement on 28 July 1965 that he would be sending ground troops into Vietnam was done in a low-key manner during a midday press conference devoted to other issues. Although the country and Congress were informed of the developments, they never had a full understanding of what the war might require and what it might cost. By stressing continuity, Johnson hoped to avoid drawing attention to his foreign policy. If he could avoid undue scrutiny, by claiming that he was merely carrying existing policy, he could then keep foreign affairs from detracting from his domestic agenda.

The incremental strategy appeared to give Johnson the flexibility to balance foreign and domestic priorities, but it fixed his position by reinforcing his reliance on policy precedents, and it worked more effectively for domestic issues than foreign policy issues. When he departed from first principles, or policy precedents, Johnson relied upon his political instincts. As president, for example, he could take innovative steps on the politically sensitive issue of Civil Rights. When he was a senator from Texas, representing the people of that state, he had been bound to the principles and precedents of segregation, but as president he could transcend these constraints.[53] In Vietnam Johnson was bound to policy precedents such as resisting aggression and honoring commitments, which in the view of his administration justified his policies. He dared not transcend those precedents because his political instincts on the issues they encompass were undeveloped.

Johnson was constrained, first of all, by the existing policy of containment. The need to contain communism,[54] deter aggression, fulfill a commitment to an ally, and, according to Dean Rusk, defend the decent world order were related examples of these principles and precedents.[55] These principles were always well supported in the debates leading up to the 28 July 1965 decision. The fear, for example, that small acts of aggression could lead to a wider war, the so-called Munich analogy, was invoked to justify increased involvement in South Vietnam.[56] Rusk was the best advocate for these first principles. If the United States were to uphold these principles in Vietnam and within the international system, it had to force North Vietnam to stop its aggression and thereby allow South Vietnam to work out its destiny. Yet this open-ended task had to be accomplished without widening or escalating the war. The strategy, designed to give Johnson flexibility, constrained him because it relied upon keeping the war limited. America had to stop North Vietnam without conducting such a massive effort that it would alarm the domestic realm or cause China to intervene. An event that required the United States to "widen the war," such as giving Vietnam its full attention, would force Johnson to confront the choice he was attempting to avoid in the first place: deepening the U.S. commitment in Vietnam by declaring war or withdrawing. Ironically, instead of giving him greater flexibility, the middle-path strategy made Johnson a captive to the extremes.

TRAVELING THE MIDDLE PATH

Johnson's attempt to chart a middle path between war and withdrawal reflected his decision-making style. His approach can be roughly described as "muddling through," a phrase borrowed from Charles Lindblom's 1959 article "The Science of Muddling Through."[57] In that work Lindblom argues that decision makers follow one of two choice models. The first is the ideal, or "comprehensive," model, but it is difficult to fulfill because of the amount of information required is great. Moreover, the model works from prior agreement on fundamental principles, yet agreement is often hard to achieve.[58] The second model is the "limited comparison" model, in which the search is for limited alternatives that offer marginal improvements. The decision process focuses on choices between marginally different alternatives rather than going to first principles and full information. Underlying the search for marginal improvements is the belief that competing positions can be reconciled. The debate focuses on marginal improvement or making marginal adjustments rather than seeking full information and determining the "best" policy choice.

Writing in 1959, four years before LBJ took office, Lindblom could have been describing Johnson's Vietnam decision-making style in 1965: "The trouble lies in the fact that most of us approach policy problems within a framework given by our view of a chain of successive policy choices made up to the present . . . An administrator enjoys an intimate knowledge of his past sequences that 'outsiders' do not share and his thinking and that of the 'outsiders' will consequently be different in ways that may puzzle both."[59]

The limited comparison model accepts the status quo, which is based upon decisions and commitments guided by the first principles as the starting point. By July 1965 Johnson was not considering withdrawal but was trying to decide whether a fast or slow increase in America's involvement would solve the problem. The assumptions, precedents, and goals eliminated questions on the soundness of the commitment, which meant the focus became what or how much should be done rather than should anything be done.

If we describe Johnson's decision-making style as resembling the limited comparison model, we can see two apparent drawbacks to it. First, it emphasized agreements rather than accepting disagreement to find the best policy. Second, the model reinforces policy precedents. The first problem, emphasizing agreement, means that the test of a good policy is the extent to which analysts agree rather than on the soundness of its first principles. Johnson often sought to create a consensus based on minimal agreement. In the case of Vietnam decisions moved forward on agreement rather than the soundness of the original commitment. The commitment's soundness was accepted, so the search was for marginal improvements rather than trying to rethink original principles. The second problem was that the method gave policy precedents an advantage. Precedents had an informational advantage, which political and strategic alternatives lacked. Actors were encouraged to accept the status quo because the lack of information discouraged efforts to examine alternatives. Internal and, especially, external critics were ill equipped to offer alternatives. Policy makers worked from a current situation, whereas critics could only argue about possible situations. Critics had to show that the positive information was inaccurate and to present a viable alternative based upon the limited information on hand to critics and outsiders. Actors could dismiss outside critics for not having all the facts or for failing to understand the political nuances beyond the immediate policy decision.

Critics who suggested alternatives faced a difficult task. They would have to overcome the dual problem of offering an alternative and finding new information. The task was to show that the previous decisions were wrong, or had failed, *and* that future decisions would not improve the situation but would lead to further problems. Moreover, their arguments were limited because they could not repudiate the first principles supporting America's post–World War II foreign policy framework. Critics had to walk a delicate line between criticizing this policy and the precedents that had led up to it. The policy makers accepted the underlying framework that led to Vietnam (containment), but critics who did not want to challenge that framework did not accept that marginal changes in the existing policy would lead to any improvements. Even if a critic attempted only a marginal adjustment, he or she faced a difficult problem created by the power of precedents. Undersecretary of state George Ball, who suggested an alternative, was hard-pressed to demonstrate that the current policies (ca. 1965) had failed but, most important, that they would fail irrespective of American efforts. In 1968 evidence existed to support this claim, but it did not exist conclusively in 1965, when the decisions were being made.

In 1965 decision makers were more aware that they wanted to avoid defeat than of what victory would look like.[60] Victory was ambiguous, but defeat was obvious. In 1963 Lindblom wrote in *A Strategy of Decision* that policy makers follow an incremental approach to decisions that allows them to avoid an "outcome" rather than achieve a goal.[61] Instead of finding agreement on the least common denominator (i.e., on issues over which there is widespread disagreement), policy makers pursuing an incremental approach seek agreement on the most common denominator (i.e., on issues over which there is little disagreement). This incremental approach focuses attention on where consensus can be reached but detracts from long-term goals that may contain disagreement.[62] Policy advisors and Johnson could see short-term gains and immediate responses to their immediate political problem, but simply avoiding defeat kept them from reassessing their fundamental commitment.

Johnson's deception and misdirection, which kept the war's cost hidden from his economic and military advisors, exacerbated the concern for avoiding an outcome.[63] Johnson's imprudence in refusing to make the initial choice strained the American regime. The crisis, created by Johnson's statesmanship, was more than a material crisis; it was also a philosophic crisis.[64] Johnson, and ultimately the entire country, could not reconcile the domestic regime—especially the material and political-philosophical limits it set—with the demands of supporting and defending a decent world order.[65]

A DANGEROUS IMBALANCE

The immediate symptoms of Johnson's foreign policy can be seen in its effect upon the economy, the American public, and Congress. These problems lead us to the more abstract level of thinking about America's international identity. As Alexander Hamilton had pointed out in *Federalist Paper*, no. 8, "It is the nature of war to increase the Executive at the expense of the legislative authority."[66] But the economic dislocations and Congress's opposition to the war were evident in late 1968, when the gold crisis and budgetary disputes revealed that Congress would not support increased spending for the war,[67] and challenged LBJ's authority. The undeclared war could not meet the external realm's rising political, economic, or military demands without disrupting domestic reforms. From the perspective of domestic politics, Johnson could not send more troops. A greater military effort would damage his domestic program, economically and politically, and put further strains on the executive-legislative relationship. The domestic realm was not willing to support the increased demands of the external realm.

Johnson wanted to avoid having to choose between domestic and foreign policy. To avoid this choice, an undeclared, limited war would be the middle path of a minimal consensus to reconcile the two policies. Recalling the decision in his memoirs, he wrote: "I was convinced that the middle ground was the right course for the United States. That was the fundamental approach of my administration, and I was not going to abandon it."[68] The balance could be held between his foreign and domestic policies only if two interconnected situations could be met. Domestic economic growth would continue to allow him to pursue consensus politics, and the military situation in Vietnam had to remain sustainable, not require a greater effort, and at the same time the international economy could not weaken the domestic economy.

The undeclared, limited war, aside from disrupting the economy, threatened to disrupt the political balance between the legislative and executive branches. Johnson argued that the dividing line between the external and internal realms no longer existed, but this threatened the fundamental demarcation between the legislative branch and the executive branch. The president, the representative of the federal government, has great latitude within the external realm. Congress, as the legislative branch, has great latitude within the domestic realm. When these branches cooperate, the power of the federal government is at its height, but, when they are divided or one overshadows the other, then it is weakened. Johnson appeared to be using the external realm to justify usurping Congress's domestic power.

Johnson tried to act as a fulcrum between the two realms, but his effectiveness depended upon his ability to centralize power and obtain Congress's approval or at least avoid its interference. He needed Congress to participate enough to give him the freedom of action needed to carry out foreign policy. Up to a certain point the president's traditional foreign policy prerogative gave Johnson room to maneuver, but his political skills kept Congress's attention diverted from foreign policy. With Congress occupied with the Great Society legislation, Johnson worked to keep Congress from scrutinizing his foreign policy even as he convinced them to support it. The problem, however, was that, instead of building a consensus with Congress, unifying the government behind his foreign policy, Johnson slowly alienated the legislative branch from his policy decisions. His approach asked, in effect, that the public and Congress accept his foreign policy by giving it their support but that they remain occupied with domestic policy. While a critic would call his actions deceptive, they reflect his political style within the domestic realm, wherein he often acted to control the timing of any decision. Moreover, he limited information and access in order to maintain that control. Yet such access to control did not exist in the external realm, in which Johnson lacked the flexibility to manage statements, adjust announcements, and coerce opponents in order to avoid a credibility gap.

Even though the gap between Johnson's rhetoric and his policies created problems, it is important to remember that Congress did in fact authorize Johnson's undeclared war through the Gulf of Tonkin Resolution. What constitutional scholars John Hart Ely and Louis Fisher, in particular, argue is that Congress failed to exercise its constitutional powers and thereby undermined the necessary separation of powers.[69] Congress later acted, through the War Powers legislation, to reassert its constitutional role, but damage was done, and the imbalance had worsened. Congress cannot be excused for failing to fulfill its constitutional responsibility. Despite the context, having a powerful president at the height of his political powers acting upon a Congress occupied with the most extensive reform legislation since World War II, Johnson dominated Congress, through his personality and political skill, like no other president. One could argue that Johnson obtained Congress's consent to carry out his domestic policies as a grand form of political judo to leverage support for his foreign policy. In this manner we can see the short-term gain from the Gulf of Tonkin Resolution; in 1964 the plenary powers to deal with aggression against South Vietnam created long-term problems over war powers and the separation of powers. Johnson's short-term leverage to defend his domestic policy from foreign policy problems laid the foundation for the long-term tension between the two realms.

The foreign policy problems mirrored the domestic realm's problems. In domestic affairs the perceived abuses of power by the president, starting with Johnson's handling of the war and domestic opposition, culminated in abuses by Richard Nixon. Slow to react to Johnson's foreign policy excesses, Congress reacted quickly to Nixon's domestic excesses by bringing impeachment proceedings against him.[70] Congress has only two ways to check an imperious president or his foreign policy: through control of the purse or through impeachment. Whereas Nixon's impeachment proceedings reflected abuses within the domestic realm, Congress acted to restrain foreign policy with the War Powers legislation. Despite these legislative palliatives to restrain the executive's power, the struggle between the executive and the legislative branches over foreign policy and war powers continues, and that struggle encapsulates the problem of reconciling the American regime to the international system.

The United States was being pulled in two different directions by its foreign policy and its domestic reforms. The foreign policy pulled America outward, while reforms focused attention inward. Johnson tried, but failed, to balance, rather than weave together, the two policies because he was caught between the competing demands. He did not give the military leaders what they wanted because he did not want a wider war, yet at the same time he did not tell his economic advisors how much he was going to spend because he did not want domestic reforms to be damaged.[71] The gap between the two policy realms created consequences that can be can be seen in three broad areas: economic dislocations, particularly higher inflation; antiwar protests, which showed Americans' opposition to the military actions being taken in Vietnam; and Congress's opposition to the war on constitutional grounds.

The economic problems created by Johnson resulted from increased defense spending and flawed fiscal policy choices, which led to inflation. The economic problems influenced the foreign policy crisis because Johnson relied upon economic prosperity to sustain the undeclared war and domestic reforms. Without a vibrant economy, the domestic realm would feel the war's economic effect more quickly and deeply. In the external realm the international economy was no longer willing to tolerate the economic policies Johnson had chosen in order to finance his war and reforms.[72]

Under the Bretton Woods system the United States dollar was a reserve currency. As the international reserve currency the United States could "export" domestic inflation. Although warning signs had existed earlier, the system was working well until 1966, when the cost of Johnson's expansive policies became apparent. The Vietnam War spending, the Great Society, and other programs created economic dislocations that worsened the balance of payments internationally. When Kennedy took office, the balance of payments was a serious concern, but Johnson's economic and political programs created an insoluble problem.[73] Members of the international system, especially France, reacted to America's changed macroeconomic position: President Charles de Gaulle charged that the United States was using its economic hegemony to force others to bear the economic cost of America's immoderate foreign policy. He challenged the United States' economic position by attacking the dollar system by converting dollars into gold.[74] Although the

French leader failed to topple America's economic dominance, the domestic response to the balance-of-payments problem and the gold crisis of 1968 had an effect because they restrained Johnson's foreign policy.

Johnson believed he could sustain the economic prosperity needed to support both realms because his economic advisors, who were unaware of his military plans, suggested that the economy could afford domestic reforms and even sustain a mild defense buildup.[75] When the buildup threatened to overheat the economy in December 1965, these advisors quickly suggested a tax increase, but Johnson resisted.[76] If Johnson raised taxes to restrain the economy or pay for the war, it would disrupt the tenuous balance he had been trying to achieve. The need for a tax increase to restrain the expanding economy eventually forced Johnson to change his foreign policy in Vietnam. As Kettl pointed out: "Johnson and his economic advisers overestimated how easy it would be to apply fiscal stimulus—and underestimated how difficult it would later be to apply restraint."[77] The politico-economic struggle over taxes mirrored the politico-military struggle in Vietnam. In the economic realm Johnson overestimated his ability to restrain the economy and underestimated his ability to stimulate the economy. In Vietnam Secretary of State Rusk and Johnson underestimated North Vietnam's resolve and overestimated the American public's patience.[78]

In Vietnam the politico-military strategy of an undeclared, limited war required the president to find the proper amount of coercion to avoid World War III but still do enough to stop North Vietnam. In the economic struggle at home the president had to find the proper mix of fiscal and monetary policy to bring inflation under control but still maintain economic growth. Although the economy grew, it could not meet the demands in each realm, which created a long-term inflation that harmed both the American and the international economies. Economic growth sustained the minimal consensus that allowed Johnson to balance the policies, but when that prosperity disappeared, because of economic constraints, the balance disappeared.

In the language of Pocock's Machiavellian Moment we can see the international economic system as part of the stream of irrational events that threatened the republic's internal structure. At the same time we can see the Great Society legislation as a response to the threat of corruption and disintegration in the domestic realm. The undeclared war trapped Johnson between two rapidly diverging policy paths: domestic reforms and an undeclared war to defend a decent world order. In Pocock's language Johnson was trying to stave off corruption (thus the need for domestic reforms) and was simultaneously trying to stave off military threats to the decent world order (the stream of irrational events).[79] Johnson's attempt to balance the two realms was ineffective because he had not woven the domestic realm to resist the external realm's pressure. A problem in the periphery of the decent world order, South Vietnam was affecting the center, the United States. As Dean Rusk warned: "If you don't keep an eye on problems in the periphery, the periphery soon becomes the center."[80] At the same time, developments at the center—the possibility of corruption and disintegration domestically— threatened to undermine the republic's ability to handle the external realm. Rusk had contributed to this problem by connecting U.S. security to the security and stability of the decent world order. Instead of resolving the ten- sion between the two realms, the policy failed because Johnson's statesman- ship divided the domestic realm rather than unified it. The undeclared war appeared to allow Johnson to have domestic reforms and a decent world order because it promised him flexibility for each. To put it in a way that merges the language of Pocock and Rusk, the center can be secured if a repub- lic's universal principles can be promoted successfully to the periphery. Yet in the language of Machiavelli this would require the republic to expand to the whole world.

The tension between the external realm and the domestic realm helps us to understand, from a philosophical perspective, why Johnson wanted to keep war protests separate from Civil Rights protests. If they became connected in the public's mind, the center, upon which Johnson had built his minimal consensus, would dwindle from dissent over foreign policy and domestic policy. The stream of irrational events in the external realm would become connected to corruption that threatened the domestic realm. Moreover, the antiwar protestors could be understood, at the philosophical level, as reacting to the apparent imbalance between foreign policy and domestic policy and between the executive and legislative branches.[81] From the perspective of the Machiavellian Moment and the fear of corruption within the regime, the anti- war protestors revealed the threat of internal corruption and disintegration.

The antiwar protests and the Civil Rights movement, in their own ways, turned attention away from an expansive foreign policy to the domestic realm. The antiwar protests—their origin, effect, and history—have been explored in depth elsewhere.[82] What they represent is the domestic realm reacting to a stream of irrational events, an expansive foreign policy, and, indirectly, the executive expanding and centralizing its power at the expense of Congress and the people. The antiwar movement reflected a public divided between a flawed foreign policy and a domestic policy that had failed to live up to the Great Society's promise. The movement's size, scope, and intensity demonstrated the extent to which Johnson had failed to weave together a lasting domestic consensus. While the protests against the war gained in size and intensity, the peaceful Civil Rights marches were giving way to violence, as riots swept through several major cities in 1967.[83] As the antiwar and race riots continued, Johnson began to see them less as an issue of domestic reforms and more as an issue of law and order that could threaten his administration's legitimacy and stability, if not the regime. Reforms, initially begun to ward off corruption, unleashed pent-up demands that threatened to split the republic. The Great Society and the undeclared war were threatening, albeit unintentionally to transform the regime by unleashing forces of corruption and disintegration rather than reform, harmony, and progress.

Johnson's statesmanship lacked the moderation needed to prioritize or restrain his policy ambitions. Douglas Adair offers an insight into Johnson's personality. While writing about the founding fathers, Adair argued that their desire for fame had led them to greatness. In the same way we can see that Johnson's desire for glory, his concern for his legacy, contributed to his immoderation.[84] Johnson wanted to be the greatest president ever, and he pursued both guns and butter, so to speak, in part because he wanted to give the people what they wanted in the domestic realm and the external realm. He wanted to achieve fame as a great president who could bring a Great Society to the American people and uphold its external commitments. His pursuit of fame blinded him to the fundamental nature of each realm. The undeclared war was designed to avoid choosing between domestic and foreign policy, but it made that choice inevitable. As an ambitious politician at the head of a republic, Johnson faced a dilemma similar to that encountered by Rome's leaders. Rome faced the need to expand its reach in order to defend the domestic realm from external enemies and to maintain its internal harmony. Whereas Rome had to extend its territory to survive, Johnson expanded the economy and the political sphere to sustain the balance between the domestic realm and the external realm. America avoided Rome's fate because Johnson's immoderate statesmanship did not lead to internal corruption, disintegration, or collapse from external pressure.

The attempt to defend a decent world order did not mean, according to Rusk, that America was expanding its imperium.[85] By equating its security with the world order, America faced an implicit choice within its foreign policy that would have consequences for its regime.[86] Would America reorganize its domestic realm in order to support the expansive foreign policy, or would it accept its constitutional limits and bring the foreign policy into balance with the domestic regime? If the two realms could be kept in balance—a task requiring vision and moderation—then what Ronald Steel has called the "imperial temptation" could be avoided.[87]

Facing the near Machiavellian Moment, Johnson and America realized that the foreign policy commitment of a decent world order was beyond the capacity of a limited, or republican, domestic regime: an unlimited commitment could not be sustained without reorganizing the domestic realm. Johnson failed to balance the two realms because the world was in motion. Johnson's enemies, both the North Vietnamese and the condition of poverty affecting so many Americans, would not allow him the stability to develop a balance between domestic and foreign commitments. Machiavelli warned about what could happen to a republic forced to expand by choice or by necessity, such as Johnson attempted to do in seeking to balance the two realms: "I believe without any doubt; that if such an entity could be held in balance this way, the result would be a true body politic and true tranquility in a city. But since all human affairs are in continual motion . . . and reason does not always lead you to the many things to which necessity leads you, so that if a republic were to be capable of maintaining itself without expansion, and necessity forced it to expand, its foundations would be demolished and it would be brought to ruin very quickly."[88]

Necessity, brought on by the deteriorating military situation in South Vietnam and the need to defend his domestic reforms, led Johnson to expand his war effort in 1965. He feared that a foreign policy failure would undermine his domestic reforms and that the international consequences would threaten the United States. Johnson's statesmanship forced the republic, which otherwise could have remained intact, to expand by necessity.

The United States avoided the fate Machiavelli had warned against, but it suffered severe consequences nevertheless from avoiding the choice. At a constitutional level Johnson's attempt to maintain the balance between two expansive policies created a problem within the regime because it led him to strengthen the executive's role. The undeclared war created a constitutional tension between domestic concerns, exemplified by the work of the legislative branch, and the political world lying beyond the nation's borders, typically the domain of the executive branch. To prosecute the war and carry out domestic reforms required a strong executive, which placed Johnson in conflict with Congress. The challenge was not over the war's constitutionality but, rather, the constitutional limits of the president's power to use force in the external realm.[89] The larger question then, as now, is whether Congress could restrain an expansive foreign policy—in this case one that required the use of force and threatened the domestic realm's balance—without damaging the president's ability to conduct foreign affairs. The answer reflects the enduring tension between the branches but also leaves open the possibility that Johnson was a special case because his previous legislative skill and experience helped him dominate the legislative branch. In an ambiguous foreign policy situation such as the Vietnam War, a skilled executive such as Lyndon Johnson could invoke the decent world order, suggesting the righteousness of an open-ended foreign policy task, to expand his powers at the expense of Congress.

The legislative and executive branches must cooperate in order to have a sustainable foreign policy. If Congress does not feel that it has a role in setting and carrying out foreign policy, then the government will become divided. Instead of weaving the two realms together, Johnson tried to claim that the line between them had been erased, but this only gave priority to the external realm, in which the executive has greater latitude. He was not the first president to rely upon his presidential prerogative to exploit the perceived constitutional gap between domestic and foreign policy, which was created and exacerbated by overlapping constitutional powers. Harry Truman was the first to exercise the presidential prerogative in foreign policy: in an act of boldness that would have been unlikely before World War II, he committed American troops to the Korean war without the consent of the legislative branch.[90] Historically, the trend toward a more powerful executive had gained its strongest impulse from Franklin Roosevelt, when he requested, and was granted, emergency powers by Congress to deal with the Depression.[91] Although these powers were granted to address a domestic crisis, they were in place when the nation entered World War II and were transformed by it. The war changed the federal government and the presidency.

Johnson had seen the problems that Truman encountered with Congress after relying on his foreign policy prerogative and tried to avoid them by including Congress in the policy process. He sought to cover his foreign policy flank by obtaining Congress's mandate through an indirect approach. Rather than presenting his foreign policy and war aims through extensive and detailed debate, Johnson took advantage of a foreign policy crisis to obtain Congress's support more surreptitiously. Congress, in this moment of uncertainty, gave Johnson a mandate to defend against aggression in Southeast Asia. At the time Johnson assured Congress that it was unlikely that he would need to use the extensive powers granted to him. He wanted Congress to support, or at least not oppose, his foreign policy in order to keep it, and specifically the war, from harming his domestic policy. Johnson had seen how war had derailed Roosevelt and Truman's domestic reforms, and he wanted to avoid the same fate.

The Gulf of Tonkin Resolution appeared to give cover to his foreign and domestic policies. By linking the two realms, however, Johnson ultimately constrained his freedom of action in each. Tactically, Johnson increased his power without relying solely on his prerogative powers or his authority as commander in chief.[92] Strategically, his indirect approach created inflexibility. He could act, but anything that threatened his domestic reforms constrained his efforts. The tension between the external and domestic realms reflects the strained relationship between the legislative and executive branches over foreign policy.

Defending the decent world order, whose security had been identified with America's security, required a unified government. If the executive and the legislative branches are in agreement on the means and ends of foreign policy, such an expansive policy is possible. When the executive does not act in concert with Congress, problems can emerge. As the Vietnam War expanded, Congress became increasingly disenchanted, but it lacked the necessary tools to counter Johnson's statesmanship. Johnson had snared the legislature in his political web by linking war and reforms. Congress's ability to criticize the war was limited by its desire for reforms, but criticism by members of Congress was depicted as unwillingness to support American troops abroad. At the same time, members' concern for domestic legislation dominated their attention. Moreover, foreign policy criticism would pay few political dividends, and it might have serious political costs. Congress was unable to resist Johnson's statesmanship directly until a combination of foreign policy reversals, domestic crises, inflation, and riots weakened the president's domestic political support. Only then did Congress, particularly through its ability to control tax legislation, which directly affected the conduct of the war, move to restrain Johnson's foreign policy.[93]

Foreign policy reversals unraveled Johnson's minimal consensus. In a declared war Congress and the people grant the president extraordinary powers, which help the executive to weather setbacks. Even if this grant is only for the war's duration, it demonstrates clear support. In an undeclared war the clear granting of powers to the president by the people and Congress does not exist. The ambiguity over the limits to consent and support leaves the situation open to manipulation, and Johnson exploited this ambiguity masterfully. He worked to keep Congress, and even his own advisors, from becoming fully and explicitly aware of the war's true cost.[94] The attempt to avoid Congress's involvement came at a price. Constitutional problems over the limits to the president's powers became apparent when Congress's constitutional war powers were in danger of being usurped.

Johnson was aware that the undeclared war could create problems with Congress. To address these concerns, he asked the attorney general, Nicholas Katzenbach, whether as president he had the authority to use force in South Vietnam. Katzenbach responded that in the case of an "undeclared war" he had the authority. This answer raised a larger question concerning Congress's cooperation. Determining that this authority rested on a narrowly defined undeclared war avoided the need for the explicit consent of Congress demanded by a declared war. Congress's cooperation added up to a minimal consensus, which demonstrated an implicit consent. A declared war would have reflected explicit consent, demonstrating full consensus. Katzenbach's narrow answer, on the legitimacy of the undeclared limited war, focused the issue on the war being limited one because a declared war would have required unlimited authority, which Johnson did not want to openly request because it would have required greater congressional involvement. Johnson, according to Katzenbach's argument, was not seeking unlimited authority but simply unlimited authority to resist aggression in Southeast Asia. Katzenbach, like Rusk, saw the president's authority as unlimited in resisting aggression but restricted by its geographical application. Unlimited authority need only be granted for a limited goal. Katzenbach's narrow answer concerning an unlimited granting of authority to handle a limited problem hid the deeper constitutional, or political-philosophical, concern for pursuing unlimited authority for a problem with no clear end, defending the decent world order. By glossing over this important issue, Katzenbach did not take into account how Johnson would manage the minimal consensus, for a limited problem, in South Vietnam, where the strategic ambiguity was demanding a greater commitment. Thus, Katzenbach argued that the president could act because he was acting in a limited manner, and, so long as he did not move to an unlimited level, he need not worry about getting the support of Congress: "I believe it fair, although not uncontroversial, summary of nearly two centuries of history to say that the power to 'declare war' is the power to confer substantially unlimited authority to use the armed forces to conquer and, if necessary, subdue a foreign nation. Unless such unlimited authority is exercised by the President, his legal position in using the armed forces is sustainable."[95]

By highlighting the difference between a limited and an unlimited war, Katzenbach avoided discussing the constitutional principles and powers concerning the use of force. His emphasis on the nature of an unlimited war, a declared war, fit Johnson's stated intention to restrict the scope of the war. Johnson's minimal consensus would support the limited goal of an undeclared limited war but would not support anything more far-reaching. The narrow constitutional position was that the president had the authority to use force in limited situations, but it left ambiguous the larger constitutional question concerning the executive's relationship with Congress over the use of force. Katzenbach touched upon this concern when he warned that, where the president's and the Congress's authority overlapped, the president had to respect Congress's prerogatives: "There is authority, however, indicating that in areas where both Executive and Congressional powers are operative, the Executive must observe the limits of any Congressional authorization that may be enacted even though, in the absence of any authorization, his Executive powers under the Constitution would clearly go beyond the Congressional grant."[96]

Johnson exploited the gap between the external and internal realms by obtaining Congress's support through the Gulf of Tonkin Resolution. This gave him political leverage when dealing with limited goals but proved insufficient when a larger war became necessary. His well-crafted minimal consensus, which had given him the initial authority to intervene in South Vietnam, unraveled when the conflict required a larger effort.[97] In the language of Ely and Fisher, Congress had failed, at the initial stages, to do its job because, in granting unlimited authority to the president to defeat aggression, it did not curb executive authority, and, in not asserting its constitutional war powers, it did not defend its constitutional prerogative. Instead, Johnson demonstrated his political mastery by obtaining Congress's consent and then exploiting it to the fullest. Although he accomplished this through political skill, Johnson, by working very closely with the Congress, had blurred the line between the executive and the legislative branches as never before. Doris Kearns suggested that Johnson worked so closely with Congress that the legislative branch was in danger of being co-opted.[98] At the same time, the electorate was preoccupied with the domestic social and economic reforms. Because it does not require debate, Congress's involvement, or the public's direct consent, an undeclared war erodes the idea of democracy.[99] In 1965 a decision to go to war had been made, but the people and their representatives had been consulted only indirectly.

In Johnson's defense it has been argued that a declaration of war could have turned a limited war into a global nuclear war. Even as he avoided one extreme, Johnson accepted another by skirting a debate and a thorough consultation with Congress.[100] The difference between an undeclared war and a declared war mirrored the tension between the American regime, whose boundaries were limited, and the decent world order, which represented an unlimited commitment. Although Johnson's statesmanship blinded him to this problem, some critics saw it.

Perhaps the most famous critic of America's Vietnam policy was French president Charles de Gaulle. Secretary Rusk and de Gaulle discussed U.S. involvement in Vietnam during Rusk's visit to France in 1964.[101] De Gaulle criticized America's military effort in South Vietnam because he believed a limited war or policy to support an unlimited commitment to a decent world order would fail, and, if the limited effort failed, it would create pressure for a larger war. Although de Gaulle did not phrase the problem in terms of the American regime, his analysis of the middle-path, limited war, was insightful. During the meeting de Gaulle warned that Johnson's middle-path policy of an undeclared, limited war was untenable. If America were determined to win, it could not sustain an ambiguous, undeclared war because the pressure would build either to fight for all of Eurasia or to withdraw.[102] Defending the decent world order would require the United States to wage a "total" rather than a limited, undeclared war.[103] The country could not succeed simply by denying North Vietnam: this goal did not make military sense and would not create a domestic political consensus.

Rusk countered by arguing that the United States could calibrate its response to North Vietnam and sustain the strategy of denial.[104] For Rusk the limited goal of denying North Vietnam victory did not require a larger war: the United States had limited goals, so only limited means were needed. A declared war, or even a wider war, would be disproportionate to the goal of defending South Vietnam by simply denying North Vietnam victory.

De Gaulle, in hindsight, better understood what was at stake in defending a world order and trying to deny North Vietnam victory. If the military goal was simply to deny victory, why expend so much effort? If one is unwilling to expend the effort needed for victory, why fight? Even if the United States did not want to wage a wider war, de Gaulle argued, trying to deny North Vietnam victory would require increasing amounts of political, military, and economic resources, and this in turn would eventually create pressure to broaden the war. Johnson and the United States were expending resources to avoid the choice between a larger war and withdrawal, but this would create a problem for the American regime. To calibrate the war effort, America required an executive with a free hand. Johnson's flexibility was curtailed by his statesmanship because he did not possess a consensus that would allow him to command greater resources.

To put the difference between Rusk and de Gaulle in the terms of the Machiavellian Moment, de Gaulle understood the problem in the language of empire. An empire, having the imperial task of promoting world order, would need to make a total effort in order to defend it. A local or regional problem becomes a threat to the state identified with that order. De Gaulle was suggesting that "victory" would require the United States to become an empire because neither a limited solution nor a limited effort would succeed. If America prioritized its commitment to the world order over its domestic structure, something Johnson wanted to avoid, then it would be accepting an imperial task. Within the realm of practical politics, domestic reform would be ignored or delayed in order to sustain foreign policy goals that could be ongoing.

Rusk approached the problem in the language of a republic. His argument for a limited effort reflected the bounded or restrained universalism within the American republic: America would undertake a limited effort for a limited goal. Even though Rusk identified America's security with the security of the world order, he did not think it required a change in the domestic realm. De Gaulle had a broader understanding because he could anticipate the geopolitical consequences from the struggle in South Vietnam. The United States' effort in South Vietnam threatened the regional balance by challenging the Soviet Union and China at their doorsteps. Neither China nor the Soviet Union would want to see the United States establish a geopolitical foothold in Eurasia. To de Gaulle the United States could attempt to win in South Vietnam only by fighting for Eurasia. De Gaulle ended the line of questioning by asking, "Then what?" Was America ready to wage World War III for South Vietnam if necessary? If it was not prepared to confront this possible situation, why make the commitment? But, then, if U.S. security was tied to South Vietnam's, then the American leaders had to treat the conflict accordingly.

Rusk's vision of U.S. support for the decent world order reflected the limits within the domestic regime. The threat to the world order, and to the

United States, was not a mortal one, so it required a limited effort. The constraints created by the limited domestic realm, one unprepared for a war, hampered U.S. efforts to defend the decent world order. The middle-path strategy, which attempted to circumvent the constraints, ended up draining resources, dividing the American public, undermining the commitment to the world order, and, perhaps most pressingly, distracting attention from the central strategic relationship with the Soviet Union. The strategy pursued by Johnson and Rusk failed to convince the American public or America's allies that U.S. security and the security of the world order were at stake.

Through the middle-path strategy Johnson avoided a declared war, but his actions created tension within the domestic structure. Either the war would expand, requiring resources that would distort domestic economic and political structures, or the war would become a drawn-out "twilight war" requiring a long-term commitment, which would create a similar demand for resources. A twilight war contained political problems for a democracy. America could face political problems similar to those faced by France in its long-drawn-out war in Algeria in the mid-twentieth century. Although the situations were different (unlike France, the United States was not defending a colonial possession or a region closely identified with its homeland), one could shed light on the other. Douglas Cater raised such questions, in July 1965, when he asked how the American public would react to a war lasting twenty to thirty years.[105] He worried that it would strain the domestic structure. Just as France's domestic structure was challenged by the war, the United States faced a similar problem. To be sure, although neither civil war nor a military coup threatened, the Algerian scenario illustrates the dangers to a democracy attempting to carry out a long, twilight war.

One can speculate about whether France's experience informed his statements, but clearly de Gaulle recognized the immoderate nature of Johnson's foreign policy. He was critical of the U.S. war in South Vietnam, where after all France had been locked in a military struggle for many years, because it exemplified America's hegemonic relationship to the international system: to him the U.S. military effort in South Vietnam threatened the system's balance.[106] Aside from his direct criticism, de Gaulle tried to redress the problem by challenging America's international economic dominance.[107] The commitment to the world order and Johnson's statesmanship raised a question for U.S. foreign policy: Would America choose the foreign policy role of a limited government, a republic, or an unlimited government, an empire?[108] Having an executive who centralizes power, like Johnson in his attempt to consolidate power in the presidency to meet the war needs and carry out reforms, at the expense of a balanced government, is, according to Pocock, a sign of empire.[109] The United States and its top leader seemed caught between an external realm that was at war and a domestic realm organized on a peacetime structure. To uphold the external realm, the executive needs increased powers to order the domestic realm for fighting a war. A war in the external realm requires a unified government, not one divided between the executive and legislative branch over the threat, the response, and the goals. A domestic realm not organized for war, balanced or divided between internal and external responsibilities, is one not fully committed to the external realm. Even though domestic politics may continue during a war, a wartime president and a wartime government are different from their peacetime counterparts.[110] Johnson had pursued a policy of war on a minimal consensus, which proved insufficient to sustain the larger commitment of resources that the war demanded, and he refused to make a choice between the realms or to go to the public to obtain more resources.[111]

Johnson's statesmanship connected the foreign policy crisis to the domestic realm. As the middle path became untenable, the question in the background was whether the domestic regime would change to support the nearly unlimited foreign policy commitment. Johnson wanted to be both a peacetime, domestic issues president and a wartime, foreign policy president, but the longer he avoided the choice between war and reforms, the more stress he placed on the regime because more resources, and therefore a more centralized government, would be needed to succeed in both realms. Moreover, fighting the struggle for a decent world order required resources that meant domestic reforms had to be delayed or discarded. The American regime was divided between sustaining the principles of liberalism at home and abroad, but there was no consensus to bind the two realms together. To make up for the lack of consensus, Johnson in effect tried to centralize more power in the executive branch by relying upon his foreign policy prerogative. Instead of relying upon consent, consensus, and debate, Johnson pursued the war through indirection, subterfuge, and decree. The attempt to be a president of war and peace created a constitutional problem for the separation of powers and the balance of powers.

Robert Tucker posed, in a slightly different manner, a similar point concerning the tension between the American domestic regime and its foreign policy in his long essay *Nation or Empire?* He argued that to create and uphold a world order is a task for an empire. Tucker pointed to Rusk's statement—

in which he identified the United States' security with the security of the world order, which was under threat in South Vietnam—to argue that the country was taking on an imperial role.[112] America, according to Rusk, was responsible for the decent world order, and that responsibility created a persistent tension within American foreign policy: republic or empire? Would America expand its commitment to South Vietnam to defend its world order, thus reorganizing its domestic realm, or would it accept a more limited role within the international system?

As a republic, the constitution limited America's ability to organize its resources to fulfill both domestic reforms and the commitment to a decent world order. Although the two goals were derived from the same source of liberalism, they created conflicting demands that set them against each other. Instead of building a consensus to connect the two realms, Johnson tried to unite them simply by blurring the line separating them. The domestic consensus that he could have sought in the domestic realm would be replaced by a demand to follow his leadership in the external realm.

Johnson's middle path did not solve his problem but only prolonged it.[113] By connecting the two policy realms, domestic and foreign, Johnson became vulnerable to any setback in either realm, which destabilized the entire program. The Tet offensive of 1968 discredited Johnson's statements on the war's progress, and the race riots in 1967, together with the ongoing antiwar protests, undermined his domestic credibility. Johnson now faced the worst of both worlds. He was caught in a mix of foreign policy setbacks and domestic dissent. His statesmanship had put him at the mercy of Fortuna's wheel.

During Johnson's years as president, the war in Vietnam and the call for social reforms had put American society on two diverging paths. If both tasks were to be completed, a stronger central government—with an especially powerful executive—was needed in order to maintain the balance between the external and internal realms. Yet the constitutional structure was not designed to allow for such centralization in peacetime or without the direct consent of Congress and through it the American public.

If the executive branch begins to dominate the legislative branch, the balance necessary to sustain the republic is threatened.[114] A powerful executive can corrupt or destroy a republic. If the people become dependent upon the executive, rather than relying on a more representative government, the republican notions of virtue and self-government become tenuous. Discretionary moves by the executive can gradually begin to replace the rule of law. In short, greater centralization of power in the executive leads to a loss of democratic identity among the public. If the executive appears to be providing benefits to the people directly through tangible reforms, it can diminish the legislature's role.

Johnson's effort to pass a large amount of legislation for the Great Society in 1964 reflected a process that Pocock described from seventeenth-century England:

> But since the crucial disturbance was no longer taking place in the relation of lords to commoners, the balance being disturbed might better be seen as one of powers rather than estates; it was the executive that threatened to encroach upon the legislature, and the problem of patronage led to a century and more of debate concerning the separation and interdependence of the power of the constitution. To qualify as corruption, however, the encroachment of the executive must be seen as more than infringement of the sphere of legislative action.[115]

To be sure, there are important distinctions between each era. The argument here is that the centralization of power toward the executive, whether in terms of the Great Society or the undeclared war, threatened the republic's constitutional balance. The imbalance between the executive and the legislature, resulting from the diverging foreign and domestic realms and differences over reconciling them, reflected a divided American society. These problems revealed the political-philosophical tension between the American regime and its commitment to a decent world order. Through Johnson's statesmanship America's foreign policy—its role within the international system—was threatening the republic's internal balance.

The Vietnam War and the commitment to the decent world order challenged America's republican identity. Johnson could not avoid this problem because he and Rusk had justified their foreign policy by identifying it with America's domestic regime. Having identified America so strongly with the security of the world order—the Korean War was cited as a valid precedent—it appeared that the principles of the domestic regime were at stake in the Vietnam War. As Tucker points out, Rusk failed to convince the public that America's involvement in South Vietnam was vital to national security. The dilemma of the Johnson administration was its apparent inability successfully to represent the war in Vietnam either as a vindication of the principles of freedom and self-determination or as a measure indispensable for American security.[116]

According to Tucker "American power and leadership were to be employed to create and maintain a stable world order, an order that would enable peoples to work out their own destinies in their own way and, by enabling them to do so, thereby insure American security."[117] In responding militarily to North Korea's invasion of South Korea in 1950, however, America was acting "within" the international system because it possessed clear support—a mandate—from the United Nations. Johnson and Rusk lacked such a mandate in South Vietnam. To its critics America was acting "outside" the international system. This difference reflects, in part, why the United States confronted, in Vietnam, the question of nation or empire. By identifying its security with that of the world order, the United States confronted the limits of its identity within the international system. Either its security was bound up with the system and it had to act accordingly, or it was not bound to that system and could refashion its position as needed.

Truman and Johnson financed their war efforts differently. Truman, in effect, went to a wartime footing to increase the government's deficit. Johnson, by contrast, tried to finance the war on a peacetime budget. To be sure, Truman had to spend extra money because the military was ill prepared for war, and Johnson was able to get by with less because the military was still at a high post–World War II strength.[118] The difference was that Johnson had a great interest in protecting his domestic reforms. Moreover, Truman was acting in a relatively clear strategic situation, while Johnson was acting in a strategically ambiguous situation, which affected their respective access to finance and support. North Korea had invaded South Korea, so there was no question about the nature of the conflict. In Vietnam the situation was less straightforward: Was it a civil war or an intrastate war? Unlike Truman, Rusk and Johnson were unable to convince Congress and the American public to support the war's aims fully.

The emerging imbalance between the executive and legislative branches can be seen in how Congress reacted to the expanding demands of the war and the Great Society. As the chairman of the Senate Foreign Relations Committee, J. William Fulbright used his position to question the principles and argument sustaining America's commitment to South Vietnam and the decent world order. Similarly, Wilbur Mills, chairman of the Ways and Means Committee, questioned the war's economic effect and the cost of the Great Society. As the war expanded in cost and commitment, Congress and the American public questioned its effect on the domestic realm. Although Fulbright gained notoriety for questioning Johnson's policy and for raising important questions about America's role in the international system, Mills proved to be more effective. He was able to demonstrate that Johnson lacked Congress's support for financing an expansive domestic and foreign policy. The domestic economy forced Johnson to choose between war and reforms. Although Mills's role has been underappreciated, it reveals one aspect of the tension between the American regime and the international system created by Johnson's expansive foreign policy.[119]

Johnson had "sold" the undeclared war as a moderate approach to the problem of defending South Vietnam and the decent world order. Instead of solving the problem, the undeclared war only delayed it. The strategy left unanswered whether America would accept the full consequences of defending the world order as an extension of its security. The Machiavellian Moment meant America had to decide whether to remain a republic or to pursue an imperial role. An imperial task involved more than invading North Vietnam or waging World War III for Asia. The challenge was subtle and therefore more dangerous. For America to commit itself fully to defending the decent world order (by agreeing to stay in South Vietnam for twenty to thirty years, if necessary) would require a profound change within the domestic regime. To sustain an open-ended commitment without a declared war would alter the balance between the executive and the legislative branches. Unlike a declared war, in which the granting of power is bound by the terms of the declaration, the undeclared war lacks such a limit, which leaves it open to abuse by the branch of government that carries it out, typically the executive. The alternative, republican position was for America to step back from identifying its security with the security of the world order.

America's dilemma was not simply a choice between foreign and domestic policy. The problem went to the heart of America's purpose within the world. How did America understand the relationship between its domestic regime and its role in the international system? Robert Tucker argued that the type of foreign policy that the United States followed would reflect and affect the domestic regime:

> The significance of the debate is not that it raises the issue whether foreign or domestic policy ought to be primary, at least, not in a general sense. Instead, it raises the issue whether a certain kind of foreign policy should continue to be affirmed on behalf of a policy that may involve the use of force to vindicate interests that, at best, are only indirectly related to the security of America (and that are increasingly held to have little relation even to the traditional purpose of America). At the root of the debate over American foreign policy is the fundamental question that has arisen

for every nation, which has achieved a certain degree of pre-eminence and relative freedom: nation or empire?[120]

The problem identified by Tucker can be seen in Johnson's inability to create a domestic consensus to support his expansive foreign policy. Johnson's failure was due in part to his methods but also to the constitutional structure. Even though the republic managed to handle this crisis, the underlying problem created by the undeclared war remains. By blurring the line between the external and internal realms, Johnson was threatening to blur the lines between the branches responsible for each. To put it in terms of practical politics, Johnson was usurping Congress's constitutional war powers.

In the domestic realm the legislative branch has dominance (the president does not make laws), and within the external realm the executive is given great latitude (the president executes foreign policy). A republic requires a sharp demarcation between the domestic, the realm of citizenship and relative stability, and the external, the realm of irrational behavior. An empire recognizes neither the distinction between the domestic realm and the external nor a concept of a divided government checked and balanced. Tucker argues that the primacy of external over internal for an empire means that a nation's security interest will determine its domestic regime as a nation or an empire. For a republic the external environment alone does not determine the choice because it tries to calibrate its foreign policy to its domestic regime.

Nor is it sufficient when dismissing the relevance of the republic-empire question simply to reaffirm that the American dream remains domestic. If there is necessarily a point—for America, as for all nations—at which foreign policy has primacy over domestic policy, the all-important issue is the manner in which the security requirements of the nation are conceived.[121]

America had to reconcile its limited domestic structure to an expansive foreign policy in the external realm. As early as the fourth century in Athens, Thucydides addressed the same problem. Although he focused on Athens and the problem of reconciling its domestic democracy with an external empire, his observations give us an insight into the problem faced by the United States. In book 8 of the *History of the Peloponnesian War* he describes how Athens became corrupted when the political logic justifying empire, the external realm, began to guide domestic politics. The politics of expediency replaced the pursuit of honor and the common good within the domestic sphere.[122] In the U.S. case critics feared that the problems created in the external realm by the war—violence, drug use, the breakdown of authority—

were filtering into the domestic realm. Although Johnson and America never faced the threat of dissolution and corruption that was faced by Athens, the antecedents to this problem—the near Machiavellian Moment—created by Johnson's statesmanship were becoming apparent.

For three years Johnson had balanced diverging foreign and domestic policy paths.[123] Yet he failed to weave together a consensus between what he believed the public wanted externally, to fight communism and defend liberty,[124] and what they wanted domestically, a Great Society and economic equality. Rather than resolving the tension between these ends or making a choice, necessity—in the form of the Tet offensive of 1968 and the concurrent domestic economic crisis—forced Johnson's hand.

After the Tet offensive Johnson made a choice. To send more troops would be to admit that previous policy had failed after so many claims of success. If he did not send more troops, the best he could hope for was that the strategic situation would stabilize. When Johnson refused to send the requested amount of troops (he did send some), he created a strategic status quo that Nixon inherited. Escalation would no longer be a strategic option and would only exist, if at all, as a short-term tactical option. Johnson implicitly accepted defeat when he decided to de-escalate. Only one strategic choice based upon the political divisions within the United States remained: withdrawal. Johnson had chosen the domestic realm, and his decisions determined his successor's choices. By choosing to decrease U.S. involvement in the war, Johnson ensured that the next president faced a nearly insurmountable task if he wanted to reverse that decision. Had Nixon wanted to escalate the conflict, he would have found it difficult, if not politically impossible, to send more troops to sustain a conflict that the American public (and Johnson, through his decision) believed to be unwinnable. Moreover, the next president would be the one to complete the withdrawal process and shoulder the burden, no matter how fast or slow it went. It would not matter who started it, all that would be remembered is who was there at the end.

3

HENRY KISSINGER:
MACHIAVELLI'S ADVISOR

In January 1968 the Tet offensive changed American foreign policy at two interconnected levels, one political, the other philosophical. At the philosophical level the liberal internationalism justifying America's commitment to South Vietnam had been discredited. The apparent failure to defend the decent world order revealed the limits of America's power. The philosophical crisis of liberal internationalism was linked, because of Johnson's failure to balance domestic reforms and foreign policy commitment, to the foreign policy crisis. America's ability to support its foreign policy was weakened, and the American public was divided between domestic goals and foreign policy responsibilities. As the gap between America's capabilities and its commitments widened, America's relationship to the international system became increasingly uncertain.

Johnson left a problematic foreign policy legacy. The Vietnam War had bankrupted the foreign policy philosophy of liberal internationalism, and foreign policy exigencies had affected the domestic realm. Liberalism, the guiding philosophy within American politics, was under attack as American society struggled to reconcile the conflicting goals of war and social reforms.[1] The foreign policy crisis left tangible problems, including domestic inflation, imbalances within the international monetary system, and a crisis in the United States' balance of payments.[2] The Vietnam War had shattered the post–World War II consensus.[3] When Richard Nixon came into office, he confronted a difficult situation because two main pillars of foreign policy—domestic political support and domestic economic vitality—were under strain. The American public, disillusioned by the Vietnam War and the inadequacy of social reforms, appeared to be turning toward disengagement, if not isolationism,[4] and the inward turn was reinforced by the domestic economic problems. The goal of widespread economic prosperity, the promise of which Johnson had used to sustain a minimal consensus and to balance domestic and foreign policy, was undermined by the inflation unleashed through the mismatched policies of war and reforms.

In late 1968 the public wanted a change in the foreign policy that had led the United States into Vietnam.[5] Richard Nixon had been elected in part because he promised to resolve the foreign policy uncertainty by ending America's involvement in the Vietnam War. He would withdraw from Vietnam without repudiating America's commitment to the international system. America's role in the world would be reaffirmed at a limited level, something that a public disillusioned by the war could more easily support. He needed public support to pursue the active foreign policy needed to withdraw from Vietnam and to reorder the nation's foreign policy commitments. Domestic support had to consist of more than just withdrawal; it had to include a complete restructuring.

Even though the United States was not on the brink of collapse, the metaphor of a business facing bankruptcy offers a thematic snapshot of Nixon and Kissinger's foreign policy philosophy. As "creditors" taking over a highly productive but mismanaged enterprise, they understood that America had become focused on one foreign policy "product line": the Vietnam War. The war was distracting the country from other productive enterprises, such as developing NATO, repairing the economy, and maintaining the central military balance with the Soviet Union. While America was preoccupied with the war, competitors in these areas had innovated and modernized. Nixon and Kissinger had to devise a policy that would sell off a wasting asset, U.S. involvement in South Vietnam, and restructure foreign policy to deal with the changed international system. Their response, the so-called Nixon Strategy, would attack the problem in two interconnected ways: through détente and through the principles of Nixon Doctrine. The public would be reconciled to a continued American presence in world affairs, albeit at a more limited level, and the "market"—its allies—would be reassured that America would meet its commitments. The Nixon Strategy would also warn competitors that America had not disengaged or given up on its productive ambitions.

To expand the business metaphor, the American public, as shareholders, had to be reassured that the new policy would reform the broken system by resolving the outstanding problem. The American public wanted Nixon to withdraw from Vietnam but still achieve an honorable and durable peace.[6] The two strands of the Nixon Strategy thus complemented each other.[7] Détente reflected the limits of the United States' power and recognized the Soviet Union's emergence as a global military rival, and the Nixon Doctrine would demonstrate that the United States remained committed to its allies and would act on behalf of global security when necessary. Rather than taking a central role, as it had in Vietnam, America would support a regional ally in a military conflict. The Nixon Strategy's two elements were designed to overcome the gap between commitments and capabilities and the gap between foreign and domestic policy that had plagued Johnson's foreign policy. Through a process of negotiations and strategic retrenchment, Nixon and Kissinger would give the United States diplomatic and military freedom of action by withdrawing from South Vietnam.[8] Yet they were well aware that dramatic changes could undermine their efforts by creating doubts about America's other commitments. If the United States withdrew too rapidly from Vietnam, it might create the impression that its other commitments were similarly vulnerable. But, if withdrawal took too long, the domestic realm would remain divided. Nixon and his secretary of state had to find a measured middle ground, an approach that would allow for gradual disengagement for the sake of maintaining U.S. credibility but which was rapid enough to appease the American public and give the administration the freedom of action it needed to pursue other foreign policy challenges.

Nixon's State of the World addresses, which Kissinger had a central role in drafting,[9] presented a dramatic break from Rusk's foreign policy philosophy of liberal internationalism. Commentators have noted that it is hard to determine where Nixon stopped and Kissinger began, yet Kissinger has insisted that Nixon was the main architect behind the administration's policies.[10] The State of the World addresses, which Nixon used to present his foreign policy philosophy, were unlike anything attempted by a previous administration. Just as Nixon's addresses presented his foreign policy philosophy, Kissinger's speeches and statements as secretary of state revealed the philosophy at work behind his foreign policy thinking. In the State of the World addresses Nixon expressed the concept of the international structure of peace, and Kissinger, as secretary of state, developed this idea. Nixon and Kissinger would restructure the international system to achieve the peace and stability that had eluded Johnson and his top advisor by accepting the limit to America's power. America could neither take responsibility for the system nor withdraw. What Nixon and Kissinger needed to find was a moderate way to extricate America from Vietnam and yet keep it involved in shaping the international system.[11]

The foreign policy consensus that supported the belief that America should intervene in the Third World to oppose communism and promote economic and political liberalism abroad was challenged by a foreign policy view that saw America as having a limited international role.[12] The problems faced within the foreign policy arena mirrored those at home, as the public continued to be divided to the point, in the word of some commentators, of unraveling.[13] The foreign policy crisis had created a crisis of confidence that raised questions about America's exceptionalism.[14] If the United States was to extricate itself from Vietnam and heal its internal divisions, it needed to change its foreign policy.

Nixon and Kissinger set forth a new foreign policy philosophy that moved away from liberal internationalism. John Lewis Gaddis argues that their innovation was to return to themes presented by George Kennan in 1947.[15] Although their approach to dealing with the Soviet Union's challenge to the United States shared similarities with Kennan, Nixon and Kissinger pursued an innovative and ambitious strategy, best exemplified by his decision to open diplomatic relations with China.[16]

The move toward greater openness with China signaled a fundamental change from Johnson's foreign policy and from the post–World War II foreign policy framework. The ideology behind containment guided Johnson's foreign policy, but Nixon and Kissinger believed it had become inflexible. Nixon argued that ideological fervor had to be lessened because "the postwar period in international relations has ended."[17] If the United States was to manage the changes in the international system and meet the Soviet Union's emerging power, it needed diplomatic flexibility. To accomplish this task, Nixon rethought ideology's role within United States foreign policy. His annual foreign policy statements developed the pragmatic approach to foreign policy that emphasized power and realpolitik, in an effort to avoid Johnson's foreign policy excesses. Unlike Johnson and Rusk, who stressed the decent world order, Nixon and Kissinger would focus on managing the central strategic balance. Their concern was with the actual underlying balance of power rather than the ideological structure of an idealized world order. Nixon would develop a new structure of peace to handle the Soviet Union. Even the contrast between Rusk's "decent world order" and the aims of Nixon's "stable structure of peace" shows the degree of difference in their views of America's role in the international system. For the sake of the decent world order America had taken a direct and unilateral approach in its defense. To achieve a stable structure of peace America would manage the structure without imposing its will or preferences.

Nixon needed freedom of action to bring the foreign and domestic realms into balance, but it required moderation. If Nixon tried to bring foreign policy into balance by withdrawing too quickly, expectations might develop a momentum that he could not control.[18] Nixon had to judge how far he could push the electorate to accept the new foreign policies, such as détente and the reorganization of American foreign policy, while maintaining the support gained by withdrawing from Vietnam.

Like Johnson, Nixon did not fully succeed in developing the stable structure of peace he envisioned because domestic challenges, created in part by his statesmanship, undermined the structure. The larger societal problems created by the Vietnam War set the stage, but ultimately it was Nixon's statesmanship that created a crisis of authority and legitimacy within the American regime. The foreign policy crisis had left America uncertain, confused, and lacking confidence in its world role, and Watergate, a domestic crisis affecting the national government at the highest levels, deepened the crisis of confidence by creating a crisis of authority. The two crises fueled each other and weakened the public's trust in the government. When Daniel Ellsberg, acting as a whistleblower, released *The Pentagon Papers* to the New York Times in 1971, its revelations put the government under close scrutiny by the press and the people.[19] Even though Nixon was responsible for his actions, it is important to remember Watergate's context within the problems surrounding the Vietnam War.[20] As the Watergate crisis unfolded, Nixon became increasingly distracted from foreign policy. His statesmanship, his use of secrecy, and the further centralization of power brought some foreign policy successes to Nixon and Kissinger, but they came at the cost of creating domestic mistrust and opposition to his methods, which undermined his ability to maintain a foreign policy consensus.[21] Without Nixon being actively involved, the stable structure of peace would be hard to sustain. To offset this potential problem, Nixon, at this critical moment, nominated Henry Kissinger to be his secretary of state.[22]

Kissinger would spend his tenure unraveling the nation's foreign policy problems and their relationship to the domestic crisis of authority. He had to uphold the foreign policy structure, resolve the immediate crisis, and sustain the domestic consensus even as the president's authority eroded. Without a strong president to lead and defend foreign policy, Kissinger faced a difficult task in trying to develop new policy initiatives. Instead of extending and see-ing through the structure in place from Nixon's first term, Kissinger worked to preserve existing initiatives. He had to rally the public's confidence to support the United States' world role and close the rift between the legisla-tive and executive branches that was created by Johnson's, and later Nixon's, imperfect statesmanship.

During his confirmation hearings Kissinger revealed his great expertise about the international problems the country faced and his strategy for deal-ing with them. He spoke of the need for more openness regarding the foreign policy process and the need to institutionalize, and thereby stabilize, it within the bureaucratic structure.[23] He attempted to placate a skeptical Congress. At the same time he sought to involve the foreign policy bureaucracy in in-stitutionalizing and formalizing the foreign policy structure. Domestically, his statements served to remind the public that the United States still had an important international role. Internationally, his statements served two functions: to reassure the nation's allies and to warn its opponents.

Kissinger defended his foreign policy approach against domestic critics and defended the structure of peace from international pressures. But his greatest challenge came in building a domestic consensus. Even though all administrations face the task of building domestic consensus and combating international pressures, Kissinger's situation was hardly typical because of the crisis of authority created by the Vietnam War and Nixon's Watergate problems. He had to have the public's support to sustain the foreign policy structure that had been developed in the first term. Even as Kissinger re-minded America of its limits, he had to encourage the nation to remain active within the international system. Vietnam had to be moved to the periphery of American foreign policy to reduce the domestic divisions that limited free-dom of action abroad: domestic dissent over foreign policy might encourage disengagement from the international system and limit America's ability to influence the central strategic balance with the Soviet Union.[24]

Nixon and Kissinger worked to bring foreign policy into balance with domestic policy, without simply sacrificing the former to the latter. Their attempt to reassert the balance rested upon a clear distinction between the two realms. As Johnson had done, Nixon treated the Constitution as a uni-tary document, wherein powers granted in the external realm were connected to those in the domestic realm.[25] Unlike Johnson, Nixon had a foreign policy consensus that was sharply differentiated from the consensus for domestic policy. Whereas Johnson had attempted to blur the lines between foreign and domestic policy and link them without first achieving consensus, Nixon created a consensus for each realm, which allowed him to calibrate policy in each. Nixon pursued a relatively liberal domestic policy that followed, with key differences in its implementation, Johnson's policies.[26] In foreign policy Nixon departed dramatically from the philosophy that had guided Johnson and his secretary of state. Although he continued and expanded Johnson's presidential prerogative in foreign policy, he pursued a more limited role for the executive branch in setting domestic policy.[27] To put the comparison simply, Johnson pursued a very active domestic policy and understood foreign policy through the prism of domestic policies; Nixon pursued a very active foreign policy and understood domestic policy through the prism of foreign policy. One could argue quite simply that Johnson's failure in Vietnam was an outgrowth of his approach to domestic policy. In contrast, Nixon's Watergate fiasco, a problem created with the U.S. executive branch itself, was an outgrowth of his approach to foreign policy.[28] Johnson and Nixon both relied upon their presidential prerogative powers, which unleashed the struggle over the limit to the executive's power and over the balance between the different branches of government that continues to this day.[29]

HENRY KISSINGER'S WORLDVIEW

What exactly was Kissinger's understanding of the international arena? Kissinger believed that the international system was undergoing a period of dramatic and fundamental change. Although Rusk had made a similar claim concerning his tenure, America's domestic weakness added a special urgency to Kissinger's claim. The Soviet Union had emerged as a superpower and a global rival to the United States. America was not only divided over the direction and content of its foreign policy, but its most powerful rival was becoming increasingly active in the international system. Beyond the central strategic balance the system was changing in other ways. De-colonization, which had begun in the early 1960s, continued to add new states to the international system. During America's involvement in the Vietnam War the international system had changed politically and economically. America's economic weakness contributed to the economic crises that were transforming the international system. The food and petroleum crises, which attacked the West's economic vitality, threatened to destabilize the world economy. Their effects demonstrated a strategically dangerous dependency on strategically valuable natural resources. America had to adjust its foreign policy to meet these challenges.

Kissinger believed that the world was on the brink of something new. The question was whether it would fall into chaos or ascend into an era of cooperation and community.[30] The main theme in Kissinger's worldview was change. A response had to be made that would restrain or contain instability and encourage order within the international system yet without requiring America to undertake a unilateral world-ordering mission. Change presented a threat and an opportunity. The threat was disorder, born of competition and America's domestic divisions, and it undermined the nation's ability to act internationally. The opportunity was the chance to develop a new structure of peace that reflected the changes in America and in the international system. A new system was needed to bring stability and avoid a new era of renewed competition.[31] A stable structure of peace would contain and channel change. Whereas Rusk had seen his task as channeling change to follow the principles of the UN Charter's preamble, Kissinger argued that change had to be undertaken along the lines of the balance of power within the international system. Rusk viewed the international system through the UN Charter, while Kissinger, through his study of history, approached the new structure of peace and how it would be implemented in a more strategic way. The test for Kissinger, as it was for the statesmen he had studied, was being able to recognize the potentialities of a situation and use them to accomplish his goals.[32]

A central question at the international level was how to manage the Soviet Union's emergence as a superpower. Nixon and Kissinger sought to use America's power to keep the Soviet Union from acting as a revolutionary state that might transform the international system. At the same time, they could not distort the international system by acquiescing or overreacting. Their structure of peace would accommodate the Soviet Union's power without involving direct conflict and by attending to the changes taking place within the United States and the international system.[33] At the domestic level the question was whether Nixon and Kissinger could develop a domestic consensus to reconcile America to the changed international system—that is, withdraw from its commitment to the decent world order—without creating further instability.

Kissinger has often said that in the post-Vietnam era American foreign policy—the relationship of the domestic realm to America's role in the world—was at a watershed.[34] The Vietnam War eroded the domestic consensus that had supported America's effort to uphold the decent world order. The nation and its role in the international system faced a profound challenge.[35] Support for an ambitious, unlimited goal, such as the decent world order, appeared to be weak at best. Instead, Kissinger worked to develop a consensus that would support an active, if limited, foreign policy to maintain America's involvement in global politics. An activist foreign policy, based upon the idea of America's exceptionalism, had been discredited in Southeast Asia. Yet America had to remain involved in the system. The nation faced a choice: it could turn inward and reduce its foreign policy activity, or it could continue a limited, although active, world role. The near Machiavellian Moment raised the philosophical question of whether America could, as it had in the past, justify its world role by its commitment to exceptionalism. America's identity both domestically and internationally had been shaped by its claims to exceptionalism. According to Kissinger, America had to accept the limits of its power and could not indulge in idealistic notions within foreign policy. Exceptionalism had a role within the United States, but it was not a guide to conducting international behavior or a basis for a stable structure of peace. Kissinger also understood that neither the awareness of the limits of power nor skepticism concerning America's moral mission could justify inaction. Refusing to act was as dangerous as acting immoderately in foreign policy.

Kissinger believed that the United States had to reassess its ability to shape the international system and work within these limits, and he continuously stressed that a stable world order could be developed if states would recognize the limits of their power to shape the international system and refrain from trying to dominate the system or change it through military force. Their self-restraint, reinforced by the external pressure created by other states, would lead to stability, but stability was not based simply upon equilibrium of power. Giving states a stake in the system's stability by conferring legitimacy would augment the equilibrium of power. A structure based upon self-restraint would last longer than one imposed by one state but would nevertheless fail if it did not give states a reason to support it. Thus, self-restraint and legitimacy would give the system stability and durability, but the approach had drawbacks. First was the difficulty of making states recognize the limits of their power. Second was to give states a stake in the international structure without undermining that hard-won self-restraint. If states did not recognize the limits to their power, conflict over the structure of the state system and their role within it would remain problematic. The key to the new structure of peace was how it handled possible changes to the system, which were, pragmatically speaking, inevitable.

Political change in the international system often results from conflict, while harmony or cooperation in achieving change is usually the exception, especially when the world is divided into rival ideological and power blocs. Instability could not be transcended by one power alone. Order could not be created by one state, a Leviathan imposing its will, because no state possessed that power. Despite the United States' great wealth and military might, it had failed to defend the decent world order in South Vietnam. Kissinger, unlike Rusk, did not see the UN world order as a viable standard to use in working through the problem of conflict and instability within the international system. Instead, he tried to address violent change by making power and self-interest as the low, but solid, foundation of the international system and the central United States–Soviet Union relationship. The conflict between these states and their respective ideologies would be dampened, according to this argument, because behavior would not be measured against the absolute standard of a decent world order. By removing or reducing the role of ideology within the international system, Nixon and Kissinger believed that conflict could be reduced and stability developed. States could then move from the question of survival, defending their ideological commitments, to questions of the quality of life within the international system. According to Kissinger: "As the world grows more stable, we must confront the question of the ends of détente. As the threat of war recedes, the problem of the quality of life takes on more urgent significance."[36]

Nixon and Kissinger would move the conflict from an abstract, although potentially absolute, level of ideology to a more practical and limited level of power. While the new level was easier to manage because it presented clear boundaries, it did not remove the underlying conflict. Attention shifted from a state's ideology to its geopolitical position. Ideology would be secondary to the geopolitical question of whether a state could take a position militarily that would undermine regional stability and threaten the system.

Geopolitics and the geopolitical relationship between the United States and the Soviet Union informed another part of Kissinger's worldview.[37] If the international system was to develop stability, there needed to be equilibrium within the central relationship between the United States and the Soviet Union. This did not simply mean equality of power; achieving equilibrium to Henry Kissinger meant establishing a situation in which no state could, or wanted to, transform the system. The move away from foreign policy guided by ideology, in which a state may continue to harbor reasons for wanting to transform the system, to a policy intended to establish equilibrium allows stability to emerge. From an ideological standpoint it was a zero-sum conflict. A geopolitical approach, by focusing on stability and equilibrium, would benefit all parties. Kissinger and Nixon, unlike those making foreign policy in the previous administration, were quite explicit about their geopolitical interests.[38] The central relationship between the United States and the Soviet Union, which now extended to all parts of the globe, guided their policies.[39] Stability and equilibrium, as policy goals within different regions and the world, would ideally demarcate the limits to America's involvement in the international system. The United States would intervene against threats to the balance of power rather than ideological threats to a decent world order.[40] According to Geoffrey Sloan, Nixon and Kissinger were pursuing a discriminating form of globalism in their foreign policy, in contrast to Johnson and Rusk's apparent pursuit of absolute globalism.[41]

Kissinger argued that ideology had made Johnson's foreign policy inflexible. By reducing its ideological content, Kissinger sought to create more room to move.[42] Even though he was less encumbered by agreeing to remain ideologically ambiguous within the realm of global politics, Kissinger still faced the problem of having to uphold a global foreign policy. Ultimately, he exchanged one form of globalism, an ideological mission, for another that was structured on the balance of power. Kissinger, like Rusk before him, still faced the task of distinguishing between core and peripheral threats. Nixon's secretary of state believed he could calibrate a correct and limited, or proportional, response because he was measuring the threats according to their urgency in terms of power, not ideology.[43] A key concern was to determine when a country in fact threatened the balance of power within the context of the structure of peace.

Measuring power and identifying core or peripheral threats was complicated because economic issues began to affect national security. Economic issues such as the price and availability of petroleum emerged unexpectedly as a national security concern. Similarly, at the military level the United States faced a bipolar world, in which they shared with the Soviet Union the rank of superpower. The economic system, however, was more complicated. The economic imbalances and rivalries reflected the changed forms of international power. Germany and Japan had developed into economic rivals to the United States, and China had emerged as a geopolitically important state. Nixon and Kissinger recognized and responded to these developments. Nixon, at one point, stated that the world had five centers of power.[44] Although he may have been overstating the case at the time, he was accurate in assessing how economic developments would have political consequences for the central relationship between the United States and the USSR. The diffusion of political and economic power was making the world more complicated for policy makers.[45]

The diffusion of power and transformative political and economic developments created economic interdependence among nations. Two economic crises, over food and petroleum, demonstrated to Kissinger that the world's increased economic interdependence was strategically significant. Although economic interdependence had always existed, America's dependence on petroleum revealed its immediate strategic consequences. The economic developments added a layer of complexity to the international system and the calculus of power within it. The Western democracies, as the major petroleum consumers, were vulnerable to an interruption in production, while a new region of interest, the Middle East, and its primary commodity, petroleum, occupied America's attention at a time when it was trying to shore up its international political and strategic position.[46] Even as Nixon tried to reduce America's commitment in Southeast Asia, the geopolitical and economic developments were demanding that America take an active role in a new region—the Middle East. The petroleum crisis was threatening the international and regional balance of power. Through the petroleum crisis the oil-producing states in the region quickly acquired vast amounts of wealth, which put a strain on the geopolitics of the region. Literally overnight these relatively poor states became immensely wealthy. This newly attained wealth would give these states the power to attempt to reorganize the region. It also created problems within the domestic realms of the newly wealthy states. Political instability occupied much of Kissinger's attention.[47] He had to focus beyond the "high politics" between the great powers to take into account the "low politics" of economics and strategic resources.

Unlike the decent world order that America had pursued in Vietnam, America's attention to the Middle East was driven by the need to defend a geopolitically important region and reflected America's economic vulnerability. Kissinger had to convince a skeptical public that the nation still needed an active foreign policy in which its interests, rather than its ideals, were at stake. Nixon and Kissinger were aided in their quest for consensus because the petroleum crisis affected all Americans. Here was a problem that was palpable to the American public. Yet Nixon and Kissinger could succeed only if their strategy did not undermine the ideals underpinning the domestic realm.

Kissinger tried to manage economic and political developments by using short-term improvements to dampen or eliminate the worst excesses being practiced by particular nations. A long-term policy had to fit within the structure of peace that was being developed within the international system. The structure would help to control the forces of change, such as revisionist states or challenges to the supply of vital resources, by giving them a mechanism, rather than relying upon ad hoc arrangements, to address any problems. Kissinger saw the structure as reflecting the balance of power within the international system. This view was reinforced by his academic writings. His work on the British foreign secretary Viscount Castlereagh, Prince Clemens von Metternich, and German chancellor Otto von Bismarck had influenced his views about international relations. In the essay "The White Revolutionary: Reflections on Bismarck" he explored how Bismarck manipulated the revolutionary elements in the European state system to achieve his policy goals.[48] Kissinger, like Bismarck, was interested in turning power into self-restraint in order to achieve stability. Stability could be achieved by understanding the "contending forces [and] [b]y manipulating competing antagonisms."[49] One way to do this was to include states that had previously tried to transform the international system. Kissinger argued that the new structure would encourage them to support the system because they would have a stake in its stability. Yet this proactive strategy could work only if an equilibrium of power existed to hold in check any states that attempted to change the system through force.

What precisely were Kissinger's goals for this world order? Establishing stability was, of course, a primary goal. In his writings and speeches Kissinger had argued that a shared concept of legitimacy and equilibrium of power were needed to create stability.[50] States seeking to change the system would be restrained by the issue of legitimacy; in other words, if a state's behavior supported the balance of power within the system, it would be considered legitimate.[51] To the extent that it was something they desired, and could lose, legitimacy could serve as a restraint. To be sure, legitimacy's power to keep all the world's nations in check depended upon how much they valued its benefits. A key question was what would be the minimum degree of adherence to legitimacy that would denote their acceptance. Kissinger saw the standard as being whether their behavior supported stability within the balance of power.

In this way the balance of power would reinforce legitimacy by restraining states that tried to change the system by force. Force, which could be used against revisionists, would be channeled by legitimacy.

Stability, a goal for the international system, would be based upon a shared understanding of the system's order and legitimacy.[52] Whereas Johnson and Rusk fought a war on the system's periphery, Kissinger and Nixon saw an order developing from the central United States–Soviet Union relationship and extending to the whole system. Order connected the center and periphery. States at the center seeking to maintain stability and legitimacy would, according to the theory, act to restrain regional problems. If stability could be achieved at the center, it would be the basis for dealing with instability in the periphery.[53] The central relationship would be stabilized by the equilibrium of power. The central powers did not have to come together from shared interests but from self-interest and self-restraint born of the awareness of the other state's power.[54] By recognizing the constraints created by the countervailing power of others, states would see that their power to change the system by force was limited. Self-restraint would lead to stability only if it was embedded within a shared concept of legitimacy.

Legitimacy was limited to the state's external behavior. Kissinger sought to separate domestic politics, in which domestic legitimacy is determined, from international politics, in which he was concerned with a state's external behavior.[55] Aware that legitimacy was important for states such as the Soviet Union, whose domestic political behavior was often criticized, Kissinger believed that such states wanted the international system to legitimate their political standing.[56] He tried to use this desire for legitimacy to modify their external behavior. How Kissinger separated domestic and international behavior reflected, in a different context, how Nixon separated domestic and foreign policy.[57] International legitimacy was a basis for states to coexist, not a device for understanding constitutional issues within other states.[58] If the international system did not condemn or threaten their existence, then they would be less likely to see the international system as a threat they needed to defeat. Self-restraint would be in their self-interest.[59] Once states realized the limits of their power to change the international system and that the system would not seek to change their domestic structure, equilibrium would develop.[60] Kissinger recognized that as a statesman his first responsibility was to guard the survival of the state, not save the souls of other states. Survival was the fundamental issue of self-interest for all of these states. Self-preservation would be the underlying motive for legitimacy and stability.

Stability in the international system was the main goal, but it was not the only goal. From stability, secondary goals, such as peace and even justice, could be developed within the international system. If peace, understood simply as stability, were the primary goal, then the system would be at the mercy of the most ruthless power. Kissinger summarized the problem of peace and its reliance on stability and self-restraint. "A world in which the survival of nations is at the mercy of the few would spell oppression and injustice and fear. There can be no security without equilibrium and no safety without restraint."[61] By making stability the primary and peace a secondary goal, Kissinger tried to avoid being held hostage by ruthless states. Yet stability would not lead to peace without a shared concept of legitimacy to create restraint through a shared sense of order.

After stability and peace, the third goal was prosperity. Kissinger's attention was divided between economic and security issues. The petroleum crisis and the closing of the "gold window" made economic issues a central concern because they contributed to the system's uncertainty and disorder. When Nixon closed the "gold window" to deal with the balance-of-payments crisis created by the Vietnam War, the economic and financial systems faced a period of uncertainty.[62] The economic insecurity and instability had consequences for the international system. Unlike the strategic problems facing the United States in Vietnam, Kissinger did not have a strategy for dealing with the economic challenges. Kissinger failed to develop a strategy because he did not have a strong grasp of economics nor did he have a mastery of the issues as he did for politico-military issues. In the oil crisis, for example, Kissinger responses covered the spectrum of international politics. First he advocated cooperation and concerted action among the consumer nations. Then, he suggested opening a dialogue between the North and South to address the related political issues. Third, he hinted at the possible use of force to solve the problem.[63] Kissinger warned that if the petroleum crisis threatened the survival of the West and was not amenable to a negotiated settlement, then military force might be needed. Kissinger's strategies reflect his better understanding of international politics than international economics.[64] Kissinger's critics argued that unlike his success with international security issues, he failed to create a structure to deal with the long-term consequences of the economic crisis.[65] Instead, Nixon and Kissinger succeeded in building a structure of peace to give America more flexibility in the international realm, yet the success of their long-term strategy remains doubtful. As William Bundy argued, their structure did not survive them because it required too much manipulation. The balance between competition and cooperation could not be maintained without their constant attention.[66]

Kissinger had a fourth goal that included, but existed beyond, the three main goals of achieving stability, peace, and prosperity. He had the goal of developing a world community. In his first address to the United Nations, Kissinger stated that if a lasting peace were to be developed, the world would have to move beyond détente to cooperation and beyond coexistence to community. Cooperation and community would enable the world to develop a just consensus in which the "aspiration for dignity and equal opportunity" could be fulfilled.[67] While these goals may appear utopian or simply idealistic, they offered a goal beyond stability and coexistence with which to motivate foreign policy. Kissinger, however, ever the realist, understood that peace, prosperity, justice, and even security would be meaningless unless there was a bedrock of stability based upon an equilibrium of power.

How would Kissinger go about achieving his goals of establishing a workable global order? First and foremost was the policy of détente,[68] which focused on reducing tensions with the Soviet Union through negotiations. This policy underlay the strategy of the Nixon White House and its formalization in the so-called Nixon Doctrine. Kissinger became the architect and spokesman for the Nixon Strategy, which represented the quintessential duality of Richard Nixon: competition and cooperation would exist side by side.[69] The Nixon Doctrine, which focused on the competitive military balance, reflected the need for America to reorganize and replenish its military capabilities; the nation had to reassess its commitments and bring them into line with its capabilities.[70] Cooperation, the other half of the duality, was represented by the strategy of détente. Negotiations and détente could only succeed, however, if they were supported by a powerful military.

Kissinger, in carrying out the Nixon Strategy, relied on negotiations to advance his world-ordering vision. He wanted to avoid any hint of appeasement, but he understood that negotiations could reduce tensions with the Soviet Union. Reduced tensions would help move the superpowers toward the stability needed to develop the new structure of peace. To offset the Soviet Union's increased power without surrendering, Nixon and Kissinger had to reorganize America's foreign policy priorities. The United States, weakened by the Vietnam War, could not sustain an extended period of confrontation. Negotiations alone would not suffice. Relying solely on negotiations would simply encourage the Soviet Union to remain intransigent in order to wrest more concessions. Stability could not be achieved by confrontation or negotiations alone but, rather, it required a proper mixture of the two. The only choice remaining was for the United States to restrain the Soviet Union without destabilizing the international system through conflict or concessions: it would negotiate even as it competed. Negotiations would help to reduce tensions within the system by giving the United States and the Soviet Union a method short of outright military conflict to manage changes in the international system and threats to their stability. Kissinger spoke to this military necessity in his 1994 book, *Diplomacy*, in which he pointed out that Nixon's foreign policy had relied upon the stability that developed from the underlying balance of power.[71]

Nixon and Kissinger believed that through negotiations and an awareness of the equilibrium of power, great powers would develop self-restraint. Self-restraint would be based upon power and expressed through negotiations. Kissinger's policy, in contrast to that of Johnson and Rusk, was one of strategic moderation. Moderation was a key theme within his diplomatic methods. Even though some of his methods may have appeared immoderate, he justified them as part of his goal of creating a structure to sustain the moderate goal of stability. In contrast to the previous administration's liberal internationalism, Kissinger sought to place his policy on the low but solid foundation of power relations.[72] Moderation would encourage stability, yet it could develop only within an international system that rewarded self-restraint and punished immoderate behavior.

One method for encouraging self-restraint and punishing incautious behavior was linkage, which worked by punishing a state in one area (e.g., trade) for destabilizing behavior in another (e.g., military aid). By alternating cooperation and competition, Nixon and Kissinger sought to encourage moderate, stabilizing behavior. In the case of the Soviet Union the goal was to bring it into the system and thereby restrain its ability or willingness to destabilize the system. The goal was not to give the Soviet Union full concessions but to convince it that it was in its interest to take part, thus linking cooperation to benefits and destabilizing behavior to costs. On the geopolitical level Nixon opened relations with China to create a point of leverage concerning negotiations over the Vietnam War and the international system. The relationship with China was linked to the United States–Soviet Union relationship. If this linkage worked, the Soviet Union would see that it could benefit by cooperating. As Coral Bell pointed out, the strategy of détente within the tripolar balance of power was based upon mutual self-interest.[73] Each party would gain from cooperation even though the underlying ideological conflict had not been removed. Kissinger understood that the Soviet Union might agree to cooperate to further its interest, but this did not mean it had fundamentally changed or would require an overhaul of its domestic political structure. The goal was to moderate the system so that states were working within it rather than trying to change it.

If détente were measured solely by its effects on the Soviet Union, Kissinger argued, it would not succeed.[74] As he saw it, temporary changes, through the benefits they conferred, would become permanent changes. Tactical adjustments, if maintained, could in time become full-scale strategic alterations. "For whether the change is temporary and tactical, or lasting and basic," asserted Kissinger, "our task is essentially the same: To transform that change into a permanent condition devoted to the purpose of a secure peace and mankind's aspiration for a better life. A tactical change sufficiently prolonged becomes a lasting transformation."[75] Détente was designed to modify the Soviet Union's behavior in the world in order to reduce international tensions in the short term and to create a long-term course of stability.

We can see the Nixon Strategy at work in the Strategic Arms Limitation Talks (SALT), which led to the anti–ballistic missile agreement signed in 1972 by the United States and the Soviet Union. These talks demonstrated the importance of negotiations and the limits to each state's ability to alter the military balance. The SALT negotiations fit within the changed foreign policy philosophy Nixon and Kissinger brought to their approach to international relations. SALT suggested that negotiations, backed by military capability, could succeed, without either side "winning" or "losing." According to Nixon and Kissinger, negotiating the limits to the number of strategic nuclear weapons would create stability as it helped avoid dangerous and costly arms buildups. Each side could still default, but doing so was discouraged by several factors. First, each side gained clear benefits from the agreements. Second, and perhaps most important, each state was aware that the other side could match its effort. Third, SALT was linked to other areas within the US–USSR relationship. Fourth, the talks were understood as a way to restrain the potential damage that could result from the use of military technological innovations.

Détente was and remains highly controversial as a foreign policy strategy. Critics argue that it was misguided and amoral, while supporters argue that it was never given enough time to succeed.[76] Although a full analysis of the policy is beyond the scope of this chapter, it is useful in giving insight into Kissinger's worldview.[77] Kissinger hoped to reduce tensions and to create stability through relatively modest tactical changes. From stability based upon these incremental changes he believed he could spark a lasting transformation that would guide the nations of the world toward cooperation. The central problem was to identify how and when a temporary change becomes a permanent transformation. In *A World Restored* Kissinger wrote that a statesman could transcend the public's experience for only a short time. Given this constraint a statesman would need to work by making tactical changes and would temporarily be outrunning the limits to his or her vision before having to reconcile it to the experiences and expectations of the public.[78] If a statesman undertakes a radical change within a state's policy, it will invariably fail from lack of support; in order to support any substantial shift, it is necessary to make many small changes. Yet if statesmen can transcend the public's expectations for only a short time, how can they transform temporary changes into a permanent change? How does one remain clear about the true nature of the various temporary changes and not confuse it with a more enduring change? Critics have suggested that Kissinger mistook a temporary fluctuation in the power balance between the United States and the Soviet Union as a permanent shift.[79]

The international situation suggested that a permanent shift was indeed occurring. The Vietnam War had weakened the United States materially and psychologically, and the Soviet Union appeared to be growing stronger.[80] One has to ask, however, whether Nixon and his secretary of state were overestimating the changes and underestimating the United States' material and psychological resources. One could suggest that Nixon and Kissinger failed to develop a lasting international structure because they built it upon the wrong premises. The structure reflected an extreme view of the United States, in the same way that Rusk's view had been extreme. Kissinger perhaps took moderation too far and misjudged its underlying basis. As J.G.A. Pocock has argued, Kissinger appeared to be playing for time in his approach to foreign policy because he believed that the nation, following its near Machiavellian Moment, was in fact in decline.[81] The United States could not avoid, but could only slow, the decline. This is not to say that the United States was losing the Cold War and the Soviet Union was winning but that the long-term strategy and the international structure were not devices that could create stability so much as merely delay the United States' eventual decline. According to Kissinger, a successful statesman, even one relying on the rudimentary principle of force, does not confuse short-term variations for long-term developments. Kissinger used the dynamics of power to create and maintain his world order.

Force, or the threat of force, was the final method Kissinger used to achieve and defend world order. The threat of force can spur negotiations and can help deter states from using force to affect the international system. Nixon and Kissinger justified some of their acts, from the covert interventions in Chile to its brinkmanship with the Soviet Union over the Middle East, by arguing that such uses of force was needed to defend stability.[82] In part, these actions demonstrated that the United States could still act decisively despite reservations in the domestic realm. Force supported international stability on two levels. On the immediate level it would deter destabilizing activity. Second, it demonstrated that the United States would act to support the international stability and back up its treaties and international negotiations should they be challenged. The threat of force could support negotiations by delimiting an issue. It likely was instrumental, for example, in aiding negotiations over the petroleum crisis. In a well-known *Business Week* interview published in January 1975 Kissinger hinted at the possibility of taking military intervention if the petroleum crisis threatened to strangle the economies of the Western democracies.[83]

What exactly was the greatest threat to the world order? For the United States, as Kissinger saw it, it was the loss, real or imagined, of the nation's will and confidence to act internationally. Without support from the American public, an active foreign policy would be extremely difficult to carry out. Kissinger, as secretary of state, had only an indirect effect upon domestic policy, but he understood that he had to address the public about the international problems if he ever hoped to convince them that his strategy was sound. In *A World Restored* he wrote that the acid test of any foreign policy is its domestic support.[84] On this test Kissinger failed. His foreign policy and his vision of the world order failed to generate adequate public support. To conservative critics his foreign policy appeared amoral and appeared to cede the strategic advantage to the Soviet Union. To liberal critics the Nixon administration's foreign policy methods, especially the reliance on secrecy and efforts to further centralize foreign policy, appeared to be antidemocratic.[85] Kissinger avoided the direct political repercussions from Watergate and the accompanying crisis of authority, but he reaped the indirect problems sown by Nixon's excesses. He had to spend time and energy defending against criticisms about the executive's unequal share of authority in making foreign policy and its propensity for secrecy . His statements and speeches stressed that he would try to build relations with the legislature and to carry on an open foreign policy. No foreign policy vision can prepare for a president's resignation, but that Nixon himself, or a president with similar international experience, was crucial to Kissinger's foreign policy philosophy indicates that it was an inflexible one. The crisis of authority had damaged the domestic consensus to the point that, under Gerald Ford, Kissinger, who had worked so closely with the embattled former president, could not succeed as the secretary of state. Just as Johnson had failed to weave together a domestic consensus that would support the nation's foreign policy, Nixon's political problems caused the domestic consensus created in the first term to unravel, disrupting Kissinger's plan for a new foreign policy. Although he provided stability during the transition from Nixon to Ford, Kissinger in time became a liability to Ford because his approach to foreign policy was seen as too closely tied to the excesses of the Nixon period.[86]

Kissinger viewed the Soviet Union, the most powerful of the so-called revisionist countries, as the United States' main threat. Even in the age of détente, the Soviet Union was in a position to change regional power arrangements and even the central balance of power. The 1973 Arab-Israeli War threatened one such region and nearly destroyed détente. Arab states closely tied to the Soviet Union launched a surprise attack on Israel, a close ally of the United States, which meant that, despite the greater stability within the central relationship that had been achieved through détente, the Soviet Union was unwilling or unable to restrain one of its "client states." Could the Soviet Union be trusted as a partner in the central strategic relationship? Why undertake the policy of détente if the Soviet Union could not restrain its regional allies? Kissinger and Nixon redressed the international problems created by the Arab-Israeli war, but the lasting damage was to American public opinion. Critics argued that events in the Middle East proved that détente had failed to modify the Soviet Union's behavior in world politics.

Kissinger was caught between domestic criticisms and international pressures. A successful middle path required a politically strong and focused president. He needed a president free of domestic political scandal who could marshal political support for a difficult foreign policy. A strong president would be able to keep both sets of pressures from feeding on each other, as Johnson had been challenged to do from 1965 to 1968. By the time Kissinger became secretary of state, Richard Nixon lacked the political strength to sustain the first term's foreign policy accomplishments.

Although Kissinger stressed stability as a foreign policy goal, "instability," understood as unregulated or undesired change, dominated the international system. Economic and political changes were constantly affecting the international landscape. In particular, instability brought on by United States–Soviet Union competition dominated the Nixon administration's foreign policy agenda. Often a perceptual problem as much as a physical problem, instability was easier to manage with a strong president who would be willing to carry out bold and timely actions to demonstrate America's confidence and ability to carry out a mission on behalf of its security. Domestically, instability in the external realm, especially in the face of claims of stability, could create doubt over the administration's effectiveness. Even its apparent success in maintaining the central strategic relationship détente suffered a serious blow from the 1973 Middle East war. To offset the perceptual problem, Nixon, along with Kissinger, sought to appear decisive when dealing with threats to stability. Yet the need to respond decisively created two further problems. How would they differentiate minor threats from major ones, and how would they calibrate their response to avoid exacerbating further conflict?

Geoffrey Sloan described the symptoms of the first problem as the challenge of discriminate globalism.[87] As a central actor in the international system, America still faced the problem of having to discern between vital and lesser interests. Nixon and Kissinger sought to avoid Johnson's problems by defining the challenge in terms of the balance of power and not in terms of the world order. The shift in emphasis from ideology to power still required being able to calibrate a proper response within the international system. The structural problem rested upon the practical question of physical resources rather than the conceptual question of commitment to an abstract standard. Without adequate material resources a policy cannot go very far. Accepting the limits of power can inhibit policy makers from taking on large-scale projects such as pursuing a stable structure of peace. Kissinger and Nixon were aware of the limits to American power as they worked to bring America's commitments in line with its resources. Even as they worked to achieve that balance, they knew it was only a means to an end. The appearance of unlimited physical resources can lead one to overact, yet appearing to lack the necessary resources can also invite inaction. Such passivity can lead an opponent to pursue a strategy to change the system through a slow but determined policy.

THE UNITED STATES' ROLE IN THE WORLD

Kissinger believed that the United States had an important role to play in the world, but his view differed markedly from that of his predecessor. Whereas Dean Rusk had viewed America through the lens of exceptionalism and saw it as an example to the world, Kissinger held a narrower view of America's role. America had changed, and so had the international system, and U.S. foreign policy had to reflect the new developments. To Kissinger the trauma of Vietnam had closed America off from the idealism expressed so optimistically in John F. Kennedy's Inaugural Address. After Vietnam America recognized that it could not go it alone, but at the same time it understood it could no longer equate its security with the security of the world order. To Kissinger America was still powerful, but there were clear limits to what it could achieve. Given the divisions within the country and Americans' disillusionment with the international system, did the United States have the will to act internationally? Nixon and his top foreign policy aide feared the consequences for the international system if America were unable to exert its power in a leadership role.[88] To Kissinger America's role as a world leader had three important and interconnected elements: political, economic, and conceptual.

The United States was a global leader in the economic and world political spheres.[89] Despite its foreign policy setbacks, America remained a central power with an important function within the international system. Kissinger was concerned that the psychological damage from Vietnam and the growing influence of the Soviet Union would undermine America's will to act. The material changes taking place within the international system were connected to the psychological changes.[90] By stressing America's leadership role, Nixon and Kissinger sought to offset, within the minds of the American public, the sense of isolationism and passivity that had resulted from the nation's losses in Vietnam War.[91] Their approach reflected a psychological and practical concern for American leadership. Psychologically, the focus on America's leadership would persuade the American public of the nation's ongoing international role. The practical aspect addressed the changes in America's relationships and continued commitment to various alliances. America had stumbled in Vietnam, but it had not fallen. By stressing its leadership, even in an altered form, it would make clear to the world that the country remained powerful, despite its misfortunes in Vietnam. America might have appeared weak and divided in the short term, but in reality it was still a very significant force leading a host of alliances in the world.

If the United States were to counter the Soviet Union effectively, it had to sustain the appearance, if not the reality, of having an active foreign policy. Doing so would require a domestic consensus that would support the management of the appearance of having power and, when needed, the exercise of that power. In their attempt to gain public support, Nixon and Kissinger missed an important lesson from Vietnam. Keeping up the appearance of having power can unravel by the very fact of trying too hard to defend it. To keep up the appearance of having power meant that even small challenges had to be met decisively lest they undermine the image.

In his first State of the World Address Nixon focused on alliances. Allies and alliances were important in their own right, but they also helped spread the burden of sustaining the appearance of power. Events and conditions at home, together with the increasingly uncertain dynamics of global politics, Kissinger sought to improve and strengthen U.S. alliances with Western European nations and Japan.[92] In the wake of the Vietnam War America had to rely upon its allies more than before. If the United States were to reinforce its negotiating position within détente, it had to rejuvenate its military strength, but America could not do this alone; it needed its allies to carry a larger defense burden against the Soviet Union.[93] Strong alliances with other nations would help the United States develop the freedom of action needed to negotiate with, or confront, the Soviet Union. Its allies could help America only if it tackled its fiscal problems and reinvigorated the underlying economic conditions needed to sustain the alliances.

America's economic health played a key part in the nation's response to the economic problems in the international system. Economic changes had accompanied the shifting political landscape of the international system, but they were not as responsive to the tools of classical realpolitik. The oil-producing states' attempt to gain political leverage against the United States showed how closely tied together the economic and political realms were. America's economic weakness was hurting its strategic situation. Kissinger saw the economic and political crises as reflective of the difficulties facing the international order. If that disorder were to be contained and reversed, America had to act decisively. The task was to develop a new international structure that could adequately address the political and economic problems.[94] America, in its leadership role, had to demonstrate creativity in developing a workable international structure.

The political system had largely been defined by East-West relations, while the economic system was defined primarily by North-South relations. A new structure of peace would have to deal with both spheres. The endemic economic problems between North and South, exemplified by the increasing leverage used by primary material producers, especially petroleum, had to be addressed. Kissinger understood that a successful structure would have to be built upon a relationship of cooperation rather than resentment be-tween these regions.[95] Reducing the North-South problems was more than an altruistic goal for the United States. The petroleum and food crises had a strategic component that could affect the United States and its alliances in critical ways. If, for one thing, the economic crisis undermined the economic strength and political unity within the United States and its allies, it would affect the central relationship with the Soviet Union. The United States re-quired domestic political and economic vitality it could use to soften the eco-nomic shocks that now seemed inevitable. It had to take the lead if it hoped to see the formation of a cooperative world economic structure.[96]

Kissinger believed that the United States had to take the lead in re-structuring and reconceptualizing the international order. A new structure of peace would address the changes from a bipolar structure, centered on the United States–Soviet Union relationship, to a multipolar structure that reflected the economic and political changes taking place in every region of the world. Kissinger saw the system as poised between two possible futures. Leaders could attempt to hold onto the old system, but they would risk hav-ing the world slide into greater disorder and conflict, or they could pursue a new order based on a cooperative future. The United States and its allies, through cooperation, would be instrumental in developing a new equilibrium needed to usher in a new structure.[97] As Kissinger saw it, America had to seize the opportunity and act decisively to bring a stable structure of peace into being. He warned Americans that domestic problems would not excuse them from carrying out their international responsibilities: "America now has an opportunity—and hence a duty—which comes rarely to a nation: to help shape a new peaceful international order. The challenge exists for us as a peo-ple, not as partisans of any cause. This is why the effort—even in periods of great domestic strain—has had bipartisan support."[98] International peace and prosperity would be possible if the United States recovered its domestic unity or accepted the duty to act within the international system. Despite these warnings concerning inaction, Kissinger and the administration were quick to point out that the United States' ability to achieve these tasks alone was limited.[99] The task was to show that the United States could act moderately as it attempted to shape the international system by retrenching its interna-tional position. The moderate statesmanship rested upon self-restraint by all actors. "There can be no peaceful international order without a constructive relationship between the United States and the Soviet Union," Kissinger as-serted in 1974. "There will be no international stability unless both the Soviet

Union and the United States conduct themselves with restraint and unless they use their enormous power for the benefit of mankind."[100] All states had to take a greater responsibility for maintaining the international system.[101]

KISSINGER'S VISION OF THE UNITED STATES

Kissinger, unlike Rusk, was an immigrant to the United States, which shaped his perception of the country. He viewed the promise of United States— it strength, prosperity, and ideals—through a prism created by his child-hood experiences in Germany. As a teenager, Kissinger had escaped Nazi Germany, and the breakdown of order within that country influenced his view of the United States and the international system. As an immigrant, Kissinger was removed from the same early nationalizing experiences of many other Americans. Before becoming secretary of state, he had not traveled widely throughout the United States but had spent most of his life on the East Coast.[102] Kissinger possessed an abstract, analytical view of the United States and its role in the world. His understanding of U.S. foreign policy was shaped more by the international system than the distinctive political features of the American regime. Instead of focusing on the principles that had long guided the American regime, Kissinger focused on the demands of power within the international system.[103]

In his confirmation statement before the Senate Foreign Relations Committee, Kissinger stressed that confidence in the United States' world role would help domestic unity and thereby support an active foreign policy: "How well we perform in foreign policy depends importantly on how purposeful we are at home. America has passed through a decade of domestic turbulence, which has deepened divisions and even shaken our national self-confidence in some measure."[104] Domestic support and domestic unity were strengthened by a foreign policy that reflected and promoted the United States' identity. To some extent all states rely upon their national identities to strengthen support for their foreign policies, but for the United States this identity plays a decisive role. Statesmen who can express foreign policy goals in terms of national identity—for example, the belief in Manifest Destiny— can tap into a deep reservoir of support. But relying for support on the draw of national identity is not without its costs and dangers. One danger is over-selling a policy; Rusk, for example, overemphasized national identity by identifying the United States' security with the security of the world order. Being aware of this danger, Kissinger argued that the previous administration's pursuit of a moralistic foreign policy had weakened it.[105] Foreign policy had been made inflexible by tying it to abstract standards rather than focusing on the distribution of power surrounding an issue. In this belief he echoed George Kennan's dislike for the legalistic-moralistic strain in previous U.S. foreign policies.[106] Kissinger was not as vehement in his disregard for American ideology as Kennan because he understood that its principles, if properly handled, could provide a valuable resource in matters of international relations. The key was to use the United States' tradition of self-confidence, based on the belief in its exceptionalism, without allowing it to dominate the policy.[107] Kissinger's foreign policy task reflected the larger problem of reconstructing the public's self-confidence.

The United States had to put its domestic house in order so it could restructure its foreign policy.[108] The divisions within the United States hindered its ability to pursue the active foreign policy it needed to meet international challenges, and Kissinger stressed this point in his confirmation statement: "These traumatic events [Vietnam and Watergate] have cast lengthening shadows on our traditional optimism and self-esteem. A loss of confidence in our own country would inevitably be mirrored in our international relations. Where once we ran the risk of thinking we were too good for the world, we might now swing to believing we are not good enough."[109] Kissinger had to balance domestic uncertainty against what he wanted to accomplish in the international system. An active foreign policy could not be sustained if public opinion switched between involvement and disengagement. America could sustain its foreign policy role if it accepted a moderate approach that did not swing between extremes. Kissinger argued that America had to remain confident even if its power was relatively diminished because it still had a purpose in the international system.[110]

Kissinger's view of the United States can be characterized as philosophically conservative. He rejected liberalism's main tenet: progress. In a 1968 essay Kissinger argued that the commitment to the liberal ideal of progress in the international arena had contributed to America's foreign policy of undifferentiated globalism.[111] Instead of progress, Kissinger focused on stability and equilibrium within the international system. Kissinger opposed drastic change or attempts at reforms that went beyond the limits of power. As he wrote in *A World Restored:* "Only the liberal leader, governed by a shallow doctrine of progress and illusion of rational reform, fails to appreciate the meaning of the limits of necessity; his efforts are bound to end in defeat."[112] America's failure reflected and in part expedited the changes within the international system's balance of power. Liberal internationalism's failure had raised questions about America's identity within the international system and the limits of its role.

Kissinger saw the United States as an ordinary country.[113] Because of the tragic consequences of the failure in Vietnam, Kissinger asserted, the United States had become more like the European great powers. In the context of the Machiavellian Moment, and in contrast to Rusk, Kissinger did not posit a difference between the Old World and the New World. For Kissinger the New World now shared the "sins" of the Old World. Vietnam had taught the United States tragic lessons about the limits of power.[114] Kissinger saw it as an opportunity to restructure American foreign policy on a more solid foundation. By recognizing the limits of power, America could better understand its possibilities.[115] The United States had to accept that a foreign policy guided by the Johnson administration's moralistic rhetoric was no longer suitable. There were limits to what it could do in the world, but, in making this point, Kissinger was also careful not to encourage isolationism. The United States could not shrink from its duty because it had an important role to play.[116] Kissinger sought to develop a balance between pragmatism, necessitated by the limits to American power, and moral purpose, needed to legitimize foreign policy and rally domestic support. While Kissinger spoke eloquently of this problem and the responsibilities of a statesman in the face of these problems, he was ultimately unable to offer a compelling solution.[117] Perhaps the problem does not have a solution, but to insist on viewing the United States as an ordinary country runs counter to its historical tradition, and clearly doing so can weaken domestic support. Even though Kissinger might have argued that a statesman must be able to transcend a nation's history and its long-standing traditions in order to chart a new path, the success of such a policy is hardly assured. Kissinger tried to sidestep a key feature of the American cultural tradition by making it a conservative power, which runs counter to the nation's founding principles, which define it as a revolutionary country, not a country that never challenges the status quo. America can be understood as a status quo power only if its revolutionary principles dominate the international system.

Kissinger seemed more at home with Kant and Spengler than with Madison, Hamilton, and Jay. For him it appeared that the American promise as an idea or a grand experiment in liberty did not carry the same resonance as it did for Rusk. America would fulfill the traditional role of a great power, thereby maintaining the status quo, rather than of a revolutionary state seeking to transform the world. As a normal superpower, the United States had to employ its limited power to manage the world system—to keep it stable and avoid the dangers that might lead to a general war. In the short term this policy worked, but it did not produce a lasting foreign policy structure. As Kissinger argued, America was no longer an exceptional country and would have to live within its own limits and within the bounds of history.

4

RUSK AND KISSINGER:
THE HIGH PRIEST OF PRINCIPLE AND
THE DARK PRINCE OF POWER

In previous chapters, we have analyzed the foreign policy philosophies of Rusk and Kissinger by posing three broad questions. The questions highlighted central characteristics of their approaches to American foreign policy by focusing on their views of the world order, of the United States' role in that world order, and of the United States itself. As this book argues, the very different answers that emerge from their respective political philosophies reflect the conceptual divide within American foreign policy created by the Vietnam War. To understand that divide, this chapter compares and contrasts those differences within a broad framework based upon Rusk's and Kissinger's views of America's exceptionalism.

The broad framework is based on what J.G.A. Pocock called the "liturgical" and the "jeremiad" modes in American history.[1] The liturgical mode celebrates America's exceptionalism and its commitment to liberalism, whereas the jeremiad mode, which is critical of these excesses, seeks to renew society and place it on a steadier path. Broadly speaking, we have seen that Rusk's speeches and his approach to the world order represent the liturgical mode. Rusk, fulfilling Kennedy's then Johnson's rhetoric, committed the United States' power and prestige, its exceptionalism, to support a decent world order under threat in South Vietnam. By contrast, Kissinger's speeches and his approach to the world order resemble the jeremiad mode. Kissinger sought to reform American foreign policy and correct the excesses within Rusk's approach. He presented a particular kind of jeremiad, however, referring in speeches to the need to reform, restrain, and rebalance affairs of state.

Kissinger sought to correct the excesses that had led to the Vietnam War and to bring America's capabilities and commitments back into balance. To achieve this end, the nation would have to accept changes within the international system and within its own system of government. Kissinger, following Nixon's lead, would retrench America's position within the international system and place it upon a comparatively limited, if stable, basis. Kissinger's approach, in contrast to Rusk, implicitly rejected the notion of America's exceptionalism by arguing that America would now behave as a "normal" power. America had to recognize and accept the limits of its power in order to shape the international system. Kissinger's jeremiad was as much about America's international identity as it was about its domestic identity. As a normal country, the external limits corresponded to internal boundaries within the regime.

The liturgical mode fits Rusk well because he celebrated American exceptionalism and its universalistic liberalism. Rusk believed that America's exceptionalism was a dynamic element in world history, and it shaped his approach to foreign policy. Rusk's speeches contain a strong sense of optimism about the United States' power to improve the world. America had helped to change the world by creating international institutions such as the United Nations and the North Atlantic Treaty Organization. These organizations reflected the optimism of Rusk's liberal internationalism. Liberal internationalism, in turn, reflected America's ideals, which had created a political system to meet mankind's aspirations.[2] Broadly understood, the ideals were translated into the international system through the UN Charter and the principle of collective security. Rusk believed that the United Nations offered the best means to avoid another general war. Moreover, he argued, America's security was bound to the international system's security because the charter reflected the United States' political principles. In other words, America's fate as an exceptional country was tied to the fate of the decent world order as expressed in the UN Charter.

When Lyndon Johnson and his secretary of state identified America with the international system, they were fulfilling the liberal internationalist framework that had shaped American foreign policy after World War II.[3] The decent world order fulfilled the liberal internationalist approach by continuing America's consistent and extensive involvement in world affairs. Although Eisenhower's secretary of state, John Foster Dulles, had shaped America's commitment to the system and to Vietnam, Rusk went beyond that commitment by arguing, through his speeches and statements, that U.S. security depended on the decent world order. America was now seeking to promote and defend a decent world order by taking responsibility for the international system's normative structure. Rusk believed that the United Nations' founding had ushered in a new era in world politics, which required America to commit its power and prestige to defend it. Vietnam, however, demonstrated the limits of that vision.

In Vietnam the defense of the decent world order proved to go beyond the limits of the American republican regime. Americans had grown weary of defending the decent world order because they recognized that they could not reform the world and the United States at the same time. When Johnson chose to de-escalate America's war effort, the nation had to accept that it had failed to defend South Vietnam and therefore the decent world order. The failure divided the United States' leadership and public over the nation's role in the world.[4] The American regime seemed unable to sustain the twin demands of expanding externally, in defense of stability in the world, and expanding internally, promoting the Great Society. Even as the pressure to turn inward grew, however, the dramatic shifts in power within the international system demanded a sustained and focused engagement. The Vietnam War not only eroded the domestic consensus supporting foreign policy, but it also weakened America's ability to sustain the delicate military balance with the Soviet Union. America had to find a way to sustain that engagement as it sought ways to limit it. The time was ripe to reassess American foreign policy.

The American public rejected Johnson and Rusk's expansive liberal internationalism; it was willing to support these principles when directly challenged, but it was unlikely to defend them wherever and whenever they were challenged. The attempt to expand America's postwar liberalism to the international system was not something that Americans were generally prepared to accept. Nixon and Kissinger stepped in to fill the gap between domestic principles and international commitments by offering to redress Johnson's immoderate foreign policy. As secretary of state, Kissinger focused on two interconnected problems created by the foreign policy crisis. He sought to address the psychological effect created by the Vietnam War as well as changes within the international system. Kissinger argued that foreign policy priorities had to be reassessed and balanced against the nation's realistic capabilities. Kissinger's argument resembled a jeremiad by stressing the need to make reforms after departing from the first principles that had long guided American foreign policy.

A jeremiad is a political sermon designed to criticize those who have fallen away from the path of righteousness. According to the literary scholar

Sacvan Bercovitch, there are two kinds of jeremiad, the American and the European. An American jeremiad promises, and is infused with the belief, that future success will occur so long as the audience accepts necessary reforms. The American jeremiad is optimistic in its promise. By contrast, the European jeremiad is pessimistic in that it does not suggest that reforms will return the righteous to the promised destination. The European jeremiad addresses the problem but offers no final salvation.[5] Kissinger's attempt to reform American policy by placing it upon a correct, if limited, basis of power resembled a European jeremiad. He did not offer the promise of future success; if, however, America reformed its foreign policy, it could avoid further decline. In effect, Kissinger was preparing the country to accept the idea of a future of limits, lacking the hope offered by liberalism. His European jeremiad would soften the psychological blow to Americans that theirs was no longer an exceptional country. By stressing that America was a normal country facing a proscribed future, Kissinger did not offer any final redemption for past foreign policy mistakes. Instead, his concern was immediate. Despite facing new limits, America needed to remain engaged in the international system; doing so would lessen international instability and strengthen America's confidence, shaken by the loss of its exceptionalism. Nixon and Kissinger's rhetorical strategy for the international system masked their attempt to create a deeper change within U.S. foreign policy.

Nixon and Kissinger worked to transform U.S. foreign policy and the international system's structure. They set out to correct the United States' overcommitment in South Vietnam. On the surface they tried to accommodate the changes in the United States and the emergence of the Soviet Union as a global rival by developing a stable structure of peace. Beyond addressing changes in the international system, they attempted a more radical goal—to shift American foreign policy away from postwar liberalism to a more pragmatic policy guided by the principles of realpolitik.[6] This is not to suggest one can draw a simple dichotomy between realism and idealism but to argue that Nixon and Kissinger brought a decidedly different view to matters of the international system and the United States' role in it. This fresh perspective led them to pursue a different role within the international system. To restructure America's position in the international system, they attempted to shift U.S. foreign policy away from its liberal foundation to a more concrete, and limited, framework built around issues of power.

The Vietnam War had weakened the United States, which amplified the changes taking place within the international system. America confronted the combined tasks of overcoming the domestic divisions created by the Vietnam War and meeting the international challenge posed by the Soviet Union's emergence as a global rival. Although they were obviously connected, the tasks required different strategies. Internationally, Kissinger and Nixon attempted to create a structure of peace that could manage the challenge presented by the Soviet Union. Domestically, they worked to rebuild a foreign policy consensus based upon achieving a stable structure of peace rather than an expansive decent world order. The Nixon administration consciously moved away from liberal internationalism to a pragmatic approach in its conduct of foreign affairs. Kissinger had the awkward task of telling Americans to be engaged in the world but only moderately. In contrast President Kennedy's ebullient optimism, which exemplified his liberalism and which he shared with Dean Rusk, his secretary of state, Kissinger came across as pessimistic. Recognizing the limits to America's power in the international system meant acknowledging limits within the United States, and it was his task to inform Americans that this had to be so.

Kissinger's foreign policy philosophy reflected the belief that the United States must act *as if* it had suffered a Machiavellian Moment. Decline rather than the possibility of renewal was America's fate, according to Kissinger, because the post–Vietnam United States was now to behave as an ordinary country. The challenge was not whether America had declined but how far it had declined and how it would respond.[7] The United States would have to live within its limits and within the confines of history.[8] Kissinger, through his speeches, stressed that the United States still had the ability to act freely and determine its future. Even if the United States was no longer expanding the sphere of liberty, it could at least preserve existing pockets of liberty. Kissinger appeared to be acting as if his task were to buy time for the United States in the face of decline and the emerging challenge from the Soviet Union.

An immediate way to correct the failed U.S. foreign policy was to disengage from the universalistic goal of Rusk's decent world order, but this cut against the strong tradition of American exceptionalism that Kennedy, Johnson, and Rusk had tapped. America's sense of exceptionalism created and informed its mission to reform the world.[9] The change from Rusk to Kissinger meant that the United States was no longer identifying itself with a mission to reform the world.[10] The task was now the more limited, although no less important, goal of surviving in an increasingly dangerous global environment. The drawback to Kissinger's approach was that it failed to develop a domestic consensus, in part because the foreign policy of limits challenged America's identity. Americans were willing to accept the reforms needed to correct its foreign policy, but they rejected what those reforms implied for the domestic realm.

The differences between Rusk and Kissinger reflect their foreign policy philosophies as much as changes within the United States during their tenures as secretary of state. At a philosophical level the continuity between Rusk and Kissinger's foreign policies, unintended though it may have been at times, resulted from liberalism's ongoing, if challenged, primacy within the United States. The crisis of liberalism in the 1960s opened the door for alternative and rival explanation to the United States' identity and history. In particular, republicanism emerged as an alternative philosophical paradigm to explain America's founding and identity.[11] Republicanism was not simply the political affiliation of the party in power, although that can be important, but it reflected a fundamental ideological or philosophical challenge to liberalism in the debate over America's founding, history, government, and identity. Republicanism emerged as an intellectual alternative but did not displace liberalism as the dominant intellectual paradigm for American history. That republicanism failed to displace the underlying liberal interpretation of the United States helps us to understand, in part, why Nixon and Kissinger's foreign policy failed to gain widespread domestic support. One can argue that Americans' unwillingness to embrace the tenets of republicanism meant that they were not ready to let the general role of liberalism within the American regime, and its particular role within foreign policy, be diminished.[12] Nixon's reassessment of American foreign policy did not extend to the domestic sphere, in which he pursued a surprisingly liberal policy.[13] Nixon and Kissinger were not seeking to transform the United States, although their foreign policy did reflect a fresh view of the United States and suggested shifts within the American regime. This is not to say that republicanism is incompatible with American exceptionalism; in fact, it seems to nurture American exceptionalism. Rather, the United States—as a normal country accepting the limits to its power—shows an affinity with republicanism, wherein the government is limited and citizenship rests upon political virtue. Domestically, republicanism stresses the limits to government power and the sphere of citizenship. To the American public raised in the post–World War II era of expansive federal governments acting on behalf of social reforms, a powerful government is nearly taken for granted. Liberal internationalism's stumble in Vietnam opened the door to Nixon and Kissinger's foreign policy reassessment, but it did not transform fundamental attitudes in the domestic realm.

CHANGING WORLDVIEWS

In 1971 Charles A. Barker argued that the Vietnam War challenged America's identity. Barker compared the war to the dilemma that Gunnar Myrdal had posed in *An American Dilemma* in 1944—that America's ideals were incompatible with racial discrimination.[14] While Myrdal focused on the domestic political structure and asked whether the United States could be both unequal and free, Barker focused on foreign policy and asked whether America could meet the demands of law and power. Could the United States, which professed a belief in supporting a multilateral world and demonstrated a respect for law, act unilaterally, thereby demonstrating a reliance on power?

The dilemma between force and law, broadly understood, captures the difference between Rusk's and Kissinger's approach to the world order because it ties into the liturgical and jeremiad modes. Rusk attempted to work within the multilateral system embodied in the United Nations Charter. By contrast, Kissinger pursued the limited goal of retaining, for a less powerful America, freedom of action in an international system. The American public and leadership would rely less upon principle and more upon power as the uninspiring, if more stable, guide to foreign policy. The dilemma, if America was willing to act within the international system, became how to negotiate the competing imperatives of power and principle. In a multilateral world Rusk was aware, as he was regarding Vietnam, that the United States had to be prepared to act unilaterally to support its principles. To fulfill the rule of law, Rusk was prepared to act beyond the limits of the system and tip the balance away from power toward principle. Kissinger, on the other hand, was aware of the multilateral nature of the world, which constrained the United States' unilateral actions. To reflect the limits of power, Kissinger appeared, in the aftermath of the Vietnam War, to be willing to sacrifice principle. The apparent imbalance between power and principle exemplified in Rusk's pursuit of the decent world order required a renewed emphasis on power. For Kissinger the international system's equilibrium reflected a balance between power and principle.[15]

Rusk's worldview was based upon a belief in universal principles of the American founding and the UN Charter. Universalism was a theme running through his work.[16] The United Nations exemplifies Rusk's universalism at two important levels: its reliance on the rule of law and the principle of collective security. The rule of law offered a measured alternative to the arbitrary rule by force. The charter offered a blueprint for a harmonious world order based upon the principles of collective security. Collective security resembled the rule of law by requiring a collective action to a particular event because peace, like the law, was indivisible. Like the rule of law, collective security was represented by a multilateral institution embodying the charter's highest principles. Rusk's commitment to the United Nations expressed his belief in liberalism. The UN Charter embodied the ideals of liberalism through the belief that rational principles could be applied to alleviate human problems and reform the international system according to constitutional principles.[17]

Rusk pursued these universal themes because he believed they offered the best chance to avoid a general war, develop stability in the international system, and create a decent world order. The charter had to be upheld to keep future conflicts from spiraling into a general war. Collective security could be seen as an insurance policy against overt military aggression. When a state seeks to change the political status quo through military force, it is in the interest of the other states to oppose it either directly or indirectly. If collective security is weakened, or fails, then other states might be encouraged to use military aggression to change the status quo.

Collective security failed to stop World War II because the democracies failed to stand up against Germany's threats of military aggression. According to Rusk, Vietnam represented a similar case. A failure of collective security there would encourage further aggression by Communist nations. The operative question was whether Vietnam truly represented a case of the need for collective security. Rusk felt that the United States had to act to support collective security because he did not see any other way to sustain global peace. If the commitment to South Vietnam failed, he worried that the United States' credibility would be undermined in other areas. Rusk would often ask rhetorically, "If the principle of collective security failed, how else could the world avoid a spiral into a general war?"[18] If international legitimacy, understood by Rusk to be the rule of law, ceased to exist, Rusk worried that states would be encouraged to resort to military force to settle their political disputes.[19] The Vietnam War, through the logic of collective security, directly challenged the international system's stability and legitimacy.

In contrast to Rusk's universalistic perspective, Kissinger presented a much more limited worldview. His jeremiad stressed America's limits and the need to accept that America was a normal country. Whereas Rusk pursued a worldview based upon the underlying principles of the UN Charter, Kissinger focused more specifically on the issue of power. Unlike ideas, power is limited in space and time. Kissinger's worldview reflected a sober assessment of the limits to the United States' power within a changed international system. The attempt to promote collective security in South Vietnam was, to Kissinger, a dangerous policy that had failed. Collective security had failed to stop the Communist victory, and pursuing collective security had weakened the United States' international position and distorted its international focus.[20] Kissinger tried to correct this problem by developing a new concept of order that rested upon the balance of power between the central states.

Two structural problems diverted Kissinger from his attempt to create stability and equilibrium in the international system. First, the Vietnam War had weakened the domestic foreign policy consensus and America's influence in the international system. Second, the international system had changed, with the Soviet Union emerging as a superpower and a global rival and Germany and Japan emerging as economic rivals. These internal and external challenges convinced Kissinger that stability and equilibrium could be developed only through a framework that accepted the changes and sought to manage them rather than reverse or minimize them. Rusk's attempt, and ultimate failure, to build a decent world order did not inspire Kissinger to redouble the effort but spurred him to redress the imbalances between power and principle. Kissinger, following Nixon's framework, worked to bring the Soviet Union and China into the international system without trying to modify their behavior to fit the terms of the decent world order. To put a key difference between Rusk and Kissinger simply, Rusk saw the world order through the filter of universal principles, while Kissinger saw the world order through the filter of power.

Kissinger's emphasis on power organized his geopolitical vision. Like George Kennan before him, Kissinger worked to balance the United States' commitments and capabilities even if it meant that important principles within the domestic regime had to be ignored within the external realm.[21] American foreign policy would reflect the demands of the international balance of power first and domestic political principles second. At a geopolitical level the main concern was the central strategic balance. Kissinger sought a global equilibrium that included the Soviet Union and China to develop stability within the international system.[22] The foreign policy task implied a new approach to world politics in that the United States would no longer indulge the belief that it could or should reform the world but would undertake management of the international system in order to protect itself. In Kissinger's view the United States was no longer an exceptional country that embodied the last best hope for the world, nor would it require that the international system created to provide global security reflect its domestic political principles. Rusk had pursued a policy that expressed a deep faith in the liberal value of progress and in the ability of an international institution such as the United Nations to reform the world. In this task he equated America's security with the security of the world order to such an extent that he believed that the country would be secure when, through the regulating influences of the decent world order, the international system should reflect America's domestic political principles. Kissinger, in pursuit of equilibrium, did not indulge Rusk's liberal faith. Kissinger argued that the belief in progress had contributed to the United States' involvement, and failure, in Vietnam.[23] Concern for a decent world order was secondary to the primary relationship between the United Sates and the Soviet Union. Although Kissinger spoke eloquently about his desire to build a world order that would meet the ideals represented by the United Nations, he understood that it required a stable international system based on an equilibrium of power.[24]

Despite the apparent difference in their outlook on the international system, Rusk and Kissinger agreed on several aspects of foreign affairs. They agreed that stability would help America be physically secure and that avoiding a general nuclear war had been a significant accomplishment for them both during their terms as secretary of state. At a fundamental level the international system could be considered stable if there were no general war. The question was what degree of instability could be tolerated within the international system and how would stability be achieved. Rusk and Kissinger used different approaches in their efforts to stabilize the international system.[25] They both understood that a successful and stable international system could be achieved through an equilibrium based upon a balance of power and legitimacy. A system based upon a concept of legitimacy would not create equilibrium because states would seek to interpret its principles according to their needs. In the same fashion a system based on a balance of power would not create a lasting equilibrium because states would always seek to alter the balance. A simple balance of power is constantly open to revision, especially in an age of rapid technological change, and is therefore inherently unstable. Without a shared concept of order based upon a common principle of legitimacy, the balance of power represents a tenuous stability.

Rusk and Kissinger viewed the principles of legitimacy within the inter-national system differently. For Rusk the main guiding principle was the rule of law.[26] If states upheld the rule of law as exemplified in the UN Charter, self-restraint, ideally, would follow from the desire to reap the benefits of being law-abiding. In contrast, Kissinger avoided an abstract standard but focused, instead, on the quality of legitimacy, defined as behavior that sup-ports stability. Coral Bell and Seyom Brown have each argued that Kissinger tried to build an order that resembled a European-style concert of power based upon shared power and an accepted principle of legitimacy.[27] State behavior that destabilized the international system would be considered ille-gitimate, and therefore discouraged, while stabilizing behavior would be pro-moted through various incentives. If the issue of legitimacy focused on a state's behavior in the international system, then states such as the Soviet Union and China, which had controversial domestic policies, did not have to adjust their behavior within their own borders. Kissinger argued that, if these states were given a stake in the international system through the principle of legiti-macy, then they would be less likely to challenge or destabilize the system.

Rusk, it appears, overlooked how the balance of power in the Security Council, at the heart of the UN system, could undermine the principle of collective security. If states, especially the five permanent members of the Security Council, believed that the UN order threatened their physical or ideological survival, they would disregard its dictates.[28] Rusk hoped to avoid this central problem by having the states accept the United Nations' common principles, thus attempting to manage political change.

Kissinger believed that stability developed from having global equilib-rium based upon a shared concept of legitimacy regarding the international order. When Kissinger began reforming U.S. foreign policy, global stabil-ity had become elusive because the Vietnam War had weakened the United States both militarily and psychologically, hindering its ability to influence the international system. The main problem appeared to be psychological be-cause the nation seemed unable, or unwilling, to mobilize its power to achieve stability. To overcome this problem, Kissinger had to develop a domestic consensus on foreign policy beyond the immediate need to leave Vietnam.[29]

Even as the domestic consensus of the United States changed, the inter-national system was being transformed. The United States faced a Soviet Union with the strategic nuclear capability to challenge it, while Japan and Germany threatened America's economic position. To develop equilib-rium within the system, the Nixon administration's strategy of combining détente and the so-called Nixon Doctrine had to be implemented.[30] The Nixon Strategy would restrain the Soviet Union and rebalance the United States' commitments and capabilities within the trilateral relationship with the USSR and the People's Republic of China. This triangular relationship helped Nixon and Kissinger achieve some key international goals. Even as the opening to China encouraged the Soviet Union toward détente, it could also work the other way. Just as détente worked to modify the Soviet Union's behavior, so too could the Soviet Union influence the United States' behavior.

As trilateral relationship between the United States, the Soviet Union, and China developed, a stable structure of peace began to emerge. These changes within the international system helped Nixon to end the nation's involvement in Vietnam. Kissinger and Nixon laid the basis for accomplishing what Rusk was unable to do: to bring China into the international system and end the Vietnam War. Nixon and Kissinger were aware that by withdrawing from Vietnam they were altering the balance of power in Southeast Asia and between China and the Soviet Union. The U.S. withdrawal signaled the end of a direct challenge by the United States to China and enabled China and the United States to work together, and it helped China improve its strategic position against the Soviet Union because, according to the theory's logic, the Soviet Union was perceived to be the greater threat.[31] Nixon and Kissinger embraced China because of issues of power rather than principle. Nixon and Kissinger were building stability on the underlying balance of power with its largest geopolitical and ideological rivals, but success could be achieved only if the emerging structure of peace continued to develop.

Stability should not be confused with the simple defense of the status quo because stability depends a great deal on how a system handles change. To Rusk change would best be directed through peaceful channels to moderate potentially revolutionary acts. Therefore, a state that preached a revolutionary doctrine of change had to be confronted. In Southeast Asia Rusk saw China as promoting a militant revolutionary ideology, which made it a force behind the Vietnam War and a challenge to a decent world order. He was reacting in large part to Khrushchev's threatened wars of national liberation. Threats to the region as well as to the system created instability by challenging the principles of the UN order. The United States, as a founder of that order as well as embodying many of its principles, had to respond to these challenges.

Rusk saw the United States taking the lead in supporting collective security and the UN Charter because it supported the rule of law as a standard of international legitimacy. If stability was to be maintained, states had to be discouraged from using military force to change the system or to settle disputes, but the system's credibility was only as good as the members' willingness to defend it. To Rusk America's effort in South Vietnam was more than a foreign policy issue because the stability of the international system was at stake as well as the decent world order's stability and credibility. But the system's stability was connected by collective security to principles of legitimacy that many states interpreted differently. Without a shared understanding of a threat, or a shared idea of legitimacy, the system would remain unstable.

The way that an international system deals with change is indicative of how it deals with issues of stability. Rusk worked to see that change occurred peacefully by attempting to channel it through international organizations and in accordance with international norms. Kissinger focused on stability, which measured change in the central strategic relationship. Rusk justified the United States' commitment to a world order based upon collective security by warning that unregulated actions in the periphery could undermine it. Focusing primarily on the key strategic relationship between the United States and the Soviet Union, Kissinger warned that changes in the periphery affected the central balance.[32] Although Kissinger's strategy for stability was based upon the limits of the United States' power, it required a high level of vigilance lest a regional disturbance affect the center. Unlike the international standard of collective security against aggression, which Rusk worked to defend, Kissinger's structure relied upon the ambiguous principles of stability and legitimacy. A stable peace based upon a foundation of power was tenuous because developments could alter the military or economic balance of power. When, for example, did a change in the periphery signal a challenge to the central balance? Constant monitoring and innovation were needed lest an opponent gain an advantage. Kissinger's system was unstable because it required constant attention to matters of instability and innovation. Moreover, Kissinger's approach meant that the system had to assume that America's ability to intervene whenever and wherever the balance was threatened would not be constrained.[33] There was little domestic consensus for an active foreign policy, however, and it required a politically strong and involved president.

Rusk saw legitimacy as adherence to the UN Charter and the rule of law it embodied. How he dealt with China's challenge to the system reflects his approach. To Rusk China presented a threat to the UN order because it was seeking to export a revolutionary doctrine throughout Southeast Asia.[34] If the UN order was to be maintained and a general war avoided, the Chinese leadership had to be convinced that it could not export its revolutionary doctrine through force.[35] Once China modified its revolutionary doctrine, then it would be accepted within the UN order. The goal was to modify China's international behavior to adapt it to the UN-led world order.

Rusk's approach to China and the Vietnam War contained a theoretical drawback because it glossed over how China viewed the region's underlying balance of power. Rusk spoke about respecting rules and modifying behavior to meet a universal principle, but China was concerned that the United States was trying to change the region's political balance. From China's perspective the United States appeared to be strengthening the anti-Communist states around China. In this regard Rusk's pursuit of a principle appeared immoderate because it distorted the balance between power and principle that was necessary for equilibrium. This is not to say that the principle that he pursued or the world order he sought to create was wrong but, rather, that undertaking a military commitment for the sake of a principle obscured the concerns for the underlying balance of power. China and the Soviet Union reacted to what they perceived as a threat to the balance of power, which compounded the instability within the system.

To meet these problems, Rusk identified the United States' security with the security of the world order, but this fed, rather than diminished, the structure's problems. Even though Rusk denied that the United States had any interest in imposing a world order beyond the borders of South Vietnam, the nation's rhetoric and behavior, by raising the specter of empire, contradicted his statements.[36] To the Soviet Union and China the United States appeared to be imposing its conception of a world order, rather than acting within the UN system. Rusk's insistence on the rule of law and the UN world order compounded the problem because it threatened the Soviet Union and China's domestic structure. Even if Rusk insisted that the United States was only defending the UN world order in South Vietnam, the principles he promoted influenced domestic regimes. Moreover, by identifying America with the system, the United States appeared to be the system's arbiter rather than simply a member. In stark contrast, Kissinger insisted that legitimacy referred solely to nations' behavior and the acceptance of the international order by all major powers.[37] Kissinger, in an essay published in 1968, went so far as to suggest that the central problem facing the international system was that it lacked such a concept of order. At a theoretical level this statement is at the very least a stark indictment of Rusk's efforts to develop his goal of world order.[38]

Kissinger understood that balancing power alone could not bring stability. Equilibrium in the system required a balance between power and the legitimizing principle.[39] Legitimacy would be based upon the mutual support for the emerging stable structure of peace. Kissinger would avoid the problem plaguing Rusk's pursuit of collective security—states interpreting and responding to threats differently. On the surface one could see a distinct difference between Rusk's and Kissinger's formulations of legitimacy, but that is not to say that Kissinger's view was without problems. Stabilizing or destabilizing behavior could be interpreted differently. As states sought to achieve an advantage outside the Central European theater, differences over stability in the periphery would emerge.[40] By giving the Soviet Union a stake in the international system through policies of détente and linkage, the United States hoped to encourage moderate behavior and address the accompanying challenges. If linkage worked as designed, denying the Soviet Union cooperation in areas it desired would punish behavior that did not contribute to stability, such as struggles in the periphery. Underlying this system would be the awareness that no state possessed the power to change the system unilaterally. States would accept the limits of their power to change the system.

In Kissinger's system détente and linkage meant that changes between the great powers would have an immediate and reciprocal effect. An essential problem with the system's structure of reciprocity was that it could be played both ways. Détente and linkage could be played to the Soviet Union's advantage as much as to the United States' advantage. Although Kissinger was at pains to argue against the idea that the Soviet Union could make gains at the expense of the United States, critics of détente stressed this potential liability.[41] Kissinger argued that whatever the Soviet Union might gain would be less than what the West achieved. If the Soviet Union now had a stake in the system, it would have to moderate its behavior to maintain that gain. Marginal cheating could be accepted so long as it did not challenge the overall structure because what was ultimately most important was the structure itself. Kissinger was also at pains to point out, however, that if the Soviet Union sought to overthrow the structure by cheating, then the West would, of course, counter such behavior. The concern with cheating by rival nations fed criticism at home, which further constrained an administration reeling from Richard Nixon's political problems. Thus, Nixon's ability to sustain the stable structure of peace according to a principle of legitimacy was undermined by his difficulties in securing political legitimacy.

TWO VIEWS OF THE UNITED STATES

Rusk and Kissinger's worldviews reflected different ways of looking at the United States. Rusk's view was based upon a belief that the UN Charter and the decent world order reflected principles found within the American regime. By contrast, Kissinger's worldview was shaped in part by the need for stability and equilibrium within the international system and the recognition that the nation faced limits to its power in trying to shape the international system. Under Kissinger America would intervene at the margins to develop a stable structure of peace rather than take responsibility for the system, as promoted by Rusk's decent world order. Rusk's view reflected the post–World War II experience wherein the United States, confident in its liberalism, its philosophical promise, its industrial wealth, and its military power had helped to found and shape the world order. The contrast with Kissinger's view is stark. Kissinger's view reflected a country that had lost confidence in its belief in its exceptionalism, its economic prosperity, and its military might. By the time Kissinger was directing U.S. foreign policy, America was a country uncertain of its political, economic, and philosophical principles, and it faced a problematic future in an international system no longer as benign or pliant as the one that had existed before.

Rusk and Kissinger's different views on exceptionalism can be characterized by the dichotomy between the New World and the Old World. Broadly understood, Rusk argued that America represented the New World alternative to the European Old World because America's founding, and the principles that formed the nation, presented an important alternative to European political traditions. Kissinger, by contrast, dismissed the dichotomy as obsolete because Vietnam had exposed the country to a challenge that required it to adapt itself to an increasingly malevolent international system. A discussion of the dichotomy between the New World and the Old World brings us back to the jeremiad and liturgical themes. Rusk and Kissinger's views of America reflected their understanding of exceptionalism and power and connect to the jeremiad and liturgical themes through the political lenses of liberalism, or a belief in progress for the world, for Rusk and conservatism, or a return to the status of ordinary nation, for Kissinger.

Rusk's view of the United States was influenced, in large part, by his background and his belief in America's institutions and ideals. He saw America as an exceptional country with a duty to defend a decent world order. To

Rusk a country demonstrates the principles of its regime by the goals of its foreign policy.[42] Rusk believed in America's exceptionalism and its mission in the world because his personal success was testament to America's promise. He had grown up in extreme poverty, but his individual talents and the opportunities open to him had allowed him to attain the powerful position of secretary of state. During his journey from poverty to the pinnacle of political power, Rusk had seen how Roosevelt's New Deal legislation had accelerated America's political and economic development. Rusk's experience of the New Deal shaped his view of the United States. For him, however, Roosevelt had not created America's promise; he had merely tapped into and developed what had been present from the time of the American founding. Rusk's faith in America and its founding principles demonstrated his abiding idealism about the country. America's founding represented the revolutionary power of ideas and institutions to shape human potential and society. Yet Rusk was not a utopian dreamer; he crafted his idealism and his belief in America's exceptionalism into his foreign policy.

Rusk's view of the United States, according to Warren Cohen, was based upon liberal exceptionalism, in which the United States through its founding embodied and fulfilled the universal promise and principles of self-government.[43] The American experiment contained a universal promise that offered hope to the rest of the world that an effective and lasting government could succeed based on consent rather than force or fraud. According to this view the rights enumerated in the U.S. Declaration of Independence are not confined to only Americans but apply to all humanity. If America is viewed as an exceptional nation, based upon its founding principles, the world must, by definition, be divided: in this case the United States, as the exception, represented the New World, while Europe represented the Old World. Within America's tradition of exceptionalism there exists the potential mission to bring its promise to the world. Even from the beginning, however, the Puritans were aware that America's power and principles could be misused because the principles contained a potentially crusading message.[44] After World War II, when the United States was at the height of its relative power, the temptation to export the nation's systems to the rest of the world was at its greatest. Rusk believed, however, that the United States had or would succumb to the temptation of power.[45] His belief in progress and exceptionalism led him to argue that America's promise and benevolence had allowed it to escape the Old World's fallen nature, as seen through two devastating world wars that had devastated Europe. Rusk was optimistic about America's ability to escape the problems of other nations because America's founding principles set it apart. In his view America and its promise, which were to be considered exceptional and were to be celebrated.

Kissinger, unlike Rusk, had immigrated to America in his youth, fleeing Nazi Germany, which shaped his view of the United States. Kissinger viewed the promise of United States—it strength, prosperity, and ideals—through a prism created by his childhood experiences; observing the catastrophic breakdown of order within Germany in the 1930s influenced his view of the United States and the international system. Having arrived in the United States as a teenager, Kissinger did not develop a deep visceral attachment to the American experience. Before becoming secretary of state, for example, he had not traveled widely throughout the United States but had spent most of his life on the East Coast.[46] Kissinger's background and experience appeared to give him an abstract, analytical view of the United States and its role in the world. His understanding of the nation seemed to be shaped more by the international system than the American regime's distinctive political features. Instead of focusing on governing principles within the American regime, Kissinger focused on the demands of power within the international system.[47]

Like Rusk, Kissinger view of the United States was shaped by a war. But Kissinger came to power in the wake of the Vietnam War, as the American public was apparently losing confidence in its world role. The confidence and hope that had infused America and its foreign policy in the early 1960s had disappeared, and uncertainty and foreboding over the future dominated the national psyche.[48] Kissinger realized that the United States had been psychologically scarred by the failure in Vietnam and that the foreign policy philosophy of liberal internationalism had been discredited. His task was to design a policy that took into account the domestic problems and the relative decline in the United States' international position while handling the international system's instability.

In his confirmation statements Kissinger argued that the United States' confidence and its ability to act decisively in the world had to be restored. The psychological problem of lost confidence influenced Kissinger's view of the United States. In contrast to Rusk's optimism, Kissinger's focus on confidence stressed the dangers that can emerge from a loss of purpose within American foreign policy. Kissinger had seen how the Vietnam War had damaged the consensus supporting American foreign policy.[49] He did not approach the United States from an optimistic belief in America's exceptionalism to guide American policy. Kissinger presented a pragmatic, some would say pessimistic, view based upon the bleaker situation he confronted. In the spirit of a jeremiad Kissinger had to remind America of its responsibility as a great power without seeking to return it to the pre-Vietnam era of foreign policy consensus and strong public support. The nation had to accommodate itself to a new role because it might have lost its mission to reform the world, but it still had to manage its responsibility in the international system and communicate that role to the public.

During his confirmation hearings Kissinger stressed the need to reform American foreign policy to restore confidence in the United States' world role, and he cited two main reasons. The first was so that it could manage the international system in this period of uncertainty. The second was that domestic unity needed to be developed to support an active foreign policy. "How well we perform in foreign policy depends importantly on how purposeful we are at home," he asserted. "America has passed through a decade of domestic turbulence, which has deepened divisions and even shaken our national self-confidence in some measure."[50]

The contrast with Rusk is stark. Kissinger argued that the previous administration's pursuit of a moralistic foreign policy had weakened its ability to act in the international system.[51] To Kissinger America's attachment to exceptionalism had created foreign policy inflexibility that appeared to ignore the distribution of power within the international system. America's exceptionalism clouded the issue and constrained foreign policy. Kissinger echoed George F. Kennan's dislike for the legalistic-moralistic strain in American foreign policy.[52] Kissinger was not as vehemently opposed to it as Kennan because he understood that America's belief in its special status was important to managing its foreign policy.[53] Yet his approach reveals Kissinger's distance from the American experience. America's self-confidence had to be reconstructed not because America was in danger of losing its belief in exceptionalism but because that self-confidence was needed to sustain American foreign policy.

America had to put its domestic house in order if it was going to restructure its foreign policy.[54] The divisions within the United States hindered its ability to pursue the active foreign policy it needed to meet international challenges. Kissinger stressed this point in his confirmation statement: "These traumatic events [Vietnam and Watergate] have cast lengthening shadows on our traditional optimism and self-esteem. A loss of confidence in our own country would inevitably be mirrored in our international relations. Where once we ran the risk of thinking we were too good for the world, we might now swing to believing we are not good enough."[55] For Kissinger an active foreign policy could not be sustained if public opinion shifted between involvement and disengagement. He argued that America could sustain its foreign policy role if it reformed its approach to the international system. In a telling passage from his memoirs Kissinger argued that America's special relationship with history was at an end. America would have to act as a normal country. In that new role, Kissinger asserted, America had to remain confident even if its power was relatively diminished because it still had a purpose in the international system. To do this, the Nixon administration would work to develop an international structure that would accommodate America's limitations but at the same time seek to avoid further conflicts.[56]

Kissinger concern for America's strategic position led him to express, at one time, the possibility that the changes in the United States and the international system signaled the crisis of Western civilization as outlined in the German historian and philosopher Oswald Spengler's major work *The Decline of the West*. Kissinger saw his role as playing for time against the impending decline because the situation looked so bleak.[57]

The contrast between Rusk and Kissinger concerning their philosophical outlooks mainly had to do with their respective beliefs about the possibility of progress. Rusk's approach to progress and his relatively optimistic view can be characterized as liberal, while Kissinger can be considered as a conservative. Optimism is a major theme in Rusk's speeches and helped formulate his view of the United States.[58] Rusk's optimism about American foreign policy and the nation's ability to improve the world reflects a theme in U.S. politics dating from the time of the Puritans. Rusk's approach tapped into America's strong strain of optimism within its political history, which is tied to a belief in mankind's potential for progress. From the Puritans onward, Americans have possessed a belief that they have a role as a redeemer or reformer nation based upon the possibility of progress. As Ernest L. Tuveson has pointed out, America represented the promise of progress: "Yet, beginning over three centuries ago a movement among a larger segment of Protestants effected a reversal of this dark belief.[that mankind's attempt to improve the world represented the height of pride.] There sprang up a hope, what might be called a 'Christian optimism' about the future of humanity and human society."[59] Rusk's outlook may have been influenced by his Protestant upbringing, but his belief in the United States reflected more than his religious background. It was derived from a belief in the nation's political principles and political institutions, which allowed individuals to flourish.[60] He invoked America's promise and principles to justify and sustain the country's involvement in Vietnam. To critics America's naïveté about the complexity of the world led it to attempt to reform the world on high-sounding principles that were empty of meaning for non-Americans.[61] As French President de Gaulle warned Rusk, things were different in Vietnam; even the communism there was different.[62] Despite such criticisms, Rusk believed that American foreign policy would succeed in Vietnam. Kissinger did not have the luxury of such a belief, however, when Nixon came to office in 1969.

In several speeches and statements Kissinger observed that the United States lacked a sense of tragedy.[63] The United States, unlike the European states, was not familiar with the tragedies and disillusionment that resulted from the exercise of power in the international system. The European states had already learned about the limits of power, and Vietnam demonstrated the limits to the United States' ability to change the world.[64] Kissinger did not possess Rusk's optimism in America's power to improve the world. Yes, he agreed, America's power was necessary to shape the international system or even guide it toward positive goals, but improving it was beyond the limits of America's power.

Rusk believed that human beings could make political and moral progress, while Kissinger seemed to accept that only technical progress, expressed through the conquest of nature or the attempt to master one's future, was achievable.[65] Rusk believed that the United States offered an example to the rest of the world. Although America had demonstrated an unprecedented ability to harness technology in the pursuit of the mastery of nature, Rusk believed that America was a worthy model simply because of the political principles of the American regime. In Rusk's view, to the extent that the rule of law existed as demonstrated by the American experiment, man had achieved progress away from the law of the jungle. Kissinger, in contrast, was pessimistic about the potential for progress.

Kissinger, in *Agenda for the Nation*, written in 1968, criticized United States foreign policy for placing too much belief in progress and the viability of its remedies. According to Peter Dickson, after seeing the horrors of Auschwitz, Kissinger could not believe in the progress of mankind, universal moral principles, or eternal values.[66] Although the death camps may have cemented his views of human nature, the empirical reasons to oppose the philosophy of progress were also supported by philosophical arguments. Progress defined by man's mastery over nature did not necessarily lead to mastery over human nature. Consequently, the problems in the international system could never be solved, only alleviated. Mankind had to confront the permanent problems for each generation and innovate as needed.[67] Whereas Rusk believed that American foreign policy could lead the world away from the law of the jungle, Kissinger argued that the most America could achieve, because of its limited power, was to conserve freedom where it existed.

Rusk was guided by a strong belief that humanity can better its situation by its own efforts and that the future holds improvements over the past.[68] In concrete terms the American economic development model offered the possibility for improving or developing the world. Idealistically, to Rusk, America was the great experiment in freedom that would allow mankind to escape the problems associated with governments founded on force and fraud and live in a realm of government based upon consent.[69]

Kissinger's view of the United States can be characterized as philosophically conservative because he rejected liberalism's main tenet: a belief in progress.[70] Kissinger argued that the commitment to the liberal ideal of progress in the international arena contributed to America's foreign policy of undifferentiated globalism.[71] Instead of progress, Kissinger focused on stability and equilibrium within the international system. Kissinger's arguments to oppose drastic change or attempts at reforms that went beyond the limits of power within the international system carried over to his view within the domestic sphere. America's claims to exceptionalism had been undermined by the foreign policy failure in Vietnam. The limits to America's power had been revealed by the failed pursuit of these ideals within the international system. What he had written years earlier, in *A World Restored*, could be applied to Johnson's approach to Vietnam: "Only the liberal leader, governed by a shallow doctrine of progress and illusion of rational reform, fails to appreciate the meaning of the limits of necessity; his efforts are bound to end in defeat."[72] America's failure reflected and, in part, expedited the changes within the international system's balance of power. Liberal internationalism's failure raised questions about America's identity within the international system and the limits of its role.

The United States was exceptional to the degree that it represented a founding in freedom. As the New World, America's promise and idealism had not yet been tainted by the apparent cynicism and realpolitik of Europe's Old World. America's success demonstrated that one need not be a captive of the Old World's pessimism. The Old World was bound by its history, which kept it from pursuing future expectations such as creating a decent world order. The issue was not that Americans were optimists and Europeans were pessimists: rather, Rusk saw America's pursuit of liberty as a way to redeem the world. If the American Revolution had succeeded, then the whole world might enjoy the same kind of freedom. The New World would redeem the Old World if America's experiment in freedom and progress were permitted to succeed.

For Rusk America's mission flowed directly from its founding principles, which were a great experiment in freedom.[73] America's experiment and its mission to expand the sphere of liberty set it apart from Europe. Through its founding America was a chosen country exempt from the Old World's corruption. Yet America's exceptionalism was tempered by a liberalism that guided it to use its advantages for the betterment of all humanity. America was an example to the world because its institutions—limited government and the rule of law—offered the best hope of freedom. America's successful revolution suggested that freedom was achievable for people of all nations, not just Americans. America had a mission to bring these principles to the world.

America's founding expressed the idea that the government derived its just powers from the consent of the governed. An innovative idea, it remains revolutionary, with nearly universal appeal. As secretary of state, Rusk saw part of his responsibility to continue the success of America's experiment in liberty and expand liberty's boundaries. To Rusk the universal principles within the American regime were to be expanded and defended abroad because they were similar to those found in the UN Charter. America represented what was best in a particular regime; hence, the United Nations represented what was best in the world order.

For Rusk America's founding was exceptional because it was dedicated to the ideas of liberty, equality before the law, and the fact that the government derived its just powers from the consent of the governed. The United Nation's founding was exceptional because it attempted to codify juridical equality for all states and offered a mechanism for resolving disputes by recourse to the law rather than force of arms. Just as equality before the law brought peace to a domestic setting, the United Nation extended such a possibility to the international arena. Therefore, America had a responsibility to extend the principles within its regime to the international system in order to affirm humanity's progress away from the law of the jungle.

Rusk's belief in America's exceptionalism reflected a strong streak of idealism. The American experience fostered the expectation that the future would be better, while Europeans often viewed such idealism as naive. Despite Europe's skepticism, Americans believed that the idea had been vindicated through America's founding and that its initial successes gave it great strength. As secretary of state, Rusk celebrated America's exceptionalism.[74]

Kissinger saw the United States through a European lens, which was more attuned to the philosophies of Kant and Spengler than those of Madison, Hamilton, and Jay. In contrast to Rusk, Kissinger did not attach the same importance to America's promise as an idea or a grand experiment in liberty. Whatever was exceptional about America was limited to the domestic sphere. In the international arena America's role was that of a traditional great power that would defend the status quo rather than act as a revolutionary state seeking to transform the world. As a "normal" superpower, the United States now had normal goals. America would employ its limited power to manage the world system—to keep it stable and avoid the dangers that might lead to a general war. America was no longer an exceptional country and would have to live within its limits and within history.[75]

Kissinger view of America's is through the lens of its limited power. America's power was not only constrained by other states; it also had to accept that it was a normal country and to act accordingly. The Vietnam War had stained America with the "sins" of power. The war had brought the sins of the Old World—power politics and quasi-imperialistic goals—to the shores of the New World. From Kissinger's perspective the Vietnam War had marked the end of the Old World—New World dichotomy that seemed to infuse Rusk's belief in America's exceptionalism. America now shared the same sense of tragedy as the Old World.[76] Whereas European statecraft had been tainted by power politics, the United States' founding principles had foresworn power politics. Unfortunately, the Vietnam War had changed that belief. According to those who criticized the war, America had spent its blood and treasure to defend the decent world order but in a conflict in which no apparent national interest, save its prestige, could be found.[77] Although arguments could be made that the United States was acting for the highest purposes, Americans had difficulty reconciling their belief in the domestic political principles to the methods and goals pursued in Vietnam. Consequently, Americans sought a circumscribed role in an international sphere fraught with uncertainty and instability.

America had to act conservatively under these new circumstances rather than pursue an unlimited mission such as maintaining the decent world order. If America had a mission, it was to manage the international system, not to reform it. America could survive a failure to reform the international system into a decent world order, but it could not survive a failure to sustain international stability. At the same time, Kissinger had to be concerned about domestic stability, which could undermine the focus needed to sustain an active, if conservative, foreign policy. The antiwar riots and the other civil unrest, coupled with growing international instability, raised the real belief that America could unravel. As a child in Germany, Kissinger had seen firsthand how domestic turmoil reinforced by international weakness had helped the Nazis come to power. If the necessities of order and security were not maintained, then the promises of prosperity and justice would never be obtained.[78]

Unlike Rusk's optimism born of a belief in America's mission, Kissinger's policies were conservative politically and philosophically. Kissinger would focus on the limited goal of pursuing stability. With its freedom of action limited, America leaders could only succeed if they innovated and managed the international system through a variety of "masterful" moves. Facing constraints, a statesman must focus on what can be achieved in the present. Survival becomes the dominant priority, pushing reform of the international system to the rank of a secondary concern. In the age of instability and the Soviet Union's growing strength, America's very survival was becoming uncertain. Whereas Rusk's foreign policy reflected a belief in America's exceptionalism, its promise, and its power, and its great advantages over its rivals and allies, Kissinger's foreign policy reflected its architect's view that America's power and position did not protect it from the problems affecting other states.

At a practical level the changes in the international economy emphasized America's dependency and ordinariness. The growing energy crisis affected the United States just as it affected Europe. The situation was less severe for the United States, but economic interdependence meant it could not avoid or forestall the storms buffeting other economies. Even without the external economic problems, the Vietnam War created domestic economic problems that undermined America's international financial position. America's balance of payments problems led Nixon to "close" the gold window and devalue the dollar.[79] Although the international monetary system's instability forced Nixon's hand, the decision had a deep psychological impact. The once mighty dollar had been devalued just as other currencies had to be devalued under the international economic system's pressure.

In the language of the Machiavellian Moment, Kissinger did not differentiate between the Old World and the New World. If the dichotomy had existed, it had vanished in the jungles of Vietnam because the New World had now tasted the corruption that beset the Old World. Vietnam taught the

United States about tragedy and about limits of power, which required a realistic, pragmatic, and therefore less moralistic foreign policy.[80] In Kissinger's view a recognition of the limits of power rather than a belief in exceptionalism should guide foreign policy. America had changed, and from now on exceptionalism would be a means to an end, rather than an end in itself. Even as he downplayed America's exceptionalism and the dichotomy between the Old and New World, Kissinger still believed in the United States' ideals and spoke eloquently about them. In contrast to Rusk, he did not see America's national interests bound up with its transcendent principles, nor were they to be identified with the international system. To Kissinger these issues only had a role to play within the domestic realm, and only through their realization in that context would they have any effect in the international realm.

TWO VIEWS OF THE UNITED STATES' ROLE IN THE WORLD

Adopting what could be called a liturgical view of the United States and its exceptionalism, Rusk guided American foreign policy by the principles outlined in the UN Charter's first two articles. For Rusk the United States would use its power and prosperity to build a decent world order and defend it wherever it was threatened. In contrast, Kissinger saw that America's pursuit of principles through its foreign policy had revealed the limits of its power. Kissinger's approach resembles that of a European jeremiad by calling on America to correct its foreign policy excess and mend its ways. In an age of diminished expectations the United States would have to reorder its foreign policy priorities and reassess whether and how it would sustain the international order created during its supremacy. Kissinger view of America's role was shaped by its acceptance of being a normal country with limited, but attainable, goals of achieving equilibrium and stability within the world.

Rusk believed that the United States had to build upon its role in developing the UN system by pursuing a decent world order because, without such a structure, the rule of law would not have any bearing within the international system. America had a mission, created by its abundant power and democratic institutions, to follow its domestic political principles and make the world a better place. America's principles gave it two interrelated roles. The first was to create a decent world order based upon the rule of law. The second was to develop a collective response against threats to the decent world order and its principles. Rusk believed that, if the United States shirked these responsibilities, the UN system might weaken to the point of failing, as had the League of Nations. The horrors of World War II convinced Rusk and many others that the United States had to take a direct role in making collective security work. Without such a commitment, Rusk worried, it would be hard to stop a regional conflict from spiraling into a general war. Collective security required America to act in the international system, guided by the UN Charter's first two articles. Blessed with power and resources, America could promote the principles of the rule of law and had to take the lead in defending the world order.

Beyond its political and military leadership, America played a central role in the international trade and monetary systems. America's economic power and position were vital to maintaining world trade and encouraging economic development. Yet, by the middle of the 1960s, the post–World War II economic advantage had been eroded. Nevertheless, the United States continued to promote growth among the world's economies because it was in the interest of the decent world order to open trade and strengthen economic development around the globe. Rusk's faith in economic development reflected a belief that free trade and a market economy were the best tools to develop an economy and improve the quality of life for a nation's citizens. From a strategic and ideological angle the United States' economic model of development presented a viable alternative to that promoted by the Soviet Union.

Rusk's foreign policy culminated in the Vietnam War. The war presented an opportunity for the United States to demonstrate that liberal internationalism could succeed against the Communist challenge and that the decent world order could indeed be defended. Rusk went so far as to identify the security of South Vietnam with the security of the United States. In doing so, the United States' involvement in the conflict in Southeast Asia was justified as being undertaken on behalf of the world community.[81] Unfortunately for the United States, the world community did not agree that its interests were threatened by the conflict in South Vietnam.

Kissinger understood the United States' role in the world to be limited in scope. The United States had reached the boundaries of its power in South Vietnam, but this awareness, while important, did not constitute the full picture. The international system had changed while the United States was attempting to create a decent world order in South Vietnam. The rise of the Soviet Union and the diffusion of economic and political power created far-reaching structural changes across the world, which appeared even greater because the United States had revealed military weakness, faced domestic disunity, and struggled with a crippled economy. America's foreign policy was as much a reaction to international structural changes as to domestic changes. The old international system, which had been built around America's primacy, was being transformed by the nation's relative decline. The emerging international system was unstable, and America's role now was to manage and contain the instability to avoid a general war. At the same time, Kissinger saw the need to avoid further decline. The United States had to remain engaged in the international system despite its weakened power. He reassured the public that, in this age of diminished expectations, the United States could nevertheless contribute to the international system.

To sustain this active, if limited, foreign policy, America had to reorder its international priorities, balance its foreign policy, and reconcile the apparent divorce between its foreign and domestic policies. Kissinger faced two tasks in maintaining the United States' active international role. The first was to educate the confused and uncertain public that, despite its limited power, the United States still had an important international function. The second task was to encourage allies and warn enemies that America was still a decisive force within the international system. The United States had stumbled in Vietnam, but it would continue to uphold its commitments and act to protect its international interests. The first task was accomplished, in part, by discarding the foreign policy philosophy of liberal internationalism, which had led the United States to overstep the limits of its power. In Kissinger's view a United States inebriated by the belief in its own exceptionalism and the possibility of progress had engaged in an open-ended commitment to South Vietnam. America's foreign policy was not to redeem the world but to achieve an immediate, if basic, goal: survival. The confidence that seemed to define American foreign policy in the early 1960s had been replaced by a wary pessimism built upon the bitter awareness that the promise of America's idealism had reached its limits.

The second task—reassuring allies—was necessary for two reasons. The first was that the United States was now weaker and could not carry the previous burdens alone. The second was that Nixon's strategy to bring stability to the international system required that the nation's allies carry a greater share of the burden. The two roles were two different sides to the same problem. The United States had to rely upon its allies because, although it was weak, it continued to possess geopolitical importance by being the main counterweight to the Soviet Union. America's lost predominance meant that it had to focus its energies on the main threat and that its allies would have to pick up the slack. The geopolitical demands on the United States, and its weakness, forced it to give diplomatic recognition to and make a strategic partnership with China. Nixon and Kissinger's approach to China demonstrates a fundamental shift from the Rusk to Kissinger eras as well as a response to the changes taking place in the United States international position. As with the need for America's allies to take on a greater burden in global politics, the U.S. relationship with China came about as a result of America's apparent weakness, not its strength.

The changes in the international system were, in part, reactions to America's failure to build a decent world order. The instability in the international system required a new structure of peace. After Vietnam the United States was not in a position to define the system because it was no longer a hegemonic power. Instead, Nixon and Kissinger would have to manipulate, manage, and massage the emerging international order in order to defend and promote U.S. interests. Unlike Rusk's approach, Kissinger did not identify America with the system but as one actor within the system. In the post-Vietnam era a superpower acutely aware of the material and psychological limits to its power could not afford to undertake a policy that placed it above other nations. America faced the complex task of retrenching its position and refashioning its policies so they relied on self-restraint, even as it maintained its commitment to stabilizing the international system.

If America did not show restraint and reform its approach, it would be unable to shape the emerging world order. Kissinger understood that the United States and its allies held the key to maintaining a global equilibrium.[82] If a stable structure of peace, based upon equilibrium, was to be created, the United States had to seize the chance. According to the Nixon Strategy, the United States had to continue its leadership role, but with its allies carrying a greater share of the defense burden. An important difficulty was America's unwillingness to back its words with deeds. It was one thing to recommend that the allies take a more independent role to give the United States freedom of action to negotiate with the Soviet Union, and it was another to accept their independent policies. The tension between these two demands was a constant problem for Nixon and Kissinger.

Kissinger, as secretary of state, stressed the idea that America could not create global stability on its own, nor could any other nation. Kissinger's concern for stability reflected the historical lessons concerning realpolitik that he had drawn from the international system. If a stable structure was to be created, it had to be based upon the limits of power that all states experienced. The international system could not be dominated or controlled to create an order governed by one power alone because the distribution of power within the system would not allow that to occur. An attempt by one state to dominate the system in order to create a world order or to create stability would only increase tensions and lead to conflict.

Kissinger saw America's new international role as reflecting its decreased power and its awareness that it was a normal country. America had plenty of resources, but essential elements of its strength, its self-confidence and sense of purpose, had been weakened. If the United States was no longer powerful enough to be able to dictate the nature of the governing world system, it was still sufficiently fit and geopolitically important enough to take the lead in managing the system's emerging structure.

5

RUSK OR KISSINGER:
CAN AMERICA BE RECONCILED
TO THE WORLD?

According to H. W. Brands, American foreign policy swings between the alternative poles of exemplarist and vindicationist, but this duality does not fit the change in foreign policy outlook from Rusk to Kissinger. To assume that the United States simply moves from one view to the other ignores what in fact binds them together and makes their differences less extreme: the notion of America's exceptionalism. The United States is the New World. What changed in the period from Rusk to Kissinger was not simply a change from an exemplarist worldview to a vindicationist one. What has occurred was a shift toward the awareness that the United States has become like the Old World and is in danger of losing its exceptionalism. Although the two men's foreign policy philosophies reflect continuity, they do represent fundamentally different views about the identity of the United States.[1] The shift that accompanied the move from Rusk to Kissinger revealed more than a change in the way the United States viewed itself; it also exposed a fundamental change in the way the United States saw the world and its role in it.

The United States could accept a more limited, Kissingerian view of foreign policy because the international system and the United States had changed. To fulfill Rusk's view would have required a fundamental change by the United States and how it viewed its world role. The public and the international system were not willing to accept the full expression of either policy's consequence. The foreign policy philosophies of Rusk and Kissinger are even more pertinent today, after the Cold War with the Soviet Union has ended. Choosing one approach, however, requires eliminating the possibility of the other. The choice will ultimately shape the American regime, making it much more difficult to revert to the other way of thinking. Yet avoiding the choice will only lead to further incoherence and ambiguity. One could say that the problem in Vietnam emerged from the founding of the United Nations in 1945 in which the United States played a critical role. The United States faced a choice of acting within the international system or transcending the system in an effort to defend it. The problem was not simply in choosing multilateralism over unilateralism because, according to Rusk, the UN system embodied the principles of the American regime and America's aims were in broad agreement with those of the international system.[2] If, however, the United States accepted responsibility for defending the UN world order, would that imply it had asserted an imperial role? The United States had to consider whether it will accept the limits of the system by seeking freedom of action within it or transcending freedom of action outside of it. The United States managed to avoid becoming an empire in Vietnam, but it has not accepted a limited republican role in the international system. Instead, the United States saw itself as acting to defend the system even if the system did not recognize the threat. America's foreign policy commitments, especially its commitment to the UN world order, even its view of the world order, force it deeper into the international system without resolving the question of whether it can reconcile itself to the international system or whether it will maintain an imperial prerogative to transcend the system by sustaining a freedom of action to act outside the United Nations.

The Vietnam War changed the foreign policy philosophy guiding the United States. In the course of the war the United States confronted the philosophical question of whether it is, or should be, a republic or an empire. The question, understood here as a near Machiavellian Moment, arose in large part as a result of Lyndon Johnson's failings as a statesman. Unable to reconcile the demands of the external realm and the domestic regime, his policies created an imbalance within the American regime. Although the United States saw the Vietnam War as a threat to the UN-established world order, the other states in the system did not see the threat in the same way. Unlike the Korean War, in which open military aggression attacked the UN principles, the Vietnam War was not perceived as such a threat to the UN world order by other states. As a result, after 1965 the views of the United States and the United Nations began to diverge as the membership changed from one that supported U.S. leadership to one that viewed it with suspicion. The international imbalance between the United States and the United

Nations over the way the international system should operate was mirrored in the domestic realm by the emerging imbalance between the executive and the legislative branches of government over war powers. The president's power, because of the simultaneous demand of war and domestic reforms, had increased at the expense of the legislative branch. The president's prerogative in foreign policy threatened to undermine the Congress's ability to act as a counterweight.

The change in foreign policy philosophy from Rusk to Kissinger can be seen in the differences in the ways each man viewed the United States, the world, and the United States' role in the world in terms of the Machiavellian Moment. Rusk's foreign policy, embodying a belief in America's exceptionalism, can be seen as a pre–Machiavellian Moment. He viewed the United States as a country that would bring freedom to the world and uphold its principles. The world had accepted the UN world order, and the United States, as its chief architect and supporter, would bring that promise to all parts of the globe. The United States' role was to support the revolution of freedom against the forces of coercion. The Vietnam War, however, obscured that idyllic vision. The war and its outcome changed the United States. The domestic realm, reeling from the demands to finance the escalating war as well as a growing number of domestic reforms, rebelled against the pace of change. As the war failed to achieve its stated purpose and the domestic reforms seemed to usher in more problems than they solved, the American public grew anxious. Was the United States unraveling? Had it reached the limits of its ability to distribute prosperity and security? Could the United States continue to support its foreign policy commitments? Henry Kissinger, serving as the foreign policy architect for Richard Nixon, sought to answer these questions.

Kissinger's approach to foreign policy can be understood as reflecting a post–Machiavellian Moment. Kissinger presented a foreign policy of limits. He set out to reassure the American public that the United States still had a mission in the world even if it was a bounded one. The American public would have to be aware that the United States was an ordinary country and could not be expected to reform the world. Nevertheless, Kissinger could not find an answer to the underlying foreign policy question: How was the United States to reconcile its domestic political principles to a world order? Although Kissinger's foreign policy philosophy of realpolitik satisfied the demand for a foreign policy that reflected the limits of power, it did not address the underlying philosophical dilemma created by the universal principles bound up within the American regime. If the United States could not export its promise to the world, did that invalidate its universality and validity for the domestic realm? Neither Rusk nor Kissinger was able to reconcile the United States with the international system. Rusk overidentified the United States' interests with the UN system and viewed it as the international system. Kissinger downplayed this identification but nevertheless could not reconcile the United States' domestic universal principles to that more limited international role. Rusk's and Kissinger's foreign policy philosophies represent an ongoing foreign policy dilemma for the United States. The United States must find a way to reconcile its domestic universal principles to an international system that does not always reflect those principles. Rusk's identification of the United States' interests with the UN system failed in Vietnam, but Kissinger's alternative of viewing the United States as a "normal" country within the international system did not work either. The near Machiavellian Moment raises two important additional questions for the United States and its role in the world.

Within the context of the question of republic or empire, Rusk and the United States faced two broad decisions. First, how would the United States balance its limited but universalistic domestic political structure, as a republic, with a universalistic foreign policy? Second, how would the United States balance its foreign policy, based on a philosophy of liberal internationalism, with a global system that is more than the UN world order? The Vietnam War forced the United States to face the limits of its power to shape the international order to accomplish the aims of its foreign policy philosophy. The dilemma was more than a question of the limits of power; it was a question of identity. In attempting to develop a decent world order and defend it in the jungles of South Vietnam, the United States confronted the limits of its republican identity. The demands of a foreign policy based on liberal internationalism could not be sustained within the limits of the domestic political structure. In other words, the limited republican government that formed the basis for the United States was slowly becoming a powerful body with many fewer constraints in its efforts to support the war and to sustain a decent world order. Would America transcend the UN system to defend South Vietnam?

The underlying tension between the United States and the international system had not been evident before the Vietnam War. America's view that the UN system and the international system were coterminous was accepted as truth, despite the fact that the Cold War rivalry with the Soviet Union clearly showed that the world, at least then, was more complicated than a single system was able to support. As a founder and the most powerful member of the UN system, the United States faced an important question in Vietnam: Did the defense of a decent world order require the nation to identify its security with that of the world order? Would America have to transcend the international system in place to defend it? The United States had to determine how far it was willing to go to defend a system it had helped to found. How would the United States relate to the UN system it had helped to found when the system did not identify the threat in the same manner?[3] Although, as it turned out, it did not have to address this concern directly, U.S. leaders were forced to come to grips with the question of whether the nation was willing to destroy the system in order, as they perceived things, to save it.

America remained within the system and accepted that it would not be able to defend South Vietnam. The effort to reform the international system, to create the decent world order, was beyond the power of the United States and its political system. The challenge of upholding a decent world order brought the United States to the limits of its foreign policy and its political regime. The imbalance between the United States' domestic structure and its foreign policy was made worse by Johnson's concurrent effort to reform the United States' regime. In effect, the United States was being pulled in two different directions, with one set of reforms pulling the United States outward and the other pulled it inward. In the end the United States was unable to reconcile its domestic regime to its foreign policy responsibility of defending a decent world order. In a sense America chose its domestic regime over its foreign policy responsibilities.

The imbalance between the domestic structure and the foreign policy can be seen in the tension between the executive and the legislative branches over the Vietnam War.[4] Until the Vietnam War, the increased presidential prerogative in foreign policy had not been a significant problem. When Johnson intervened in Vietnam, the tension became a crisis. The United States' domestic sphere was forced to react to the increased foreign policy demands created by the war, and conditions at home worsened. This in turn created an even greater imbalance between the United States' foreign policy and the international system. The confluence of these two crises brought the United States to a near Machiavellian Moment.

In the domestic realm the legislative branch reacted to the executive's increased foreign policy power and enacted the War Powers Act late in Nixon's presidency. The federal government had widened its role in the everyday life of U.S. citizens, and Congress feared that the executive branch was becoming dangerously close to undermining citizens' capacity for self-rule. The powerful federal government threatened the very idea of a limited republican government.

The crisis facing the executive domestically mirrored the crisis facing the United States within the international system. The crises were connected by the perceived need for a strong executive. Whereas LBJ had brought the Great Society to Americans, the United States was bringing a decent world order to the international system. Vietnam, as a test of this ideological viewpoint, created a dangerous overextension of the United States' position. Just as the executive's role in the domestic regime was ultimately scrutinized and restrained, so too was America's position in the international system. The imbalance between the foreign policy and the international system was an essential problem that Johnson and Rusk left to Nixon and Kissinger.

The Nixon administration responded to the multitiered crises it faced in dealing with the rest of the world by reordering U.S. policy, returning a measure of balance to its foreign policy as well as the country's relationship with the international system. It was a moderate goal but nevertheless required extraordinary means. The United States had to maintain its freedom of action yet remain within the bounds of the international system, and with Kissinger's guidance it managed to do so by agreeing to participate as an actor within the system, rather than identifying itself directly with the system. The changed view of the United States' role in the international system helped make the withdrawal from Vietnam palatable and possible. Nevertheless, Nixon and Kissinger were not ultimately successful in resolving the problem of the United States' relationship to the international system; they simply changed the focus from reforming the system to managing it.

Unlike his predecessor Dean Rusk, as secretary of state, Henry Kissinger was not interested in reforming the international system. Instead, he sought to refine the United States' position within the international system. The United States would fit into the international system by accepting the role of manager, with limited power to change the system. Kissinger's foreign policy philosophy did not relate the new role to the United States' reformist or revolutionary founding principles. By giving up its universalistic foreign policy aspirations, which were fueled by the domestic political structure, the nation faced a danger that those principles might also become invalid for the domestic regime. Kissinger's calls to be aware of the limits of power within foreign policy had a spillover effect on domestic opinion. A crisis in confidence emerged in part because it appeared to the public that an unexceptional foreign policy meant an unexceptional domestic regime.

To be successful, a statesman must weave together the discordant threads of domestic and international politics to create a web of politics that protects the state. This web of state operates on two levels: the domestic level, combining domestic policy and foreign policy; and the external level, which balances the foreign policy with the international system. These two levels must work together to deal with events but without disrupting each other. When the two realms are working in harmony, the nation's security is maximized because it is being reinforced, rather than restrained, by the larger world-governing system. In Vietnam the system restricted the United States rather than reinforcing its goals and efforts. Even the apparently limited goal of managing stability can tempt a state to overextend itself. The United States still wrestles with finding a way to balance its original role as a leading architect of the UN system with its updated role as manager. The United States can act outside the international system for brief periods, but in doing so it risks creating imbalances in the domestic realm and a reaction from the international system.

Having a strong executive is critical to having an active foreign policy, despite the fact that it can lead to instability and disharmony within the regime. As the size, and hence power, of the federal government has swelled— since the Great Depression and World War II—American society has had to wrestle with the question of whether to accept greater centralization by the government as a necessary by-product of having greater security. Nevertheless, a statesman in a role as powerful as U.S. president must be able to weave together domestic and foreign policy to achieve a sustainable relationship with the citizens as well as other nations; it is not sufficient to have one or the other or to allow them to converge. The domestic crisis created by the Vietnam War shows what can happen when these realms converge and domestic principles blur into the external realm. The backlash against Nixon and Kissinger in 1973 and 1974 demonstrates what can happen when they diverge.

Further research on the Vietnam War will undoubtedly place the war within the context of liberalism given that the foreign policy crisis abroad has been closely linked to the political crisis of liberalism at home. This book only touches upon the domestic context, but further research is merited to explore how changes in the United States' identity and in its domestic structure have influenced foreign policy. One could argue that the Vietnam War expressed what had been implicit within the trend toward a greater centralization of power after World War II. Foreign policy decisions affect the domestic structure; an expansive foreign policy, for example, requires a strong executive and thereby a more powerful federal government. It is worth examining how the foreign policy of the Vietnam War years, which reflected that liberalism, brought changes to the domestic structure. From a constitutional point of view the war led to increased power for the presidency and the federal government, which has not diminished. Although his work focuses on the process rather than the philosophical questions created by the increased power of the federal government and the executive, here it is useful to consider the constitutional question raised by Gordon Silverstein's work. He examines how the balance of power between the branches of the government and the states has been changed. Uday Mehta's book *Liberalism and Empire* explores how the philosophical concept of liberalism is distorted when it is used to justify an expansive foreign policy.[5] In his discussion of Edmund Burke, Mehta touches upon the problem as a statesman tries to reconcile the domestic political regime against its foreign policy. Future research would have to examine the theoretical issues of blending liberalism and foreign policy with attention to the constitutional problems created by the perceived need to have a powerful executive branch to support an active foreign policy. Can a liberal regime pursuing liberal internationalism abroad sustain the powerful president needed to execute that policy?

The future of U.S. foreign policy will rest upon how it balances its past role as a founder of the UN order with its current role as the most powerful country within that order. Supporting the UN system can help the United States manage its position indirectly and thereby avoid the internal and structural dangers created by taking on challenges such as the Vietnam War. But at the same time this closeness with the UN system constrains the United States and emboldens it. Although Kissinger spoke of limits, being held back from pursuing what it perceives is the best course of action is not what he had in mind. According to Kissinger, any restraint in the nation's dealings with other nations would at first glance be self-restraint because states would see the benefits of the system. At second glance force would be needed to persuade states that did not accept such restraints. At the same time, the United States is emboldened by such a system of indirect control because it wants to take direct action to make the system work to its principles. The foreign policy of limits that Kissinger developed for Nixon was designed to create stability and to manage the system so that any attempt to bring domestic principles into the international system could be resisted or deterred. The foreign policy task was to find freedom of action within that system and manage it to achieve stability, which would be unlimited by an approach explicitly based on or guided by exceptionalism. The challenge for both Rusk and Kissinger was when the limits either to one's power or of one's rivals no longer constrained foreign policy. What happens to foreign policy when it appears that the state has enough power to promote its principles?

The end of the Cold War presented the United States with a philosophical and political dilemma. When the Soviet Union disintegrated, the United States no longer faced a major rival that might constrain its freedom to act in the international sphere. Even as the United States gains a new freedom of action, the UN system is no longer strained by the ideological rivalry of the Cold War. The United States now confronts the possibility of pursuing a foreign policy that essentially transcends Rusk's or Kissinger's foreign policy philosophy. If the United States chooses to follow Rusk's approach, it will work within the UN system and emphasize the rule of law, which was so frequently thwarted or restrained by the ideological conflict between the United States and the Soviet Union. If the United States follows Kissinger's lead, it will exploit its freedom to take action to manage the international system to its advantage. This would require the United States to develop concepts of legitimacy and equilibrium that reflect its interests in maintaining stability. A choice between the two, however, is a zero-sum game. Pursuing one option means doing without the other. The two can be reconciled but not in their pure forms. What appears at present, with the current disarray in the UN system, is the possibility for the United States to transcend the UN system and act unconstrained so that it can shape the global system to its domestic regime's universal principles.

What links Rusk's and Kissinger's views is that they both must be in balance. There is a need for balance within the United States but also within the world order. Can the United States sustain moderation in both areas yet act outside the limits when necessary, and how should the United States affirm its international role? The United States is of course not the United Nations, though its foreign policy supports the institution that it helped to found. If the United States is powerful enough to circumvent the system and rely for security, instead, on its own resources and that of its alliances, how will it reconcile the demands of that role to its republican identity? The question for future American statesmen is to find a moderate path through the temptations of power.

6

APPLYING THE MACHIAVELLIAN
MOMENT TO THE PRESIDENCY OF
GEORGE W. BUSH

In his 1995 study of Lyndon Johnson and the Vietnam War, *Pay Any Price,*
Lloyd Gardner detailed the administration's strategy of escalating the war
while remaining attentive to the perceptions of the American people:

> On the same day that the President announced the troop buildup, Douglas
> Cater [the president's special advisor on domestic policy] ... invited Bundy
> [the national security advisor] to a meeting to discuss the government's in-
> formation program, "primarily as it pertains to the domestic audience." The
> "home front" was a real front line in this war, said Cater, and he attached
> an outline of what was to be discussed. The basic assumption they would
> work from, he wrote, was that "we are going to have a 10 to 20 year period
> of 'twilight war.'" That situation required a "sophisticated consensus of the
> American people" to avoid the dangers of "polarization and extremism."[1]

The passage depicts the shared if different challenges faced by Lyndon
Johnson and George W. Bush to develop and sustain a domestic consensus
needed to support their foreign policy. Whereas LBJ did not pursue this approach and suffered the consequences of a minimal consensus, Bush has undertaken a sustained program to maintain support for his foreign policy.

Like Johnson, and others before and after him, Bush has had to try to
reconcile America's domestic universal principles to the international system.
Although events in the external realm have prompted Bush to reassess U.S.
foreign policy and the nation's relationship to the international system, Bush's
statesmanship faces challenges similar to those faced by Johnson. Whereas

Johnson was in Vietnam to uphold a decent world order, Bush has also committed the United States to creating order within the international system. One of Bush's stated strategies is to promote liberty by defeating tyrannical regimes if necessary, not to contain or deter tyranny, as NSC-68 was designed to do.[2] His global democratic revolution has embraced and transcended Johnson and Rusk's defense of a decent world order. Whereas they were constrained by the Cold War, the associated technological, political, and military limits to American power, and their belief in the UN system, Bush has had access to unprecedented power and freedom of action. Although events at home and in the world remain in flux and his administration, in its second term, is still ongoing, it is difficult to gauge Bush's overall success at managing the interrelationship of foreign policy and domestic support. The question to consider is whether Bush can avoid the pitfalls that hampered Johnson.

To examine Bush's statesmanship in light of that of LBJ, it is useful to ask two broad questions. First, how has Bush woven *virtu* and virtue together to protect the republican regime from internal and external threats? Second, how has Bush used that web of politics to reconcile the republican regime to the international system?

FRAMING THE ISSUE

Bush's war on terror and the global democratic revolution present a challenge for the United States because they force the country to confront its identity within the international system. Just as Johnson's statesmanship was tested over his handling of issues, Bush must wrestle with the tenacious question of the nation's identity within the international system: Will the United States remain a republic, or will it become an empire?

If we understand the Machiavellian Moment as a clash between virtue and *virtu* within the republic, then we can ask how Bush has reconciled the two elements.[3] To pursue virtue, reforming the domestic realm, Johnson tried to develop the Great Society so that all citizens could participate in the American dream. At the same time, he pursued *virtu*, understood as military skill, by demonstrating U.S. resolve against Communist aggression through the undeclared limited war in Vietnam. Whereas Johnson tried to expand both realms to keep them in balance, Bush appears to have balanced the two realms by weaving together a domestic consensus to support his foreign policy. An essential difference between Bush and Johnson in this regard is that Bush's consensus was built upon a nationally unifying event, the attacks of 11 September 2001. At the time of the attack, Bush was pursuing a relatively modest domestic legislative agenda. The attack and the aftermath allowed Bush to put his activities in the domestic realm on hold, stabilize it, and instead pursue an expansive foreign policy. He was thus able to avoid the challenge of developing a middle path between war and reforms, but Bush's challenge remains as great as Johnson's. The question for Bush is whether the demands of *virtu*, sustaining America's military will to fight the war on terror *and* promote the global democratic revolution, will come at the expense of virtue. In this sense Bush's statesmanship appears moderate because he has avoided taking a middle path between his domestic policy and foreign policy. Yet in terms of the philosophical question of republic or empire, the crux of Pocock's Machiavellian Moment, Bush's foreign policy may in fact be immoderate. The pursuit of *virtu*, the military power to prosecute the war on terror, may unleash an ambition unrestrained by prudence. If his use of military power to change the international system unleashes this ambition, then it may undermine the essential balance within the domestic realm. The challenge for the republic is to harness its ambition to redirect it from a pursuit of glory to the pursuit of fame.[4]

We can consider an apparent difference between Johnson and Bush as the difference between the pursuit of glory and the pursuit of fame. Johnson was keen to surpass previous presidents, such as Roosevelt, and expressed concern about his legacy. He pursued glory by trying to bring the Great Society to America and to defend the decent world order in Vietnam. Bush does not appear similarly concerned about his legacy, and if this is indeed the case his ambition may be bound up with, rather than separate from, the republic. Obviously, these observations are tentative. Bush's legacy will rest as much on what he does or does not achieve now and throughout the remainder of his presidency as on the later consequences of his policies. The issue of fame or glory will no doubt be debated for years to come, but in any case it will depend on Bush's statesmanship in sustaining his domestic consensus and reconciling America's republican regime to the international system.

THE CHALLENGE OF *VIRTU*

Johnson displayed his *virtu*, generally, through the policy of containment of the Soviet Union and, specifically, through the undeclared limited war in Southeast Asia. Johnson's undeclared limited war in Vietnam followed a muddled middle path between his domestic policy and his foreign policy and between his foreign policy and the international system. The undeclared limited war was designed to give him the flexibility to expand both realms simultaneously, but he could not keep them in balance. Johnson tried to balance the two realms by blurring the distinction between them, but this move threatened to bring the foreign policy crisis into the domestic realm; he tried to centralize power to sustain this middle-path strategy, but, ultimately, the legislature resisted the president's appropriation of power. Johnson's failure reflected a larger crisis within the regime. The American regime, limited and balanced, was being asked to sustain an unlimited, open-ended commitment through an undeclared war.

Bush demonstrated his *virtu* in his response to the attacks of 11 September 2001 and the subsequent war on terrorism as well as in the war in Iraq. He faces a very different situation from Johnson in that at the turn of the twenty-first century U.S. military power allows him to sustain an open-ended commitment. Bush's *virtu* raises the question of whether his ambition has led him to pursue immoderate goals in the international realm that threaten the moderation at the heart of the America regime. Herein lies a major test of Bush's statesmanship. So far, he has been effective at convincing a majority of Americans to support his war on terror. If that consensus holds, the next question is whether the pursuit of a global democratic revolution could destroy that consensus. The war on terror may reach a short-term equilibrium in which the United States is free of immediate threats but has to accept continual instability. The pursuit of global democratic revolution may indeed require a commitment that goes beyond the nation's collective republican will.

Johnson pursued an undeclared limited war in July 1965 to avoid the perceived policy choice between an all-out escalation of the war and withdrawal. He tried to protect his domestic programs and meet his foreign policy commitments through the undeclared limited war, which would allow him to avoid a sustained debate over his foreign policy aims. Bush, by contrast, has not faced the same choice or tried to pursue both goals simultaneously. On the surface it appears that he has chosen foreign policy over domestic policy. Like Franklin D. Roosevelt, who was forced to respond to military aggression against the country, Bush has used the 2001 attacks on the United States to build a domestic consensus for his war policies in Afghanistan and Iraq. What remains to be seen is whether he can or will continue to sustain that strategy. For, unlike Roosevelt, Bush has not gone from having an exclusively domestic focus to one concerned only with foreign policy. Consequently, Bush, like

Johnson, has appeared to blur the distinction between foreign and domestic policy because he wants to be able to appear at war and peace at the same time.

Does Bush's response to the attack on 11 September 2001 suggest that he has pursued *virtu* at the expense of virtue? One could point to his reliance on U.S. military power in responding to international events, but this would be only part of the story. First, we need to consider whether Bush's commitment to the external realm has come at the expense of the domestic realm. Bush's limited domestic agenda stems from constraints created by presidents Johnson's and Reagan's policies. LBJ's Great Society created a number of social welfare programs that the federal government continues to fund. Reagan's tax cuts limited the federal government's ability to develop similar programs. Thus, without significant changes to the status quo, subsequent presidents must follow a limited domestic program.[5] A year into his second term, despite growing opposition to the war in Iraq and difficulties in responding to domestic emergencies such as Hurricane Katrina, Bush's foreign policy had not curtailed his domestic agenda, and the demands of the domestic realm have not constrained his foreign policy. Second, we need to consider whether the America's military power is equal to Bush's ambition in the external realm. Does Bush possess the necessary *virtu* to succeed in the external realm? This question remains open for several reasons. First, the United States may not be able to translate its military predominance into political success because the public consensus that currently supports it was not formed for that mission. Unless the public has the appetite to fulfill the global democratic revolution through a long twilight war, military force will be rendered useless. Second, the open-ended commitment to the external realm may create challenges within the domestic realm. The longer the twilight war lasts, the more domestic issues, such as the vast social needs let loose by Hurricane Katrina, will emerge. Finally, Bush's *virtu* may not be sufficient to move from the war on terror, which entails reforming the international system, to the global democratic revolution, which requires managing the system.[6] In any case either Bush or his successors will need to moderate the war on terror to avoid confusing it with the global democratic revolution.

Although George W. Bush may have avoided Johnson's tactical dilemma of guns versus butter, he has not escaped the strategic problem of whether the nation will remain a republic or will veer toward empire. Power may be centralized within the executive for the short term to fight the war on terror, which presents a long-term problem at the strategic level because something as ambitious as a global democratic revolution could last for generations.

Moving from a tactical short-term military commitment to an ongoing strategic political and diplomatic commitment may require Bush and his successors to blur the line between the external and internal realms beyond what Johnson attempted.[7] The danger is that Bush and his successors may have to become permanent peacetime and wartime presidents simultaneously. In this case the *virtu* needed to sustain international ambitions, the power gained to fight the war on terrorism in the short term, corrupts the domestic balance in the long-term by creating dependence on an expanding executive branch. For example, in response to the attacks of 11 September 2001, a new cabinet-level Department of Homeland Security was formed in March 2003, an amalgamation of twenty-two formerly independent agencies. Its existence attests to the executive branch's propensity to expand in a foreign policy crisis, which in turn extends the federal government. In mitigation Bush's apparent philosophy of pursuing limited government may restrain the domestic dependence upon the federal government so that the foreign policy does not inhibit the republican nature of self-rule.

If Bush has avoided the challenge created by *virtu*, he has done so because he was able to achieve a domestic consensus to support his foreign policy. To weave together the factions that focus inward and those that focus outward, the statesman must educate the people to understand the problem and the policy response required. Through speeches and deeds a statesman educates the public, and in Bush's case the attacks on the American homeland, which came only eight months after he took office, helped him to create and sustain a domestic consensus. Bush's handling of *virtu* has been very different than Johnson's, and, unlike his predecessor, he has been more willing to address the public about the nation's alternatives. In contrast to Johnson, Bush and his team appear to have adequately prepared the public for the long twilight war.

THE DEMANDS OF VIRTUE

In large part Johnson's failures resulted from his inability to balance the domestic and external realms in pursuing an undeclared limited war. Bush's National Security Strategy of 2002 and associated speeches direct American foreign policy with a clarity and purpose free of the vicissitudes of domestic politics. Through a series of speeches, statements, and addresses to the public, Bush has presented a clear vision of what he is trying to achieve. Over time policies and strategies will need to be adjusted, and these adjustments need to be guided by a resolute vision that a statesman must supply. Johnson failed to articulate a clear strategy to Americans and educate them about the critical choices they faced as a nation. Instead, he tried to modulate his foreign policy against his domestic policy by following a middle path. Bush, by contrast, has not needed to modulate his foreign policy to his domestic policy because the consensus built following the attacks of 11 September 2001 gave him extra capital with which to move forward on his policy decisions. Bush's strategy, clarity of vision, and sense of purpose emerged from a situation that Johnson never faced, the attack on the American homeland.[8] Ultimately, however, Bush's statesmanship has not been determined by events alone but also by his philosophy and personality. His response to the attacks on the United States, though influenced by powerful members of his administration, was his alone.

At the broadest level Bush does not face the challenge of an alternative worldview as Marxist-Leninism posed for LBJ. Bush, unlike Rusk, does not confront an alternative ideological or philosophical world order that is potentially attractive to strategic parts of the world, which gives him a certain freedom of action. In his introductory letter to the National Security Strategy, created early in his first term, Bush stated there is only one model for success. While at the time the document spoke as though there was not an alternative worldview that challenged the nation in the way that communism had, Bush's handling of the international system has not avoided criticism and its share of challenges both at home and abroad.[9]

Within the American regime Bush has been forced to sustain the debate about the nation's foreign policy. Even if Americans have disagreed with his style or the quality of debate around important legislation, such as the Patriot Act, they have generally been made aware of the choices involved. Moreover, the national election campaign of 2004 provided the president with an extended opportunity to address the public about the alternatives facing American foreign policy. One could argue that the election was a referendum on his foreign policy. By speaking publicly about these issues, he has demonstrated moderation, which Johnson lacked. Johnson did speak about the Vietnam War and the issues involved in it, and he did try to convince the public about his policies, but he never undertook a sustained national debate over his foreign policy before carrying it out, in part because he inherited his policy positions and in part because his manner of statesmanship did not seem to him to require it. Consequently, Johnson achieved only a fragile domestic consensus, which reinforced his need to modulate his foreign and domestic policies.

How has Bush educated the public about the alternative policy choices? In part he has done this through a number of major addresses and speeches and through the National Security Strategy, a formal blueprint for U.S. foreign policy published in 2002. In President Bush's first major public address following the 9/11 attacks, on 20 September 2001, he told the American public the United States would respond with a global campaign without a specific end: "Our war on terror begins with al Qaeda, but it does not end there. It will not end until every terrorist group of global reach has been found, stopped and defeated." Later in the same address he warned that it would be a long campaign: "Americans should not expect one battle, but a lengthy campaign, unlike any other we have ever seen."[10] A few months later, during the State of the Union Address in January 2002, Bush reiterated that this campaign could last for generations: "Our war on terror is well begun, but it is only begun. This campaign may not be finished on our watch—yet it must be and it will be waged on our watch."[11] He also warned in his 2002 National Security Strategy that the war on terror had an uncertain duration: "The war against terrorists of global reach is a global enterprise of uncertain duration."[12] In 2005 he repeated this theme in his Second Inaugural Address: "The great objective of ending tyranny is the concentrated work of generations."[13] In addition to warning Americans about the long campaign ahead, Bush educated the public about the nation's strategic challenge.

In June 2002 Bush used a speech before the West Point academy to prepare the country for changes within the U.S. strategic framework, which would be developed in the National Security Strategy. "For much of the last century," he asserted, "America's defense relied on the Cold War doctrines of deterrence and containment. In some cases, those strategies still apply. But new threats also require new thinking. Deterrence—the promise of massive retaliation against nations—means nothing against shadowy terrorist networks with no nation or citizens to defend. Containment is not possible when unbalanced dictators with weapons of mass destruction can deliver those weapons on missiles or secretly provide them to terrorist allies."[14] When Bush's National Security Strategy emerged, it contained a number of important foreign policy statements. Its introductory letter, for example, stated that there is a single model for success: "The great struggles of the twentieth century between liberty and totalitarianism ended with a decisive victory for the forces of freedom—and a single sustainable model for national success: freedom, democracy, and free enterprise."[15]

Bush has solved short-term problems in a way that Johnson could not, by educating the public, and thereby has demonstrated superior statesmanship. Yet he may still fail in the long term, as a consequence of his actions, because he has set the country on a path it cannot sustain without changing the very nature of the U.S. government. Johnson transformed America through the Great Society but lost Vietnam; is Bush in danger of transforming the international system but losing America?

WEAVING TOGETHER THE UNITED STATES AND THE INTERNATIONAL SYSTEM

A successful statesman weaves together the divergent threads within the regime to create a web of politics to protect it from the vicissitudes of the international system. By ably balancing the two levels, the statesman can keep events in the external realm from disrupting the domestic regime. In Bush's case U.S. security has been reinforced, rather than restrained, by the global system. Bush has benefited from having a domestic consensus to bolster his foreign policy agenda, and the international system has, in a qualified sense, been supportive. Yet there are underlying problems in how Bush has woven the web of politics together.

One danger that exists is that an executive might try to find a shortcut to consensus by removing or blurring the differences between the domestic and foreign realms; the unlimited external realm can intrude into the balanced and limited domestic realm. A republic relies upon a limited, balanced government within the domestic realm, in which issues are divisible. A republic requires an unlimited, unitary government in the external realm, in which issues are indivisible. The government is limited in the domestic realm because citizens seek to protect themselves from its possible excesses, while in the external realm they want the government to be unified and unfettered in its efforts to defend them against external threats. If the distinction between the two realms is blurred, then the logic of the external realm may dominate the domestic realm or the domestic realm may bleed into the external realm.[16] In either case the regime would be threatened. In the first case the threat would come from corruption brought on by a fearful citizenry that is willing to accept the rule of a single person in an unfettered, unbounded government in order to feel protected. In the second case a limited government abroad would be unable to defend the regime from external challenges.

Two questions arise when considering how Bush has woven *virtu* and virtue together. First, does Bush's approach blur the distinction between the foreign and domestic realms? To address the first question, we need to consider two secondary problems that characterized Johnson's flawed statesmanship and see whether Bush shares the same flaws. Has the executive relied upon foreign policy powers to justify changes in the domestic realm? A second problem was Johnson's attempt to act as peacetime domestically and a wartime president externally. Has Bush attempted the same? The challenge is that the two realms require two different types of government, and a government at war abroad, for which it needs unitary control, has a hard time sustaining stability in the domestic realm, in which it relies upon a government made up of legislators, citizens, and other influential bodies.

Second, in evaluating how Bush has woven *virtu* and virtue together, does the political logic at work in the external realm threaten to undermine the fundamental principles of limited government on which the domestic regime rests? Thucydides had raised a similar question with the Athenian thesis, whereby immoderation exhibited externally in time infects the domestic realm.[17] I am not arguing that America has acted as an empire abroad and has therefore invalidated its republican principles at home.[18] Nevertheless, it is useful to ask whether Bush's foreign policy goals or how they are executed contain an immoderation that could threaten the domestic realm. One may find that his administration's foreign policy goals are such that they can only be achieved by altering the domestic realm. Does Bush's foreign policy contain this challenge? In other words, has America faced a Machiavellian Moment in responding to 11 September 2001?

When considering this point, I believe it is important to stress that George W. Bush did not create this problem. As I argued with Lyndon Johnson, Bush has faced the same problems as any other executive. Although he may have demonstrated moderation by developing a domestic consensus, what remains to be seen is whether that difference is of degree or kind. A Machiavellian Moment will occur if the other branches of government and, ultimately, the people accede to it willingly or through indifference. In either case the people have a choice. The challenge for the people is to retain their republican virtue against an executive who, because of the necessity created by the external threats, threatens to corrupt the domestic realm. The public may be willing to accept a short-term disruption yet will likely not approve if that short-term disruption becomes a long-term change. How much uncertainty and instability is the public willing to tolerate in the external realm? If security issues take precedence over matters of social justice at home, then fear rather than virtue can come to dominate the domestic realm. Thus far the problem has not emerged, but the longer the war on terror continues the greater is the possibility that a U.S. president will face a Machiavellian Moment.

Bush and his successors must be aware that even if America moves from reforming the international system through such efforts as the war on terror to the goal of managing the system by promoting the global democratic revolution, the republic's integrity still faces a threat. Bush's domestic consensus for the war on terror may simply not extend to managing the system through the global democratic revolution. Carrying out this policy may require more effort than the current consensus is willing to accept. Moreover, such a task may be beyond America's resources as a republic. In effect, the question may arise as to who decides when the war on terror has ended? If the war on terror is without end, can the republic sustain such a war footing without changing the constitutional balance between the branches of the federal government?

President Bush has gone beyond Dean Rusk's pursuit of a decent world order by viewing the United Nations as part of that international system rather than coterminous with it. Whereas Rusk had emphasized the United Nations' promise over its performance, Bush has stressed the opposite. In 1989 the Cold War ended, and to a number of U.S. leaders the United Nations was found wanting. In this regard Bush has viewed the United Nations as part of the nation's foreign policy problem because the organization failed to live up to its promise and has furthermore inhibited U.S. actions meant to enforce order within the international system.[19] UN Secretary-General Kofi Annan has recognized the United Nation's flaws and suggested ways to reform the system to prevent future failures to uphold its principles and power, such as occurred in Rwanda and Kosovo during the 1990s. From Bush's perspective America has had to take on a greater share of responsibility for maintaining the international order, and the United Nations is one element of the global system. For Bush the United Nations may be an important part of the system, but it is only a part.

In the short term assuming the role of reformer is sustainable, but eventually the United States must turn to managing the order. As a reformer, the country can act freely to shape the system to its interests because of its broad access to power. Freedom of action in the international system can come at a price domestically, however, because it may demand more resources than the regime can sustain. (How long can the U.S. constitutional system sustain an exception?) If America wants to manage the system, it will need multilateral institutions such as the United Nations to help export its vision. Bush and his team, however, have not given the United Nations primacy in constructing their vision of the international system. Instead, they have sought to reform the system to their interests. Nevertheless, Bush has recognized that international organizations are important to sustaining international security.[20] The challenge for him as an American statesman is to turn from the global war on terror to the global democratic revolution and then find a way to transfer responsibility for the broad-reaching revolution into the UN system. The question will be whether the world body and Bush's global democratic revolution are converging or diverging and for how long. Also if America goes this route, will it reduce the nation's responsibility for maintaining the system without diluting its own agenda?

The end of the Cold War presented the United States with a philosophical and political dilemma. The United States no longer faced a major rival that might constrain its freedom of action. Although the United States appears to confront a choice between following Rusk's or Kissinger's foreign policy philosophy, it may be that Bush has transcended both of them. It appears that Bush has gone beyond Rusk's pursuit of a decent world order. To this extent he has rejected the limited approach suggested by Kissinger. In contrast to both former secretaries of state, Bush faces an era in which the nation's primacy allows it to exploit its freedom of action to shape the international system to its advantage. Whereas Kissinger argued that America had to be able to act freely for the sake of establishing international limits, Bush has been able to act freely because of its relative power. Kissinger's view of limits led him to develop concepts of legitimacy and equilibrium to achieve stability. Bush, by contrast, has developed a concept of legitimacy that challenges the status quo and causes instability because it requires fundamental changes to the global order. Rusk talked of defending the decent world order, whereas Bush talks of creating it. Moreover, Bush's foreign deeds, both in Afghanistan and Iraq, match his rhetoric of bringing about regime change. If America and the United Nations view the threats to the system in the same way, their interests will find common ground. In this case Bush may yet approach Rusk's position.

America's success in the international system will depend upon the balance within the regime and the balance between the regime and the international system. Without domestic support the president has limited strength to sustain an active international role. For Bush, as it was for Johnson, America's success within the international system will depend on the balance between its domestic and foreign policies. It appears that, unlike Johnson, Bush has not attempted to balance both realms by expanding them, nor has he attempted to fight an undeclared limited war. Instead, he has pursued a relatively limited domestic policy while undertaking an expansive foreign policy. But how long can Bush's expansive foreign policy, which relies on the 11 September 2001 consensus, last?[21] Can a domestic realm organized for peace support a long-term campaign to promote a global democratic revolution? So long as the American regime is based upon a limited government at home, it cannot sustain the expansive and unlimited task of maintaining a world order indefinitely.

The international system may be changing in ways that reduce the strain on the republican regime. The debates within the United Nations over issues of national sovereignty and the organization's responsibility to protect nations under threat from hostile forces raise the possibility that the interests of international system are converging with those of the Bush administration.[22] In other words, if the Bush Doctrine is based upon holding national regimes to account, then the changes this would entail in the international system are reflected, even if indirectly, in the emergence of the idea of responsibility to protect. The responsibility to protect refers to the idea that states have a responsibility to their citizens, and if they fail in their responsibilities, other states may intervene. If that proves to be the case, then Bush's foreign policy does not appear to be as immoderate as Johnson's. In the words of Colin Gray, the international system appears to accept America's role as a sheriff.[23] Similarly, John Lewis Gaddis has pointed out that the question is not why do people hate America but why so many love it.[24] Bush may be able to reconcile the domestic regime to the international system because the two could be converging.

Although a complete treatment is beyond the scope of this chapter, we can only understand Bush's statesmanship set against the changes in the international system. Bush faces a choice as dangerous as the one Johnson had to confront because his foreign policy explicitly seeks to expand America's domestic principles to the world. Although Johnson's failure led the United States to abandon South Vietnam to its fate, it did not compromise the American regime. Bush's success or failure, however, could transform it. An attempt to transmit the bounded universal principles within the regime into a universal system will require an increasingly centralized national government and a more powerful executive. Even without actually achieving that goal the regime risks being transformed.

In the international system the convergence of the United Nations and Bush's global democratic revolution would require the United Nations to shift from a status quo organization to one that supports reform. This does not mean that the United States should control the United Nations or that the policies and preferences of the United Nations should be subordinated to U.S. interests. What needs to be considered is whether the interests of the United Nations and the United States can find commonality and whether the American public will continue to support that arrangement. Can the American public sustain its support for the high military costs until the global democratic revolution is complete? If Bush is able to use the nation's predominance to change the international system, thus freeing America from its burden, he will have succeeded where Johnson failed, but this success will only come about if he can maintain the domestic consensus.

For the American regime the long-term question is how to restrain the executive's power during a long twilight war without hindering its ability to succeed. In this regard the international system may not change sufficiently because the public fears the domestic consequences of an executive empowered to assert order within the international system. The public may tolerate the executive's prerogative in the external realm simply because it has not yet encroached on the domestic realm. Eventually, the problem and the choice it entails will emerge. The problem is a powerful executive that threatens the domestic political balance. The choice will be between the domestic regime and the international system. Whereas during the early years of Johnson's presidency the public had turned away from involvement in the external realm, in part because people were focused on the promise of the Great Society programs and also because they were wary of the high costs of the task, for Bush the situation is very different: America may not be able to stop supporting the global democratic revolution.[25] Moreover, the long campaign may end up corrupting the nation's long-standing republican virtues as the public becomes habituated, out of necessity, to accepting the executive's increased powers because they seek security. In this regard the desire for security begins to corrupt citizens' republican virtue and creates dependence among them, making them subservient to a powerful leader.

AMERICAN STATESMANSHIP IN THE EMERGING INTERNATIONAL SYSTEM

Will the domestic consensus that Bush has been able to sustain extend to long-term public support for the global democratic revolution? Has Bush presented America with a Periclean strategy, which, after he leaves office, could become unmanageable? If the mission in Iraq represents the beginning of a new era, how will it be sustained? Or does the war in Iraq stand as a marker to demonstrate U.S. willingness to apply that rule to other states? America possesses the military power to undertake future regime changes, but can it arouse the same level of public support to undertake future actions without a similar provocation? Moreover, does Iraq represent a limit, serving as an example to encourage other states to undertake reforms? If Bush's approach to Iraq pointed the way toward changing the international system and fulfill Bush's rhetoric, can this strategy last? What, and where, is the next step? The questions are fundamental to the future of the American regime.

The public, which benefits directly from the efforts in the domestic realm and only indirectly from the external realm, may choose to support the domestic realm. The republican virtue may already be corrupted, however, as the people have come to expect big government at home, and only the appetite for government programs at home restrains the executive's power in the external realm. At a grand strategic level Bush may be unable to fulfill the global democratic revolution. Ronald Reagan's tax revolution has had the lasting effect of restraining the growth of government, and the substantial social programs put in place by Lyndon Johnson continue to absorb an increasing share of the government's resources, which leaves a smaller share for pursuing an expansive foreign policy. What Bush may try to do is restrain government at home so that he can use its power abroad. This, however, would require a change in the public culture and a reordering of the public's relationship to the federal government. In sum, Bush would have to reverse the behavior and expectations of big government built up over the past sixty years of social welfare legislation. In his first year in office Bush had already begun to undertake these moves to transform the American regime. He also spoke of changing the American culture following the attacks of 11 September 2001; as he said in the 2002 State of the Union Address: "This time of adversity offers a unique moment of opportunity—a moment we must seize to change our culture."[26] In his 2005 State of the Union Address he spent considerable time talking about reforms to the Social Security system.

The problem is that big government at home relies upon big government abroad. The federal government has grown dramatically since 1932 in large part because of the demands of national security. The response to the attacks on 11 September 2001 represents the latest step in that development. As Bush stated in the introductory letter to his National Security Strategy, the attack led to the largest and most extensive restructuring of the country's national security structure in the nation's history. At the same time, the federal government's increased power and scope have brought important benefits, and these cannot be overlooked, nor should they be overturned. Nevertheless, the Machiavellian Moment may arrive through the small series of changes demanded by the external realm and accepted in the name of security. These changes would be made palatable to the public because they would be incremental and accompanied by clear benefits. These benefits over time could begin to undermine Americans' self-government by making them dependent upon the state.[27] If the public becomes habituated to the power of the government for the sake of greater security and comfort, it may not realize what it is losing in terms of civil rights or even national identity. Bush has not yet faced a Machiavellian Moment, but the nation he is leading—by ignorance, choice, or necessity—may be on the path toward that destination.

The American regime must reconcile its greater role in the international system without giving more power to the federal government, and particularly the executive branch. The challenge in the current war on terror is deciding when the mission has ended or at least eased so that the sense of urgency has abated. Is this a matter for the executive to decide? As long as the regime is set on a war footing, power continues to accrue to the executive, and the legislature tends to be less willing to challenge it. Although it may appear balanced and moderate overall, has Bush's statesmanship set the United States on a long twilight path toward empire? Has Bush set the regime on a goal that is even more immoderate than anything contemplated by Johnson? Rusk's defense of the decent world order in South Vietnam was not open-ended because it was not, for example, part of a greater plan to roll back tyranny and because the Great Society constrained finances. By contrast, Bush's war on terrorism has no apparent limit because, one could argue, the fate of the international system is at stake, and there is no pressing domestic agenda occupying his attention. For Dean Rusk, South Vietnam exemplified the defense of the decent world order, but it was not the final test; when South Vietnam was overrun, the decent world order did not end. What is the alternative to Bush's mission? He has set America the task of transforming the international system to win the war on terrorism. Bush's foreign policy ambition reveals an inherent immoderation within the regime not checked by a domestic policy ambition. Although issues at home such as the destruction created by Hurricane Katrina have raised domestic policy challenges for Bush, they are not of the same magnitude as those of the Great Society. Johnson had understood the costs of building the Great Society, whereas many of the costly social undertakings that have begun during Bush's tenure were not planned.

How much does the American regime need to change to sustain its commitment to the global democratic revolution? One choice is to try to force other states to change by undertaking future wars for regime change. This would be an open-ended goal. A second choice would be to intervene only under exceptional circumstances. If other states change their systems of government because of the Iraq example, it appears that U.S. foreign policy will not undermine the necessary balances within the republican regime. If other nations of the world continue to resist the global democratic revolution, the central question will be how long before the unlimited foreign policy commitment conflicts with the priorities of the nation's republican government.

The challenge for American statesmen is to use the nation's military superiority prudently in seeking to transform the international system in order to enhance America's interests, principles, and purpose without creating resentment and possibly engendering an alternative world order.

NOTES

INTRODUCTION

1. The term *decent world order* refers to the principles contained within the UN Charter, which Dean Rusk understood as the principle of the rule of law and the belief that political change should come through peaceful means, not military force. Upholding the rule of law was a goal that Rusk restated at nearly every occasion at which he invoked the UN Charter. On the role of international law within the United States' conception of the world order, see Francis A. Boyle, *Foundations of World Order: The Legalist Approach to International Relations (1898–1922)* (Durham: Duke University Press, 1999). An attempt to define the term *world order* is found in Torbjorn L. Knutsen, *The Rise and Fall of World Orders* (Manchester: Manchester University Press, 1999).

2. In 1972 Kissinger stressed in Nixon's annual foreign policy message to Congress, the State of the World Address, which Kissinger had written, that the foreign policy philosophy of the United States had changed. See Henry Kissinger, *White House Years* (Boston: Little, Brown, 1979), 159.

3. See Thomas W. Zeiler, *Dean Rusk: Defending the American Mission Abroad* (Wilmington, Del.: Scholarly Resources, 2000). Warren Cohen described Rusk's view as liberal exceptionalism. See Warren I. Cohen, *Dean Rusk: The American Secretaries of State and Their Diplomacy*, ed. Samuel Flag Bemis (Totowa, N.J.: Cooper Square, 1980), 1. See also Patrick L. Hatcher, *The Suicide of an Elite: American Internationalists and Vietnam* (Stanford: Stanford University Press, 1990). On the philosophical understanding of liberal internationalism, see Michael Joseph Smith, "Liberalism and International Reform," in *Traditions of International Ethics*, ed. Terry Nardin and David R. Mapel (Cambridge: Cambridge University Press, 1992), 201–24.

4. See Robert Tucker's analysis that an imperial state identifies the security of the world order with its own security (*Nation or Empire? The Debate over American Foreign Policy* [Baltimore: John Hopkins Press, 1968]). On the issue of the United States and the

world order in Vietnam, see George Liska, *War and Order: Reflections on Vietnam and History* (Baltimore: Johns Hopkins Press, 1968). On the different typologies of empire, see Michael W. Doyle, *Empires* (Ithaca: Cornell University Press, 1986). See also J. S. Richardson, "*Imperium Romanum*: Empire and the Language of Power," *Journal of Roman Studies* 81 (1999): 1–9.

A republic is not a unitary state but one that has a compound or mixed government. See, for example, Alexander Hamilton, James Madison, and John Jay, *The Federalist; or, The New Constitution*, ed. Max Beloff (Oxford: Blackwell, 1948), nos. 10, 39, 40, and 51. In this regard a mixed government, a government of checks and balances, is under threat as power becomes centralized when the government fights an undeclared war to support a commitment to a decent world order.

5. Tucker's observations follow the work of George Liska, who, in examining ancient empires, defines an empire as "a state exceeding other states in size, scope, and salience, and sense of task . . . The scope of its interests and involvements is coterminous with the boundaries of the system itself, rather than with a narrow security zone or habitat . . . Finally, the sense of task which distinguishes the imperial state is typically that of creating, and then maintaining, a world order the conditions and principles of which would harmonize the particular interests of the imperial state with the interests of the commonweal." Qtd. in Tucker, *Nation or Empire*, 9. See also Liska, *War and Order*.

6. Tucker, *Nation or Empire*, 50.

7. The same question can be seen in Thucydides' *History of the Peloponnesian War*, in which Athens attempted to overcome the tension between its domestic regime (liberty) and its external regime (tyranny). On the tension between the two realms and its effect upon foreign policy, see Timothy J. Galpin, "The Democratic Roots of Athenian Imperialism in the Fifth Century B.C.," *Classical Journal* 79 (1983–84): 100–109. See also Christopher Bruell, "Thucydides' View of Athenian Imperialism," *American Political Science Review* 68, no. 1 (1974): 11–18; and Clifford Orwin, "Justifying Empire: The Speech of the Athenians at Sparta and the Problem of Justice in Thucydides," *Journal of Politics* 48, no. 1 (1986): 72–85.

8. For an interesting discussion of the dangers of veering away from republican principles as an American problem during the Vietnam War, see Raymond Aron, *The Imperial Republic: The United States and the World, 1945–1973*, trans. Frank Jellinek (Englewood Cliffs, N.J.: Prentice-Hall, 1974). See also Stanley Hoffmann, *Gulliver's Troubles; or, The Setting of American Foreign Policy* (New York: McGraw-Hill, 1968); and Jerome Slater, "Is United States Foreign Policy 'Imperialist' or 'Imperial'?" *Political Science Quarterly* 91 (1976): 63–87. Two other works that shed light on these questions are Sidney Morgenbesser, "Imperialism: Some Preliminary Distinctions," *Philosophy and Public Affairs* 3, no. 1 (Fall 1973): 3–44; and Robert L. Beisner, "1898 and 1968: The Anti-Imperialists and the Doves," *Political Science Quarterly* 85, no. 2 (June 1970): 187–216. Alexander Hamilton made an early effort to address how this problem might challenge the United States, exploring the possible ways in which the American republic could be an "empire" without threatening the liberty within it. Hamilton expressed this new form of empire in *Federalist Papers*, no. 1. He believed that the United States could be a republican empire and

overcome the problem of expansion, normally an act of imperialism, by basing expansion upon consent by the republic's citizens. See Karl-Friedrich Walling, *Republican Empire: Alexander Hamilton on War and Free Government* (Lawrence: University Press of Kansas, 1999).

9. Hadley Arkes, *Bureaucracy, The Marshall Plan, and the National Interest* (Princeton: Princeton University Press, 1972), 6. Arkes discusses how a regime embodies the rules, laws, and norms of a society. See also Joseph Cropsey, "The United States as Regime," in *The Moral Foundations of the American Republic*, ed. Robert Horwitz, 3d ed. (Charlottesville: University Press of Virginia, 1986).

10. In understanding the functions and qualities of statesmanship, this book relies upon Wendell John Coats Jr., *Statesmanship: Six Modern Illustrations of a Modified Ancient Ideal* (Selinsgrove, Pa.: Susquehanna University Press, 1995). Coats attempts to develop a theory of statesmanship based upon the ancient understanding of the ideal and to apply it in modern contexts. In particular, he looks at three skills that a statesman must possess in order to be successful: "First is the distinctly statesman like skill, following the ancient Greek view of politics as the master, or architectonic art, of judging when to employ and develop the other 'arts' (e.g., diplomatic, financial, military, and so on) . . . [The second set of skills upon which the first relies is] some substantive knowledge of the subordinate activities and professions involved—legal, commercial, military, parliamentarian, etc. A third distinct area of skills contributing to success in the art of statesmanship concerns those expressly useful in building alliances or bases of support: for example, ability at public and private persuasion, diplomacy, endurance, and a working knowledge of the types of human beings afoot, including what is likely to be persuasive and motivating for each type, under varying circumstance, from normal to extreme" (28–29). These skills relate to statesmanship's aims, scope, and means. Coats looks at statesmanship generally, whereas here I examine it within the realm of foreign policy with some attention to its impact within the domestic realm. A full understanding of Johnson's statesmanship would encompass his efforts within the domestic realm and the external realm.

11. William Appleman Williams also argued that America's expansion abroad would have domestic consequences. Along with Tucker, he understood this essential dilemma for U.S. diplomacy but, unlike Tucker, he was concerned with the role of economics in encouraging the nation to take on external responsibilities. William Appleman Williams, *The Tragedy of American Diplomacy* (New York: Norton, 1988); Williams, *The Roots of the Modern American Empire* (London: Blond, 1970); and Williams, *Empire as a Way of Life: An Essay on the Causes and Character of America's Present Predicament along with a Few Thoughts about an Alternative* (Oxford: Oxford University Press, 1982); David Noble, *The End of American History: Democracy, Capitalism, and the Metaphor of Two Worlds in Anglo-American Historical Writing, 1880–1980* (Minneapolis: University of Minnesota Press, 1985), 136–39. Noble argues that the root of Williams's complaint with American foreign policy is that he is preaching a conservative jeremiad in trying to reconcile American democracy with American capitalism. Thus, Williams seeks to restrain the utopian aspect of American politics for fear that the United States, through a belief in its status as a redeemer nation, will bring us to the brink of Armageddon.

12. Tucker, *Nation or Empire*, 52.

13. Tucker, *Nation or Empire*, 53.

14. Cohen, *Dean Rusk*, 128.

15. See, for example, the statement by Lyndon Johnson: "We are in South Vietnam not only for he South Vietnamese but for ourselves, not only to preserve the freedom of the South Vietnamese but to preserve the freedom of others and ultimately of our own." Qtd. in Tucker, *Nation or Empire*, 14.

16. A globalist foreign policy means that the nation in question has interests around the world that it must protect. The Roman Empire at the end had such a policy but was unable to meet all the threats to its various interests and thus collapsed. See Joseph A. Schumpeter, *Imperialism and Social Classes*, trans. Heinz Norden, ed. Paul M. Sweezy (Oxford: Blackwell, 1951), 66. A system of collective security such as NATO faces a similar problem because a challenge to that system, if it goes unaddressed, can undermine the credibility of the system and render it powerless. The failure to uphold collective security before World War II had catastrophic consequences for much of the world; the post–World War II international system was carefully designed to avoid such breakdowns of order in the future.

17. John B. Hall II and William Espinosa, "The Tragedy of Dean Rusk," *Foreign Policy* 8 (1972): 172. "He equated American diplomacy with the aims of the UN. He would frequently read the Preamble of the UN Charter and proclaim, 'I have also just read to you the essential foreign policy of the United States.'"

18. Tucker, *Nation or Empire*, 37–38; also see, for example, Richard W. Van Alstyne, *The Rising American Empire* (New York: Norton, 1974), 1–27.

19. J.G.A. Pocock, *The Machiavellian Moment: Florentine Political Thought and the Atlantic Republican Tradition* (Princeton: Princeton University Press, 1975), vii. See also Pocock, "The Machiavellian Moment Revisited: A Study in History and Ideology," *Journal of Modern History* 53 (March 1981): 49–72.

20. See *Federalist Papers*, nos. 48 and 67.

21. Mark Jurdjevic calls this "Machiavelli's republican paradox" because a republic can only survive by expanding, but the roots of decay are born in expansion. See Jurdjevic, "Virtue, Commerce, and the Enduring Florentine Republican Moment: Reintegrating Italy into the Atlantic Republican Debate," *Journal of the History of Ideas* (2001): 728.

22. On the problem of corruption in republican politics and how it relates to the regime's health rather than simply its political behavior, see S. M. Shumer, "Republican Politics and Its Corruption," *Political Theory* 7, no. 1 (February 1979): 5–34.

23. Pocock, *Machiavellian Moment*, 3.

24. Karl von Clausewitz, a Prussian general and military strategist during the Napoleonic Wars, is well known for his proposition that war is "merely the continuation of policy by other means." See Wendell John Coats Jr., "American Democracy and the Punitive Use of Force: Requiem for the McNamara Model," *A Theory of Republican Character and Related Essays*, 78–118 (Selinsgrove, Pa.: Susquehanna University Press, 1994).

25. Johnson financed the war on a peacetime budget, which necessarily limited the war effort. To put it differently, Johnson did not have the same economic support for the

war as Truman had for the Korean War. See Leonard B. Taylor, *Financial Management of the Vietnam Conflict, 1962–1972* (Washington, D.C.: Department of the Army, 1991).

26. Robert M. Collins, "The Economic Crisis of 1968 and the Waning of the 'American Century,'" *American Historical Review* 101 (April 1996): 396–422.

27. A contemporaneous approach to the problem of America's role within the international system can be seen in Charles O. Lerche, "The Crisis in American World Leadership," *Journal of Politics* 28 (1966): 308–21.

28. See Lyndon B. Johnson, *The Vantage Point: Perspectives of the Presidency, 1963–1969* (New York: Holt, Rinehart and Winston, 1971), 443.

29. On Johnson's political style, see Philip L. Geyelin, *Lyndon B. Johnson and the World* (New York: Praeger, 1966). On Johnson's desire to avoid a debate over Vietnam and his middle path policy, see Robert Dallek, "Lyndon Johnson and Vietnam: The Making of a Tragedy," *Diplomatic History* 20, no. 2 (1996): 148–55.

30. Gordon Silverstein, *Imbalance of Powers: Constitutional Interpretation and the Making of American Foreign Policy* (Oxford: Oxford University Press, 1997), 25–30. Silverstein emphasizes the rise of the executive prerogative after World War II to explain the imbalance between the executive and the legislative branches. His analysis depends largely upon the belief that the Constitution must be read as a unitary document so that powers granted to foreign policy also serve domestic policy. This interpretation runs counter to Justice George Sutherland's, which focuses on natural rights and reads the Constitution differently as it pertains to foreign affairs versus domestic affairs. For an alternative view of the question, see Hadley Arkes, *The Return of George Sutherland: Restoring a Jurisprudence of Natural Rights* (Princeton: Princeton University Press, 1994). Arkes argues that the two realms can be reconciled by returning to a natural rights understanding of the Constitution and the role of the executive branch.

31. Arkes, *Return of George Sutherland*.

32. See, for example, *Federalist Papers*, nos. 48 and 67.

33. Dean Rusk, *The Winds of Freedom: Selections from the Speeches and Statements of the Secretary of State Dean Rusk, January 1961–August 1962* (Boston: Beacon Press, 1963), 5 and 16.

34. Paul M. Kattenburg, *The Vietnam Trauma in American Foreign Policy, 1945–1975* (New Brunswick, N.J.: Transaction Books, 1980), 71.

35. Rusk firmly believed, as noted earlier, in the benefits that America's fight for freedom could bring to the rest of the world. Unlike his predecessor Dean Acheson, who, according to Rusk, "did not give a damn about the brown, yellow, black, and red peoples of the world," Rusk did care. Rusk, as told to Richard Rusk, *As I Saw It* (New York: Norton, 1990), 422. Acheson argued that the European, or Atlantic, relationship was the most critical to the United States and therefore more important than the Pacific relationship. Rusk believed, however, that other nations besides those of the Atlantic region also deserved the blessings of liberty. As a result, his foreign policy outlook shifted from the Atlantic to the Pacific and relied heavily on the principle of universalism.

36. John Lewis Gaddis, *Strategies of Containment: A Critical Appraisal of Postwar American National Security Policy* (New York: Oxford University Press, 1982), 200–202

and 208–10. See, for example, Rostow's work on economic modernization as a counter to the communist theories of modernization. W. W. Rostow, *The Stages of Economic Growth: A Non-Communist Manifesto* (Cambridge: Cambridge University Press, 1960).

37. Gaddis, *Strategies*, 217–18.

38. Thomas J. Schoenbaum, *Waging Peace and War: Dean Rusk in the Truman, Kennedy, and Johnson Years* (New York: Simon and Schuster, 1988), 369–70.

39. Shoenbaum, *Waging Peace and War*, 149. Warren I. Cohen, *Dean Rusk*, vol. 10 of *The American Secretaries of State and Their Diplomacy*, ed. Samuel Flag Bemis (Totowa, N.J.: Cooper Square, 1980), 10–12.

40. Schoenbaum, *Waging Peace*, 206–7.

41. Schoenbaum, *Waging Peace*, 200–201.

42. For a discussion of Rusk's argument for how the United States should deal with China's aggression and the need to keep China from receiving a political reward for military aggression, see *FRUS* 7 (1950): 1327.

43. See Yeung Fong Khong, *Analogies at War: Korea, Munich, Dien Bien Phu, and the Vietnam Decisions of 1965* (Princeton: Princeton University Press, 1992), 45. The Korean War was the analogy used most frequently in the foreign policy decision making of 1965. According to Khong, Rusk used historical analogies more than the other participants. His historical analogies can perhaps be attributed to his firsthand experience with the danger of failing to resist military aggression. He was in Germany during the rise of the Nazis in 1933 and was undersecretary of state for Far Eastern Affairs at the outbreak of the Korean War.

44. See Stephen E. Ambrose, *Rise to Globalism: American Foreign Policy since 1938*, 4th rev. ed. (New York: Penguin Books, 1985). See also Akira Iriye *The Globalizing of America, 1913–1945* (Cambridge: Cambridge University Press, 1993).

45. See Lloyd Gardner, *Pay Any Price: Lyndon Johnson and the Wars for Vietnam* (London: Ivan Dees, 1995), 244.

46. See, for example, Gardner, *Pay Any Price*, 186. Johnson connected the Civil Rights movement to international events and, with his advisors, saw the interrelationship between the domestic and international realms in regard to Vietnam (253–56).

47. Transcript, Dean Rusk Papers, interview 2, 26 September 1969, by Paige E. Mulhollan, Internet copy, LBJ Library, 17.

48. See Coats, "American Democracy."

49. On this question, see Michael H. Hunt, *Lyndon Johnson's War: America's Cold War Crusade in Vietnam, 1945–1965* (New York: Hill and Wang, 1996), 87–88. See also Chen Jian, "China's Involvement in the Vietnam War, 1964–1969," *China Quarterly* 142 (June 1995): 356–87. On the promise to intervene, see 360–61; on the U.S. reaction, 367; and on the amount of men and material, see 372–79.

50. See for example, Brands, *Wages*, 4 and 234. See also Doris Kearns, *Lyndon Johnson and the American Dream* (New York: Harper and Row, 1976), 252–54. Johnson spoke of having bad dreams and feared being called a coward by Robert Kennedy for betraying JFK's legacy.

51. Moya Ann Ball, "The Phantom of the Oval Office: The John F. Kennedy Assassination's Symbolic Impact on Lyndon B. Johnson, His Key Advisers, and the Vietnam Decision-Making Process," *Presidential Studies Quarterly* 24 (Winter 1994): 105–19.

52. For an excellent insight into Johnson's other foreign policy issues and how Vietnam influenced them, see Thomas Alan Schwartz, *Lyndon Johnson and Europe: In the Shadow of Vietnam* (Cambridge, Mass.: Harvard University Press, 2003).

53. For a very interesting analysis of virtue and *virtu* within Machiavelli's work, see Harvey C. Mansfield Jr., *Machiavelli's Virtue* (Chicago: University of Chicago Press, 1996).

54. See Gardner, *Pay Any Price*, 253.

55. Hans J. Morgenthau argued that China would not allow this and would have required a war that we could neither win nor afford to lose. Morgenthau, *Vietnam and the United States* (Washington, D.C.: Public Affairs Press, 1965).

56. Harry W. Brands, *The Wages of Globalism: Lyndon Johnson and the Limits of American Power* (Oxford: Oxford University Press, 1995), argues that Johnson's foreign policy, aside from Vietnam, was successful. For a contrary view, see Gaddis, *Strategies*.

57. Gaddis makes this point repeatedly in *Strategies* and argues that Nixon and Kissinger returned American foreign policy to its original limits as suggested by Kennan's initial writings. See Gaddis, *Strategies*, 308.

58. For a fuller understanding of how Machiavelli envisioned the perfect advisor to a prince, see chaps. 22 and 23 of Niccolò Machiavelli's *The Prince*.

59. See Peter W. Dickson, *Kissinger and the Meaning of History* (London: Cambridge University Press, 1978), 83–116.

60. Joanne Gowa, *Closing the Gold Window: Domestic Politics and the End of Bretton Woods* (Ithaca: Cornell University Press, 1983). See also M. Stephen Weatherford, "The International Economy as a Constraint on U.S. Macroeconomic Policymaking," *International Organization* 42, no. 4 (Fall 1988): 611–25, esp. 615–23.

61. Gardner, *Pay Any Price*, 35.

62. For a good overview of the relationship between the United States and the United Nations, see Gary B. Ostrower, *The United Nations and the United States* (London: Twayne, 1998).

1. DEAN RUSK

This chapter relies heavily upon Dean Rusk's public statements within the *Department of State Bulletin* (*DOSB*) as well as material from the few books written on Rusk: Dean Rusk, *As I Saw It*, as told to Richard Rusk, ed. Daniel S. Papp (New York: Norton, 1990); Thomas J. Schoenbaum, *Waging Peace and War: Dean Rusk in the Truman, Kennedy, and Johnson Years* (New York: Simon and Schuster, 1988); see also Thomas Zeiler, *Dean Rusk: Defending the American Mission Abroad* (Wilmington, Del.: Scholarly Resources, 1999); Warren I. Cohen, *Dean Rusk* (Totowa, N.J.: Cooper Square, 1980).

1. See for example Kennedy's Inaugural Address: "We observe today not a victory of party but a celebration of freedom—symbolizing an end as well as a beginning—signify-

ing renewal as well as change"; and "Now the trumpet summons us again—not as a call to bear arms, though arms we need—not as a call to battle, though embattled we are—but a call to bear the burden of a long twilight struggle, year in and year out, 'rejoicing in hope, patient in tribulation'—a struggle against the common enemies of man: tyranny, poverty, disease, and war itself." *DOSB*, 6 February 1961, 175–76.

2. See, for example, Robert Dallek, *Flawed Giant: Lyndon B. Johnson, 1960–1973* (Oxford: Oxford University Press, 1998); Lloyd Gardner, *Pay Any Price: Lyndon Johnson and the Wars for Vietnam* (Chicago: Ivan Dees, 1995).

3. Johnson's first speech was titled "Let Us Continue," which stressed that the United States would keep its commitments from South Vietnam to Berlin.

4. Lyndon B. Johnson, *The Vantage Point: Perspectives of the Presidency, 1963–1969* (New York: Holt, Rinehart and Winston, 1971), 443.

5. See Gardner, *Pay Any Price*, 186; Doris Kearns, *Lyndon Johnson and the American Dream* (New York: Harper and Row, 1976), 251.

6. Rusk had faced a similar dilemma over Korea. There America had to find a middle path between total war and abject surrender. The solution in Korea was different from Vietnam, however, because there the effort had been sanctioned by the United Nations, whereas in Vietnam it had not. Moreover, the Korean conflict was not waged as an undeclared limited war whereby the administration sought to avoid a full debate on the war effort for fear of the social and economic consequences of doing so. See U.S. Department of State, *Foreign Relations of the United States, 1950*, vol. 7: *Korea*, 1327 (hereafter cited as *FRUS*).

7. Rusk, *As I Saw It*, 456.

8. Johnson, *Vantage Point*, 112–53.

9. See *FRUS, 1964–1968*, vol. 2: *Vietnam (January–June 1965)*, 95–97.

10. Hans J. Morgenthau, *Vietnam and the United States* (Washington, D.C.: Public Affairs Press, 1965), 84–87.

11. See *DOSB*, 13 May 1963, 727-35.

12. Leo Strauss, *What Is Political Philosophy? and Other Studies* (Glencoe, Ill.: Free Press, 1959). Strauss argues that all political action is either for preservation or change and is guided by the good. The forces for change see the good they pursue as better than the good pursued by the forces for continuity. In either case the contestants see their positions as designed to maintain the good.

13. See transcript, Dean Rusk Papers, interview 2, 26 September 1969, by Paige E. Mulhollan, Internet copy, LBJ Library, tape 2, 17: "We learned the lessons from World War II and wrote them into the United Nations Charter and into our great security treaties. The principal lesson we learned from World War II is that if a course of aggression is allowed to gather momentum that it continues to build and leads eventually to a general conflict."

14. Thomas J. Schoenbaum, *Waging Peace and War: Dean Rusk in the Truman, Kennedy and Johnson Years* (New York: Simon Schuster, 1988), 206–7.

15. Schoenbaum, *Waging Peace*, 200–201.

16. See, for example, Dean Rusk, "The President," *Foreign Affairs* 38, no. 3 (April 1960): 353–69. As he would say later, he was a strong admirer of George Marshall and hoped to emulate his approach to the position. In Dean Rusk's words, "He never let any blue sky show between he and the president." Rusk, *As I Saw It*, 516.

17. Brands, *Wages of Globalism*, 5–6.

18. See *FRUS, 1950*, vol. 6: *Korea*, 752.

19. See Thomas Zeiler, *Dean Rusk: Defending the American Mission Abroad* (Scholarly Resources, 1999). Warren Cohen described Rusk's view as liberal exceptionalism. See Cohen, *Dean Rusk*, 1. See also Patrick L. Hatcher, *The Suicide of an Elite: American Internationalists and Vietnam* (Stanford: Stanford University Press, 1990). On the philosophical understanding of liberal internationalism, see Michael Joseph Smith, "Liberalism and International Reform," in *Traditions of International Ethics*, ed. Terry Nardin and David R. Mapel (Cambridge: Cambridge University Press, 1992), 201–24.

20. See Rusk, *Winds of Freedom*.

21. G. G. Gutierrez, "Dean Rusk and Southeast Asia: An Operational Code Analysis," paper presented at the 1973 annual meeting of the American Political Science Association New Orleans, September 1973.

22. See *DOSB*, 31 July 1961, 175–83; and Rusk, *Winds of Freedom*, 11.

23. See transcript, Dean Rusk Papers, interview 4, 8 March 1970, by Paige E. Mulhollan, Internet copy, LBJ Library, 29.

24. See Peter Rodman, *More Precious than Peace: Fighting and Winning the Cold War in the Third World* (New York: Scribner's, 1994). Rodman argues that after the arenas of Europe and the delivery of nuclear weapons had become stalemated, the new arena for the Cold War would be the Third World. This change occurred in the 1960s with Khrushchev's wars of national liberation and the attempt to turn the United States' and the West's flank.

25. See Ronald J. Stupak, "Dean Rusk on International Relations: An Analysis of His Philosophical Perceptions," *Australian Outlook: Journal of the Australian Institute for International Affairs* 25, no. 1 (April 1971): 13–28.

26. See Cohen, *Dean Rusk*, 128. Rusk shifted the geopolitical view away from the Atlantic to a more global perspective. The change in geopolitical focus is also indicative of the changed philosophical outlook.

27. Transcript, Dean Rusk Papers, interview 2, tape 2, 26 September 1969, by Paige E. Mulhollan, Internet copy, LBJ Library, 17–18.

28. See Rusk, *Winds of Freedom*, 1–8.

29. See W. W. Rostow, *The Stages of Economic Growth: A Non-Communist Manifesto* (Cambridge: Cambridge University Press, 1960).

30. *DOSB*, 17 August 1964, 217.

31. Rusk testified thirty-two times before Congress on behalf of foreign aid. See transcript, Dean Rusk Papers, interview 3, tape 1, 2 January 1970 by Paige E. Mulhollan, Internet copy, LBJ Library, 28.

32. See Rusk, *As I Saw It*, 398–407.

33. See *DOSB*, 2 December 1963, 842.

34. As Ronald Stupak points out, Rusk was not averse to employing "realism" in the manner of Kennan or Morgenthau, but he used it to achieve an idealistic world order. American foreign policy would actively seek this end and not simply wait for it to occur by fortune: "One must invariably remember that this 'official realism' was based on his consuming belief that the United States must *actively* pursue an international system based on the principles of the United Nations Charter. In effect, basic philosophical value judgements probably reflect more accurately the driving force behind a Rusk stance on a foreign policy issue than does an understanding of the realism of a Morgenthau or an Acheson" (Stupak, "Dean Rusk on International Relations," 25).

35. See transcript, Dean Rusk Papers, interview 2, tape 1, 26 September 1969, by Paige E. Mulhollan, Internet copy, LBJ Library, 3–4. "The credibility of the President of the United States at a moment of crisis and the fidelity of the United States to its security treaties are both of the utmost importance in maintaining peace in the world" (4).

36. See Khong, *Analogies*, 57.

37. See Schoenbaum, *Waging Peace*, 50–51, 61.

38. See *DOSB*, 6 March 1951, 335; and Rusk, *As I Saw It*, 82–83.

39. Dean Rusk Papers, tape PPPPP, 28. Rusk says that Kennedy firmly believed in making collective security a top priority.

40. Kenneth W. Thompson, *Tradition and Values in Politics and Diplomacy: Theory and Practice* (Baton Rouge: Louisiana State University Press, 1992), 273–79, esp. 279, in which he discusses the ambiguity of collective security in Vietnam.

41. Brands, *Wages*, 241. Johnson tried to visualize what the world would look like if the United States did not intervene.

42. On Rusk's negotiating efforts, see Rusk, *As I Saw It*, 459–74.

43. The point was reinforced by Rusk's belief in Lin Piao's statement in the *Peking Review* concerning the people's wars against U.S. imperialism. Lin Piao, "Long Live the Victory of People's War," *Peking Review* 8, no. 36, 3 September 1965.

44. Rusk did not believe that the United States had developed then, or now, an adequate strategy for dealing with insurgencies. Dean Rusk Papers, tape XXX XXX, 8.

45. See Henry Kissinger, *White House Years* (Boston: Little, Brown, 1979), 69.

46. In his Inaugural Address Kennedy pointed out that the United States would have to compete with communism but that this was not the sole justification for his undertaking particular programs: "Not because the communists may be doing it, not because we seek their votes, but because it is right."

47. W. W. Rostow, *The View from the Seventh Floor* (New York: Harper and Row, 1964), 14.

48. Gaddis, *Strategies*, 200.

49. Chen Jian, "China's Involvement," 360–61.

50. Rusk, *As I Saw It*, 456.

51. See, for example, Dean Rusk, *The Winds of Freedom*, ed. Ernest K. Lindley (Boston: Beacon Press, 1963), 1–9.

52. Cohen, *Dean Rusk*, 1.

53. Cohen, *Dean Rusk*, 133. See Ernest Lee Tuveson, *Redeemer Nation: The Idea of America's Millennial Role* (Chicago: University of Chicago Press, 1968); Anders Stephanson, *Manifest Destiny: American Expansionism and the Empire of Right* (New York: Hill and Wang, 1996). See also Albert K. Weinberg, *Manifest Destiny: A Study of Nationalist Expansionism in American History* (Chicago: Quadrangle Books, 1963).

54. Rusk was not committed to the traditional U.S. ideal of progress; in fact, he doubted that modern man was somehow morally superior to primitive man. His concern was that underlying modern humanity's successes in attaining peace and prosperity was the ever-present possibility that human beings themselves could destroy those gains. See Schoenbaum, *Waging Peace*, 265.

55. See, for example, Rusk, *As I Saw It*, 532.

56. Rusk, *Winds of Freedom*, 8.

57. While the word *progress* also contains a moral element, the meaning here is in economic terms. Progress in the economic sphere does not imply progress in the moral sphere, and Rusk would never equate the two. He would, however, stress the importance of sharing progress from one nation—ruled by a government that derives its just powers from the consent of the governed—to other nations, following that principle. In this regard Rusk was a believer in political progress. Moreover, he believed that economic progress and political progress go together.

58. Nisbet, *History of the Idea of Progress*, 4.

59. Christopher Lasch, *True and Only Heaven: Progress and Its Critics* (New York: Norton, 1991).

60. Lyndon Johnson, *My Hope for America* (New York: Random House, 1964), 90.

61. Rusk, *Winds of Freedom*, 43.

62. Rusk, *Winds of Freedom*, 17.

63. Rusk, *Winds of Freedom*, 1.

64. See, for example, *DOSB*, 30 December 1963, 993; and 28 October 1963, 654–58.

65. The failure in Vietnam became particularly dangerous because it threatened to undermine that idealism. Despite a high number of casualties, the United States and its institutions escaped from Vietnam relatively unscathed, but the imbalance between the president and the Congress, as exemplified in the War Powers legislation, is an ongoing legacy of the war. See Gordon Silverstein, *Imbalance of Powers: Constitutional Interpretation and the Making of American Foreign Policy* (New York: Oxford University Press, 1997).

66. See Rusk, *Winds of Freedom*, 58. Rusk's view of the United States and its role in the world bears a striking resemblance to the idea of the Puritans' errand into the wilderness used by Perry Miller. See Miller, *Errand into the Wilderness* (Cambridge, Mass.: Belknap Press of the Harvard University Press, 1964), 1–15.

67. *DOSB*, 20 July 1964, 77. "We owe these things [economic and social reforms] to ourselves. I am interested in them as a citizen, but also as Secretary of State. For whatever improves our national life also strengthens freedom in the world struggle in which we are engaged. We are the trustees, the leaders, of the cause of freedom. Our enemies rejoice in our blemishes. The friends of freedom, who are a great majority of mankind, expect us to set a splendid example."

68. *DOSB*, 8 February 1965, 166. "We have to be concerned with the whole world. We can be secure only to the extent that this planet is safe for freedom." See also *DOSB*, 10 May 1965, 699; *DOSB*, 28 June 1965, 1032; and *DOSB*, 6 July 1964, 3.

69. *DOSB*, 22 March 1965, 399. "When we talk about 'the rule of law,' we are talking about the difference between rational behavior and the regime of the jungle. We know that law enlarges the area of freedom by making it possible to predict with greater confidence the behavior of others."

70. *DOSB*, 27 September 1965, 511 and 513.

71. *DOSB*, 22 March 1945, 399. "The goals and our policies grow out of our interests as a nation and our basic commitment to the people—commitment to freedom and human dignity."

72. See *DOSB*, 17 April 1961, 547; and Cohen, *Rusk*, 128.

73. Cohen, *Rusk*, 128.

74. Rusk could understand why Americans would be skeptical of collective security since, in supporting it, they had suffered over six hundred thousand dead and wounded, and the United States had supplied 90 percent of the forces in Korea. See Rusk, Dean Rusk Papers, tape T.

75. See transcript, Dean Rusk Papers, interview 2, tape 2, 26 September 1969, by Paige E. Mulhollan, Internet copy, LBJ Library, 17.

76. Andrew Rotter, *The Path to Vietnam: Origins of the American Commitment to Southeast Asia* (Ithaca: Cornell University Press, 1987). Japan was an important ally and a key part of the world economy, and it depended economically upon Southeast Asia.

77. See Gaddis, *Strategies*, 109–13.

78. Geoffrey R. Sloan, *Geopolitics in United States Strategic Policy, 1890–1987* (Brighton: Wheatsheaf, 1988), 143–44.

79. Sloan, *Geopolitics*, 142.

80. See Douglas J. Macdonald, "The Truman Administration and Global Responsibilities: The Birth of the Falling Domino." In *Dominoes and Bandwagons: Strategic Beliefs and Great Power Competition in the Eurasian Rimland*, ed. Robert Jervis and Jack Snyder (Oxford: Oxford University Press, 1991), 112–44.

81. Rusk, *As I Saw It*, 495–96.

82. Sloan, *Geopolitics*, 150.

83. See Rodman, *More Precious than Peace*.

84. Gordon H. Chang, "China, JFK, and the Bomb," *Journal of American History* 74, no. 4 (March 1988): 1290.

85. Chen Jian, "China's Involvement in the Vietnam War, 1964–1969," *China Quarterly* 142 (June 1995): 356–87.

86. See, for example, *DOSB*, 6 April 1964, 534: "We dare not falter. For unless the world is made safe for freedom, our own freedom cannot survive"; and again *DOSB*, 6 July 1964, 3: "Today, we can be secure only to the extent that our total environment is secure—and by 'total environment' I mean the land, waters, and earth of the entire world and adjacent areas of space."

87. For an interesting analysis of the theory of exceptionalism and its application to U.S. foreign policy, see Joseph Lepgold and Timothy McKeown, "Is American Foreign Policy Exceptional? An Empirical Analysis," *Political Science Quarterly* 110, no. 3 (Fall 1995): 369–84. Although their study suggests that U.S. foreign policy is not exceptional, it does explore the New World–Old World dichotomy as part of America's self-image as an exceptional country. My book explores the connection between the foreign policy crisis and the crisis of exceptionalism within the United States.

88. See, for example, *DOSB*, 4 June 1962, 896.

89. See Tony Smith, *America's Mission: The United States and the Worldwide Struggle for Democracy in the Twentieth Century* (Princeton: Princeton University Press, 1994).

90. Rusk, *DOSB*, 9 March 1964, 361.

91. See Tuveson, *Redeemer Nation*; and David Noble, *The End of American History: Democracy, Capitalism, and the Metaphor of the Two Worlds in Anglo-American Historical Writing, 1880–1980* (Minneapolis: University of Minnesota Press, 1985).

2. LYNDON JOHNSON'S FLAWED STATESMANSHIP AND THE NEAR MACHIAVELLIAN MOMENT IN AMERICAN FOREIGN POLICY

1. On the foreign policy crisis, see Eugene V. Rostow, "Great Cases Make Bad Law: The War Powers Act," *University of Texas Law Review* 50, no. 5 (May 1972), 899. On the constitutional crisis, see George McGovern, "Indochina: The Constitutional Crisis," *Congressional Record—Senate* 15419 (13 May 1970).

2. This chapter focuses on the political-philosophical context for the decision rather than offering a comprehensive account of the decision. Several excellent diplomatic histories already exist of that tumultuous month. See, for example, William C. Gibbons, *The U.S. Government and the Vietnam War*, pt. 3: *January–July 1965* (Princeton: Princeton University Press, 1989); Larry Berman, *Planning a Tragedy: The Americanization of the War in Vietnam* (New York: Norton, 1982); Lloyd C. Gardner, *Pay Any Price: Lyndon Johnson and the Wars for Vietnam* (Chicago: Ivan Dee, 1995).

3. J.G.A. Pocock, *The Machiavellian Moment: Florentine Political Thought and the Atlantic Republican Tradition* (Princeton: Princeton University Press, 1975), vii. See also Pocock, "The Machiavellian Moment Revisited: A Study in History and Ideology," *Journal of Modern History* 53 (March 1981): 49–72.

4. See *Federalist Papers*, nos. 48 and 67.

5. Pocock, *Machiavellian Moment*, 3.

6. See Harvey C. Mansfield Jr., *Taming the Prince: The Ambivalence of Modern Executive Power* (Baltimore: John Hopkins University Press, 1993). See also Niccolò Machiavelli, *The Prince*, Rethinking the Western Tradition, trans. and ed. Angelo M. Codevilla (New Haven: Yale University Press, 1997), chap. 18. In particular, Machiavelli stressed the point that a prince had to be able, as necessity required, to adapt his approach to finding a middle path by balancing the duality (see chaps. 15–19, which focus on the statecraft required of a successful prince).

7. See Plato, *The Statesman*, trans. J. B. Skemp (London: Routledge and Kegan Paul, 1952).

8. By statesmanship, I follow the concept sketched by Plato in *The Statesman* and elaborated by Wendell Coats Jr. in *Statesmanship: Six Modern Illustrations of a Modified Ancient Ideal* (Selinsgrove, Pa.: Susquehanna University Press, 1995). According to Plato, finding a moderate middle path that can weave together both the aggressive and the peaceful elements within a society is the task of a statesman. See Plato, *Statesman*, 306a–311c. See also Stanley Rosen, *Plato's Statesman: The Web of Politics* (New Haven: Yale University Press, 1995), 179–90; and Joseph Cropsey, *Plato's World: Man's Place in the Cosmos* (Chicago: University of Chicago Press, 1995), 141–44.

9. Coats, *Statesmanship*, 123.

10. See Coats, *Statesmanship*, 113.

11. This problem is perhaps at the crux of the debate over war powers and who controls foreign policy. Although Congress has a constitutional role to play in designing and enacting foreign policy, it tends to shun direct action in this area because its members prefer to avoid the political pitfalls associated with setting foreign policy. An examination of the compelling debate between the executive and legislative branches is beyond the scope of this book. What I hope to show, however, is that Johnson's mishandling of the relationship threatened the regime. The war powers controversy is but one example of the instability created by Johnson's flawed statesmanship. For more on the idea that the war powers are shared by Congress and the president, see Maj. Geoffrey S. Corn, "Presidential War Powers: Do the Courts Offer Any Answers?" *Military Law Review* 157 (October 1998): 180–255.

12. See Sutherland's opinion in *United States v. Curtiss-Wright Export Corp.*, 299 U.S. 304 (1936). Hadley Arkes touches on this issue in *The Return of George Sutherland: Restoring a Jurisprudence of Natural Rights* (Princeton: Princeton University Press, 1994).

13. Johnson believed he could pay for the war and the Great Society at the same time. See, for example, Donald F. Kettl, "The Economic Education of Lyndon Johnson: Guns, Butter, and Taxes," in *The Johnson Years*, vol. 2: *Vietnam, the Environment, and Science*, ed. Robert A. Divine (Lawrence: University Press of Kansas, 1987), 54–78. Of particular interest is Kettl point that at the time guns and butter seemed possible and his citation of Gardner Ackley's 30 July 1965 memo (54, 58). In the memo Ackley suggests that there is room in the economy to handle a defense buildup.

14. See *Public Papers of the Presidents of the United States: Lyndon B. Johnson*, vol. 1: *1965* (Washington, D.C.: Government Printing Office, 1966), 794–803, (hereafter cited as *PPP LBJ*).

15. See Lyndon B. Johnson, *The Vantage Point: Perspectives of the presidency, 1963–1969* (London: Weidenfeld and Nicolson, 1972), 443.

16. Lloyd C. Gardner, *Pay Any Price: Lyndon Johnson and the Wars for Vietnam* (Chicago: I. R. Dee, 1995). See also Joseph A. Califano Jr., *The Triumph and the Tragedy of Lyndon Johnson: The White House Years* (New York: Simon and Schuster, 1991), 37, 106–14. See also Johnson, *Vantage Point*, 443.

17. See Henry William Brands Jr., "Johnson and Eisenhower: The President, the Former President, and the War in Vietnam" *Presidential Studies Quarterly* 15 (1985): 589–601.

18. Machiavelli, *Prince*, chap. 18.

19. Roosevelt cast a long shadow on all the presidents who have followed him, and Johnson wanted to surpass him. See William E. Leuchtenburg, *In the Shadow of FDR: From Harry Truman to Ronald Reagan*, rev. ed. (Ithaca: Cornell University Press, 1989). On Johnson's desire to be better than Roosevelt, see Kearns, "Johnson's Political Personality."

20. On the example of the prudent archer, see Machiavelli, *Prince*, chap. 6.

21. On this analysis of the economy, see Tom Riddell, "The Vietnam War and Inflation Revisited," in *Lyndon Baines Johnson and the Uses of Power*, ed. Bernard J. Firestone and Robert C. Vogt, Contributions in Political Science no. 221 (New York: Greenwood Press, 1988), 225. The Vietnam War took place at a time when the United States' economy was booming; Johnson had helped to create that boom with a tax cut in 1965.

22. Geyelin, *Lyndon B. Johnson*, 11.

23. See, for example, George C. Herring, *LBJ and Vietnam: A Different Kind of War* (Austin: University of Texas Press, 1995), 25–62.

24. Johnson was politically skillful enough to be able to cover his tracks and make a minimal consensus work that a later scholar could claim that Johnson had kept Congress and the public fully informed concerning the nation's Vietnam policy. It may be true, up to a point, that the public was unwilling to listen fully to what Johnson was saying, but this argument overlooks the fact that LBJ was particularly skilled at telling the public what they wanted to hear and what he thought they wanted to hear. Johnson may have been seen as a peace candidate by a naive and trusting public, but it is also true that he worked quite hard to make himself appear as such. A good politician works within the realm of appearance and image making, and his or her support for an issue can change according to the audience. Johnson tried to manipulate appearances on such a large scale in simultaneously pursuing war and domestic reforms that there was little room to calibrate his message as needed.

25. See Conkin, *Big Daddy*, 192.

26. Kearns, *Lyndon Johnson*, 216.

27. See Kearns, *Lyndon Johnson*, 254. See also Moya Ann Ball, "The Phantom of the Oval Office: The John F. Kennedy Assassination's Symbolic Impact on Lyndon B. Johnson, His Key Advisers and the Vietnam Decision-Making Process," *Presidential Studies Quarterly* 24, no. 1 (Winter 1994): 105–19.

28. See *PPP LBJ*, vol. 2: *1965*, 7 April 1965, 395, 397–98.

29. Orrin Schwab, *Defending the Free World: John F. Kennedy, Lyndon Johnson, and the Vietnam War, 1961–1965* (Westport, Conn.: Praeger, 1998).

30. See *PPP LBJ*, vol. 2: *1965*, 794.

31. Tom Wicker, *LBJ and JFK: The Influence of Personality upon Politics* (New York: Morrow 1968), 208.

32. See Brian VanDeMark, *Into the Quagmire: Lyndon Johnson and the Escalation of the Vietnam War* (Oxford: Oxford University Press, 1991), 216.

33. Wicker, *Personality*, 185. The book is devoted to exploring the influence of personality upon politics; Wicker suggests that "Kennedy *could* have had an alternative, while Johnson had none whatever" (185).

34. See Denise M. Bostdorff and Steven R. Goldzwig, "Idealism and Pragmatism in American Foreign Policy Rhetoric: The Case of John F. Kennedy and Vietnam," *Presidential Studies Quarterly* 24, no. 3 (Summer 1994): 515–30. The article argues that Kennedy sought to balance idealistic arguments and pragmatic arguments in his foreign policy. The authors suggest that if Kennedy had lived he would have encountered problems similar to those Johnson faced over Vietnam. While the authors do not attempt to connect the rhetoric to a policy strategy, they do suggest that Kennedy was walking a middle path as he tried to blend and balance idealistic and pragmatic arguments: "To comprehend the President's Vietnam rhetoric more fully, one has to understand both types of arguments and the way in which Kennedy intertwined them" (525).

35. Gardner, *Pay Any Price*, 98.

36. Kenneth W. Thompson, *Traditions and Values in Politics and Diplomacy: Theory and Practice* (Baton Rouge: Louisiana State University Press, 1992), 269.

37. See Jeffrey W. Helsing, *Johnson's War / Johnson's Great Society: The Guns and Butter Trap* (Westport, Conn.: Praeger, 2000).

38. Fredrik Logevall, "Vietnam and the Question of What Might Have Been," 19–62, in *Kennedy: The New Frontier Revisited*, ed. Mark J. White (New York: New York University Press, 1998).

39. Gardner, *Pay Any Price*, 156. In the 1965 State of the Union Address Johnson stated that there was no longer a dividing line between foreign and domestic. This approach also reflects Johnson's political training within domestic politics. See Bostdorff and Goldzwig, "Idealism and Pragmatism," 515–30.

40. See Johnson's 1966 State of the Union Address, in which he stated that America could have a Great Society and keep its international commitments (*PPP LBJ*, vol. 1:*1966*, 3–12).

41. Geyelin, *Lyndon B. Johnson*, 154.

42. See Califano, *Triumph and Tragedy*; Kearns, *Lyndon Johnson*, 256.

43. Kearns, *Lyndon Johnson*, 212.

44. See Johnson, *Vantage Point*, 443. According to Johnson, the two streams of American life came together at that moment, and he had to follow them wherever they led.

45. See Stanley Hoffmann, *Primacy or World Order: American Foreign Policy since the Cold War* (New York: McGraw-Hill, 1978), 107.

46. *FRUS, 1964–1968*, vol. 2: *Vietnam, January–June 1965*, 213.

47. See Dallek, *Flawed Giant*, 84–91; Geyelin, *Lyndon B. Johnson*, 15–21.

48. Kearns, *Lyndon Johnson*, 256.

49. Geyelin, *Lyndon B. Johnson*, 15, 21.

50. See McGeorge Bundy, "The End of Either/Or," *Foreign Affairs* (January 1967): 159–201.

51. Rowland Evans and Robert Novak, *Lyndon B. Johnson: The Exercise of Power: A Political Biography* (London: Allen and Unwin, 1967), 550; Geyelin, *Lyndon B. Johnson*, 187.

52. Leo Strauss, *Thoughts on Machiavelli* (Glencoe, Ill.: Free Press, 1958), 264.

53. See T. Harry Williams, "Huey Lyndon and Southern Radicalism," *Journal of American History* 60, no. 2 (September 1973): 267–93.

54. See, for example, Fred I. Greenstein and Richard H. Immerman, "What Did Eisenhower Tell Kennedy about Indochina? The Politics of Misperception," *Journal of American History* 79, no. 2 (September 1992): 568–87, esp. 568.

55. See Hugh M. Arnold, "Official Justifications for America's Role in Indochina, 1949–67," *Asian Affairs: An American Review* 3, no. 1 (1975): 31–48.

56. See Khong Yuen Foong, *Analogies at War: Korea, Munich, Dien Bien Phu and the Vietnam Decisions of 1965* (Princeton: Princeton University Press, 1992).

57. The term comes from an article by Charles Lindblom, "The Science of Muddling Through," *Public Administrative Review* 19 (1959): 79–88.

58. Lindblom, "Science of Muddling Through," 81–82.

59. Lindblom, "Science of Muddling Through," 88.

60. The idea that avoiding losses can drive a decision maker's approach is explored by prospect theory, and Johnson's decisions concerning the 1965 escalation are ripe for such an analysis. For more on prospect theory and how the desire to avoid losses can shape foreign policy decisions, see Barbara Farnham, ed., *Avoiding Losses / Taking Risks: Prospect Theory and International Conflict* (Ann Arbor: University of Michigan Press, 1994).

61. David Braybrooke and Charles E. Lindblom, *A Strategy of Decision* (New York: Free Press, 1963), 74.

62. Braybrooke and Lindblom, *Strategy of Decision*, 134.

63. Halberstam, *Best and the Brightest*, 736. Kettl, in "Economic Education of Lyndon Johnson," attempts to downplay Johnson's apparent deceptiveness by stressing the political and economic impediments that a tax increase faced. Allen J. Matusow, in *The Unraveling of America: A History of Liberalism in the 1960s* (New York: Harper and Row, 1984), makes a similar argument, but the key problem remains that Johnson's advisors, both military and political, did not know the true economic costs of the war. Much of the blame has fallen on Secretary of Defense McNamara, but ultimately it rests with Johnson, who as chief executive was responsible for all final decisions.

64. If Johnson had succeeded in getting a declaration of war, which he avoided, he could have placed the United States and its economy on a war footing. The possible resources at Johnson's disposal then could have enabled him to fight the war indefinitely. Whether Johnson could have or even wanted a declaration of war is another matter entirely. The point here is to suggest that the United States could have afforded the war if it had undertaken the necessary adjustments. For a further discussion of the gap between resources and commitments, see Samuel Huntington, "Coping with the Lippmann Gap," *Foreign Affairs* 66, no. 2 (Winter 1987–88): 453–77.

65. Pocock, in *Machiavellian Moment*, 543, makes the argument that the United States was unable to expand the sphere of credit and virtue in Vietnam and that this failure has doomed the United States to become an imperial government. The point I am trying to make is that perhaps the United States' "failure" was not in that realm but in the physical realm. The "failure" in South Vietnam did not spell the end of the United

States. In one sense United States' "expansion" ended because it lost an important ally on the Eurasian landmass. Yet the nation continues to expand, albeit philosophically, by promoting the ideas of democracy and equality as well as acting as an example for other nondemocratic states. If the UN system, which perhaps best epitomizes the United States' philosophical ambitions, fails because the United States becomes corrupt, is defeated, or fights a world-destroying war, then the Machiavellian Moment will have arrived. In other words, the United States has never attempted a Pax Americana because it has replaced its ambitions for a world order with a UN world order. In Vietnam it inverted that relationship, experienced its failure, and has for the most part since that time exhibited caution about undertaking large-scale foreign policy interventions that are driven by liberal internationalist views.

66. For a fuller discussion of the imbalance between the president and Congress, see Gordon Silverstein, *Imbalance of Powers: Constitutional Interpretation and the Making of American Foreign Policy* (New York: Oxford University Press, 1997).

67. An example of this can be seen in how Wilbur Mills, the Senate Ways and Means Committee chairman, restrained the federal government's ability to finance the war and domestic reforms. This had the effect of changing Johnson's domestic strategy from expanding the Great Society to preserving it. See Robert M. Collins, "The Economic Crisis of 1968 and the Waning of the 'American Century,'" *American Historical Review* 101 (April 1996): 412-22.

68. Johnson, *Vantage Point*, 443.

69. Louis Fisher has written extensively on this issue; see, for example, "Congressional Abdication: War and Spending Powers," *Saint Louis University Law Journal* 43, no. 3 (Summer 1999): 931–1012.

70. See Barbara Jordan's speech before the House Judiciary Committee (*Testimony before the House Judiciary Committee, Texas Journal of Women and the Law* 5 [1996]).

71. See Helsing, *Johnson's War / Johnson's Great Society*.

72. See Johnson's instructions to Secretary of the Treasury Fowler concerning the impact that the international economic situation could have on his strategy. See *FRUS, 1964–68*, vol. 8, 171–74.

73. See Collins, "Economic Crisis of 1968," 396–422.

74. See Gavin, *Gold Crisis*. See also Bozo, *Two Strategies for Europe*.

75. On 30 July 1965 Gerald Ackley sent a memo to Johnson suggesting that the United States economy had room to handle a defense build up. See Kettl, "Economic Education," 58.

76. David Halberstam, in the *Best and the Brightest*, argues that Johnson intentionally hid the cost of the war from his economic advisors (736). Kettl offers an alternative assessment that suggests that Johnson's activities were prompted less by deviousness and more by uncertainty. The section draws heavily on the work of Kettl, Kauffman, and Matusow.

77. Kettl, "Economic Education," 56.

78. Rusk, *As I Saw It*, 419.

79. Pocock, *Machiavellian Moment*, vii. On the meaning of political corruption, see J. Patrick Dobel, "The Corruption of a State," *American Political Science Review* 72, no. 3 (September 1978): 958–73. See also Christopher Nadon, "From Republic to Empire: Political Revolution and the Common Good in Xenophon's *Education of Cyrus*," *American Political Science Review* 90, no. 2 (June 1996): 361–74.

80. See *DOSB*, 22 May 1961, 763.

81. One is tempted to analyze the domestic unrest through a Lockean lens. According to Locke, if there is a conflict between the executive and the legislature, the people will decide the matter. How will they do this? By acting in a variety of ways "including public opinion, general willingness to remain obedient to government actions, elections when those are relevant, and, finally, revolutions." See Michael P. Zuckert, "Hobbes, Locke, and the Problem of the Rule of Law," in *The Rule of Law*, ed. Ian Shapiro (New York: New York University, 1994), 75.

82. See, for example, Melvin Small, *Johnson, Nixon, and the Doves* (New Brunswick: Rutgers University Press, 1988); and Charles Debenedetti and Charles Chatfield, *An American Ordeal: The Antiwar Movement of the Vietnam War*, Syracuse Studies on Peace and Conflict Resolution (Syracuse: Syracuse University Press, 1990).

83. Although the first riots began in 1964, they climaxed in the long, hot summer of 1967. The civil unrest posed a severe domestic political problem for Johnson and, like the tension between the undeclared war and domestic reforms, appeared to be an issue for which he could not make the necessary choices to resolve it satisfactorily. Kenneth O'Reilly, "The FBI and the Politics of the Riots, 1964–1968," *Journal of American History* 75, no. 1 (June 1988): pp. 91–114, esp. 113–14.

84. The material concerning fame and the founding fathers, especially as it relates to the war powers, is drawn from William M. Treanor, "Fame, the Founding, and the Power to Declare War," *Cornell Law Review* 82, no. 4 (May 1997).

85. The United States was not seeking to expand its rule over another people as suggested in the word's original meaning. It was attempting, in fulfillment of the Truman Doctrine, to help South Vietnam determine its future free from the threat of physical coercion. See J. S. Richardson, "*Imperium Romanum:* Empire and the Language of Power," *Journal of Roman Studies* 81 (1991): 1–9.

86. Joseph A. Schumpeter argued that Rome's interests expanded because even if the empire's direct interest was not at stake, then the interest of an ally was at stake, which would bring Rome into the conflict. See Schumpeter, *Imperialism and Social Classes*, trans. Heinz Norden, ed. Paul M. Sweezy (Oxford: Blackwell, 1951), 66.

87. See, for example, Ronald Steel, *Temptations of a Superpower* (Cambridge, Mass.: Harvard University Press, 1995).

88. Machiavelli, *Discourse*, 1.6.37.

89. The tension between the executive and legislative branches over foreign policy has existed in the United States since the founding. For an interesting view on this problem and an example of this tension before the Gulf of Tonkin Resolution and the War Powers legislation, see Stephen A. Garrett's work on the Bricker Amendment, "Foreign Policy

and the American Constitution: The Bricker Amendment in Contemporary Perspective," *International Studies Quarterly* 16, no. 2 (June 1972): 187–220. For a good overview of this issue as well as a good list of leading articles, see David Gray Adler, "The Constitution and Presidential Warmaking: The Enduring Debate," *Political Science Quarterly* 103, no. 1 (Spring 1988): 1–36.

90. Edward S. Corwin, *The President: Office and Powers, 1789–1984: History and Analysis of Practice and Opinion* 5th rev. ed., ed. Randall W. Bland, Theodore T. Hindson, and Jack W. Peltason (New York: New York University Press, 1984).

91. See, for example, Walter LaFeber, "American Empire, American Raj," in *America Unbound: World War II and the Making of a Superpower*, ed. Warren F. Kimball (New York: St. Martin's Press, 1992), 56.

92. Arthur M. Schlesinger Jr., *The Imperial Presidency: With a New Epilogue* (Boston: Houghton Mifflin, 1989), 115.

93. Collins, "Economic Crisis."

94. See Matusow, *Unraveling of America*, 155–79.

95. *FRUS, 1964–1968*, vol. 2: *Vietnam*, 752.

96. *FRUS, 1964–1968*, vol. 2: *Vietnam*.

97. *FRUS, 1964–1968*, vol. 2: *Vietnam*. Katzenbach's memo suggested, indirectly, that the Gulf of Tonkin Resolution, until it is reversed or suspended, can be used to justify the president's actions so long as they do not infringe on Congress's right to declare war. See also Silverstein, *Imbalance of Powers*.

98. Kearns, *Lyndon Johnson*, 222.

99. See Brien Hallett, *The Lost Art of Declaring War* (Urbana: University of Illinois Press, 1998).

100. See Jacob K. Javits, "The Congressional Presence in Foreign Relations," *Foreign Affairs* 48 (January 1970): 226. See also Cecil V. Crabb and Pat M. Hold, *Invitation to Struggle: Congress, the President, and Foreign Policy* (Washington D.C.: Congressional Quarterly Press, 1980), 45.

101. Rusk to State Department, 16 December 1964, Johnson Papers, NSF, Subject files, box 23.

102. Gardner, *Pay Any Price*, 155.

103. Hew Strachan, "Essay and Reflection: On Total War and Modern War," *International History Review* 22, no. 2 (2000): 341–70, esp. 355.

104. See Coats, "American Democracy," for a critique of Shelling's limited war theory.

105. See Gardner, *Pay Any Price*, 253.

106. On De Gaulle's view of the United States and the international system, see Anne Sa'adah, "Idées Simples and Idées Fixes: De Gaulle, the United States, and Vietnam," 295–317, in *De Gaulle and the United States: A Centennial Reappraisal*, ed. Robert O. Paxton and Nicholas Wahl (Oxford: Berg, 1994).

107. For an interesting analysis of De Gaulle's economic moves against the United States, see Jonathan Kirshner, *Currency and Coercion: The Political Economy of International Monetary Power* (Princeton: Princeton University Press, 1995); see also David P.

Calleo, "De Gaulle and the Monetary System: The Golden Rule," in Paxton and Wahl, *De Gaulle and the United States.*

108. See Pocock, *Machiavellian Moment,* 361–74.

109. Pocock, *Machiavellian Moment,* 391 and 510.

110. The issue is explored in more depth by Martin Sheffer, "Does Absolute Power Corrupt Absolutely? Part I. A Theoretical Review of Presidential War Power," *Oklahoma City University Law Review* 24, nos. 1–2 (Spring–Summer 1999): 233–302.

111. Doris Kearns gives an excellent analysis of Johnson's personality in an attempt to find the sources for his inability to address necessary choices. While her essay seeks the sources for Johnson's personality, this book focuses on its political-philosophical consequences. Kearns, "Lyndon Johnson's Political Personality," *Political Science Quarterly* 91, no. 3 (Fall 1976): 385–409.

112. See, for example, *DOSB,* 6 April 1964, 534. "We dare not falter. For unless the world is made safe for freedom, our own freedom cannot survive."

113. In many ways Johnson was in a situation similar to the one faced by Stephen Douglas prior to the Civil War and exposed quite brilliantly by Abraham Lincoln during their famous debates. Douglas was trying to fight antislavery measures in the North and pro-slavery measures in the South because he did not want slavery to be made a test of political orthodoxy. In that regard Douglas feared a civil war more than he believed that slavery was an evil that had to be defeated. See Harry V. Jaffa, *Crisis of the House Divided: An Analysis of the Issues in the Lincoln–Douglas Debates* (Seattle: University of Washington Press, 1973), 58–62.

114. George Carey, "Separation of Powers and the Madisonian Model," *American Political Science Review* 72 (1978): 151–64.

115. Pocock, *Machiavellian Moment,* 420.

116. Tucker, *Nation or Empire,* 17.

117. Tucker, *Nations or Empire,* 20.

118. See Helsing, *Johnson's War,* 191–93.

119. See Collins, "Economic Crisis."

120. Tucker, *Nation or Empire,* 39.

121. Tucker, *Nation or Empire,* 47.

122. See Steven Forde, *The Ambition to Rule: Alcibiades and the Politics of Imperialism in Thucydides* (Ithaca: Cornell University Press, 1989), 142. A key difference, however, is that Athens was corrupted when its domestic politics began to reflect its empire; domestic politics were conducted differently than the outward-looking politics of empire, Whereas the United States did not attempt to conduct its foreign relations much differently from its domestic politics. While the United States recognized a difference between the two realms, it followed similar principles in both areas.

123. See Otto Eckstein, "The Economics of the 1960s—A Backward Look," *Public Interest,* no. 18 (1970): 91; and *The Great Recession: With a Postscript on Stagflation* (Amsterdam: North-Holland, 1978), 33–36. See also Matusow, *Unraveling of America.*

124. One could argue that America's liberal internationalism and its connection to the public's imagination can be seen in the number of volunteers for the Peace Corps, an

organization built upon those values. In 1965 and 1966 the number of participants peaked. It has never matched those levels even thirty years later. Elizabeth Cobbs Hoffman, *All You Need Is Love: The Peace Corps and the Spirit of the 1960s* (Cambridge, Mass.: Harvard University Press, 1998), 262.

3. HENRY KISSINGER

For a fuller understanding of how Machiavelli understood the relationship of an advisor to the prince, see chaps. 22 and 23 of *The Prince*. For a similar view of advisors, see Xenophon, *The Education of Cyrus*, Everyman's Library, trans. H. G. Dakyns, ed. Ernest Rhys (London: J. M. Dent and Sons, 1914), bk. 7, chap. 5, 59–62.

1. See, for example, Robert M. Collins, "The Economic Crisis of 1968 and the Waning of the 'American Century,'" *American Historical Review* 101 (April 1996): 396–422.

2. See, for example, Collins "Economic Crisis of 1968," 396–422; Joanne Gowa, *Closing of the Gold Window: Domestic Politics and the End of Bretton Woods* (Ithaca: Cornell University Press 1983). See also Benjamin J. Cohen, *Organizing the World's Money: The Political Economy of International Monetary Relations* (London: Macmillan, 1977); Lloyd C. Gardner, *Pay Any Price: Lyndon Johnson and the Wars for Vietnam* (Chicago: Ivan R. Dee, 1995), 410–14; M. Stephen Weatherford, "The International Economy as a Constraint on U.S. Macroeconomic Policymaking," *International Organization* 42, no. 4 (Fall 1988): 605–37.

3. Richard A. Melanson, *American Foreign Policy since the Vietnam War: The Search for Consensus from Nixon to Clinton* (Armonk, N.Y.: M. E. Sharpe, 1996).

4. See Henry Kissinger, *White House Years* (Boston: Little, Brown, 1979), 56–60. See also William Safire, *Before the Fall: An Inside View of the Pre-Watergate White House* (Doubleday: New York, 1975), 135–42.

5. See, for example, Charles Gati, "Another Grand Debate? The Limitationist Critique of American Foreign Policy," *World Politics* 21, no. 1 (October 1968): 133–51.

6. On the apparent contradictions in public opinion between withdrawal and letting the Communists win, see John E. Mueller, *War, Presidents, and Public Opinion* (London: Wiley and Sons, 1973), 99–102 and 97.

7. Anthony Hartley, *American Foreign Policy in the Nixon Era*, Adelphi Paper no. 110 (London: International Institute for Strategic Studies 1975). On the connection between the Nixon's foreign policy and the policy of détente, see Litwak, *Détente and the Nixon Doctrine*, 50–75.

8. See also Kissinger, *White House Years*, 54–70, 128–30, 192–94, 226–38. See also Richard M. Nixon, *RN: The Memoirs of Richard Nixon* (London: Sidgwick and Jackson, 1978), 343.

9. See Richard M. Nixon, *U.S. Foreign Policy for the 1970s: A New Strategy for Peace*, report to the Congress, vol. 1 (Washington, D.C.: Government Printing Office, 1971); *U.S. Foreign Policy for the 1970s: Building for Peace*, report to the Congress, vol. 2 (Washington, D.C.: Government Printing Office, 1972), *U.S. Foreign Policy for the 1970s: The Emerging Structure of Peace*, report to Congress, vol. 3 (Washington, D.C.: Government Printing Office, 1972), *U.S. Foreign Policy for the 1970s: Shaping a Durable Peace*, report to Congress, vol. 4 (Washington, D.C.: Government Printing Office, 1973).

10. See, for example, Morris, *Uncertain Greatness*. Other views of Kissinger's success within the Nixon White House can be found in Seymour Hersh, *The Price of Power: Kissinger in the Nixon White House* (New York Summit Books 1983). William Bundy, in *A Tangled Web: The Making of Foreign Policy in the Nixon Presidency* (New York: Hill and Wang, 1998), 511, suggests that Kissinger simply executed the plans designed by Nixon. Kissinger gave extensive credit to Nixon; see, for example, *White House Years; Years of Upheaval*, 414–17; and *Years of Renewal*. William Safire offers an insight into the Nixon-Kissinger relationship in *Before the Fall*, 497. See also Bruce Mazlish, *Kissinger: The European Mind in American Policy* (New York: Basic Books, 1976), 211–62.

11. Gaddis, *Strategies*, 277, makes the point that Kissinger wanted to give foreign policy a "philosophical deepening," but the kinds of changes suggested here represent a wholesale shift in underlying foreign policy philosophy. See, for example, the second State of the World Address, in which Kissinger made the claim for a change in philosophy; see also Kissinger, *White House Years*, 159. In his testimony to the Senate Committee on Foreign Relations on 1 October 1973 Kissinger asserted: This means an open articulation of our philosophy, our purposes, and our actions. We have sought to do this in the President's annual reports to the Congress on foreign policy" (*DOSB*, 1 October 1973, 427).

12. See, for example, Tony Smith, *America's Mission: The United States and the Worldwide Struggle for Democracy in the Twentieth Century* (Princeton: Princeton University Press, 1994).

13. See Allen Matusow, *The Unraveling of America: A History of Liberalism in the 1960s* (New York: Harper and Row, 1986). See also Daniel Bell, "The End of American Exceptionalism," *Public Interest* 41 (1975–76): 193–224.

14. Bell, "End of American Exceptionalism," 204.

15. See John Lewis Gaddis, *Strategies of Containment: A Critical Appraisal of Postwar American National Security Policy* (London: Oxford University Press, 1982), 283. See also Geoffrey R. Sloan, *Geopolitics in United States Strategic Policy, 1890–1987* (Brighton: Wheatsheaf, 1988), 170.

16. Although Nixon was not the only one thinking along these lines, he had the courage and the opportunity to carry out the strategy.

17. Nixon *New Strategy for Peace*, 4.

18. Keeping this balance was a test of Nixon's statesmanship. The withdrawal had to occur fast enough to calm domestic opinion but not so fast as to create a dangerous vacuum of power in Southeast Asia. As Machiavelli noted, the most dangerous time for a prince is during a period of reform because he makes enemies of those who had benefited from the old policies without having yet secured the support of those who will benefit from the new policies (*Prince*, chap. 6).

19. For an analysis of Watergate as it relates to the corruption of republican politics, see Shumer, *Republican Politics*, 28–31.

20. Kissinger, in *Years of Upheaval* (Boston: Little, Brown, 1982), 72–127, points out how the Vietnam War created, indirectly, the conditions that led to Watergate (see esp. 81–89); to him it was a matter of personalities and the political context. Arthur M. Schlesinger Jr., in *Imperial Presidency* (Boston: Houghton Mifflin, 1974), 208–17,

argues that the problem was institutional and stemmed from the greater centralization of power.

21. See, for example, Bundy, *Tangled Web*, 519–20. Bundy argues that the problem was not directly caused by secrecy and centralization but that Nixon misrepresented his policies to the public and thereby eroded the trust necessary for a successful foreign policy.

22. In his book *Years of Upheaval*, 414–49, Kissinger presents an insightful analysis of why Nixon appointed him secretary of state. The details as well as the strategy and tactics of the appointment take us away from the present discussion, but they are well worth reading for their insights into Nixon and Kissinger.

23. *DOSB*, 1 October 1973, 427 ff. Kissinger's statement to the Senate committee expressed his desire to control the process so that it could be routinized and thus avoid the appearance that it was "out of control" or simply in the control of the White House. See also Robert Strong, *Bureaucracy and Statesmanship: Henry Kissinger and the Making of American Foreign Policy*, Credibility of Institutions, Policies and Leadership vol. 9, series ed. Kenneth W. Thompson (Lanham, Md.: University Press of America, 1986).

24. Strong, *Bureaucracy and Statesmanship*, 56, on isolation; and 112–62, on the relationship with the Soviet Union.

25. Gordon Silverstein, *Imbalance of Powers: Constitutional Interpretation and the Making of American Foreign Policy* (New York: Oxford University Press), 25–30.

26. Richard P. Nathan, "A Retrospective on Richard M. Nixon's Domestic Policies," *Presidential Studies Quarterly* 26, no. 1 (Winter 1996): 155–64.

27. Nixon believed that domestic policy could be handled without much presidential involvement and was an area in which the Cabinet could play an important role. Foreign policy was the sole preserve of the president and required his attention. In this realm the president was the dominant actor, and the Cabinet, when it was involved, would only play a subordinate or consultative role. See, for example, Morris, *Uncertain Greatness*, 64–67.

28. Nixon attempted to defend the Watergate cover-up on the ground that revealing the content of the presidential tapes would threaten national security. In a general sense Nixon here invoked his foreign policy prerogative, and responsibility, to defend domestic acts.

29. Silverstein, *Imbalance*, 83–122. In contrast to Johnson, Nixon pursued a different type of imperial presidency. Johnson understood the Constitution as an inclusive document that relied on a strong government both abroad and at home, and his foreign policy was a direct outgrowth of his Great Society vision for domestic policy. Nixon similarly believed that he could use the executive powers that had developed over the years in office to deal with foreign policy in the domestic realm, but he drew a distinction between the two realms. He did this in order to focus his attention more closely on the problems of foreign policy. The difficulty for Nixon was that the techniques he used in foreign policy—centralizing power and practicing secrecy—were problematic when applied to the domestic realm.

30. As Kissinger put it: "The world stands uneasily posed between unprecedented chaos and the opportunity for unparalleled creativity. The next few years will determine

whether interdependence will foster common progress or common disaster" (*DOSB*, 17 February 1975, 197).

31. *DOSB*, 1 October 1973, 426.

32. See Henry Kissinger, *A World Restored: Metternich, Castlereagh and the Problems of Peace, 1812–22* (Boston: Houghton Mifflin, 1957), 325.

33. See Raymond Aron, *The Imperial Republic: The United States and the World, 1945–1973*, trans. Frank Jellinek (Englewood Cliffs, N.J.: Prentice-Hall, 1974), 114. "With the urgent task of finishing with Vietnam there combined another long-term and ill-defined task, that of restraining an international system in which the United States would not reign supreme and which, without ruling out a clash of interests or even disputes, would constitute, if not a balance comparable to that of the Concert of Europe, at least relations of a traditional kind between all powers, including the revolutionary powers."

34. For a fuller discussion of Kissinger's philosophy of history, see Peter Dickson, *Kissinger and the Meaning of History* (Cambridge: Cambridge University Press, 1978).

35. Dickson, *Kissinger*, 84.

36. *DOSB*, 15 October 1973, 471. While Dickson makes much of the fact that Kissinger's first and penultimate official addresses as secretary of state were to the United Nations and contained explicit Kantian themes, I do not share his analysis. These ideas were secondary to the initial and continuing question of power. The balance between the power blocs could live only in a stable peace, but given that the world was divided on that basis, nothing could be built on it. To put it directly, Kissinger's power structure provided stability because the powers confronted each other rather than struggling over an agreed-upon standard such as the rule of law. In Kissinger's structure states could live only on the continually tenuous power balance, not a stable standard enforced by a moderating international body. His international system would never be ordered in the same way as domestic politics.

37. See Kissinger, *White House Years*, 65, for more on this theme.

38. See Sloan, *Geopolitics*, 166–67.

39. Hartley, *American Foreign Policy*, 15. "From 1969 onwards the achievement by the Soviet Union of a degree of nuclear parity with the United States and strategic mobility for her armed forces (principally by the expansion of her Navy and her airlift capability) had increased her capacity for military intervention at the same time as American public opinion was acting as a brake on any similar action by the United States."

40. Gaddis, *Strategies*, 284–85. By downplaying ideology, Nixon and Kissinger viewed threats to their interests in a different manner, but they still faced the problems of globalism, albeit in a different form.

41. See Sloan, *Geopolitics*, chaps. 5 and 6, for more on the difference between these two eras.

42. Kissinger, *Diplomacy*, 676.

43. Sloan, *Geopolitics*, 178.

44. See *DOSB*, 26 July 1971, 96. See also Osgood, *Retreat from Empire*, 1–22.

45. See W. W. Rostow, *The Diffusion of Power: An Essay in Recent History* (New York: Macmillan, 1972).

46. See Brown, *Crises*, 107–22.

47. See Seyom Brown, *The Crises of Power: An Interpretation of United States Foreign Policy during the Kissinger Years* (New York: Columbia University Press, 1979).

48. See Henry Kissinger, "The White Revolutionary: Reflections on Bismarck," *Daedalus* 97 (Summer 1968): 888–937.

49. Kissinger, "White Revolutionary," 890, on self-restraint; and 888, on manipulating contending forces.

50. See, for example, *DOSB*, 12 April 1976, 483 "We must recognize that no world order will be stable over the last quarter of this century unless all its participants consider that they have a stake in it and it is legitimate and just." See also *DOSB*, 15 October 1973, 469–70; and 29 October 1973, 527–30.

51. Alastair Buchan, "The Irony of Henry Kissinger," *International Affairs* (Royal Institute for International Affairs) 50, no. 3 (July 1974): 369.

52. See Henry Kissinger, "Central Issues in American Foreign Policy," in *Agenda for the Nation*, ed. Kermit Gordon (Washington, D.C.: Brookings Institution, 1968), 588.

53. Brown, *Crises of Power*, 12.

54. See Kenneth W. Thompson, *Traditions and Values in Politics and Diplomacy: Theory and Practice* (Baton Rouge: Louisiana State University Press, 1992), 289. "Peace in Nixon's view can never be based on mutual friendship. Its sole foundation must be 'mutual respect for each other's strength.'"

55. On the separation of domestic and international spheres, see John D. Montgomery, "The Education of Henry Kissinger," *Journal of International Affairs* 29 (1975): 51.

56. A case in point is the Helsinki Accords that the Soviet Union signed. The Soviet Union promoted these negotiations and signed the accords because they legitimized the territorial borders of the Soviet Union. See Bundy, *Tangled Web*, 480–84.

57. Silverstein, *Imbalance*, 89–100.

58. See Bell, *Diplomacy*, 32; see also Kissinger, *World Restored*, 1.

59. Bell, *Diplomacy*, 31.

60. A central ambiguity in Kissinger's approach was determining when a state was acting legitimately or illegitimately within the international system. How did one differentiate a minor disturbance from a precursor to a large-scale attempt to revise the system? See Litwak, *Détente and the Nixon Doctrine*, 60–61. Kissinger's understanding of the geopolitical balance faced a similar obstacle in that one had to have a global presence in order to respond to changes in regional politics that might signal a shift in the central balance of power. See, for example, Sloan, *Geopolitics*, chap. 6.

61. *DOSB*, 13 October 1975, 546.

62. Collins, "Economic Crisis of 1968," 396–422; Gowa, *Closing of the Gold Window*; and Weatherford, "International Economy," 605–37.

63. On the "threat to use force," see *DOSB*, 27 January 1975, 101. The quotation appeared in an interview in *Business Week*, 13 January 1975.

64. For an interesting analysis of the economic and political trends that culminated with the Nixon administration and how they influenced U.S. foreign policy, see Aron, *Imperial Republic*.

65. See Mazlish, *Kissinger,* 257–61; see also Bundy, *Tangled Web,* 452–60.

66. See Bundy, *Tangled Web,* 510–22, on the failure to build lasting structures.

67. On the move from détente to cooperation see *DOSB,* 15 October 1973, 470. On the aspiration for dignity and equal opportunity, see *DOSB,* 13 October 1975, 552.

68. On the connection between the Nixon's foreign policy and the policy of détente, I follow the analysis of Litwak, *Détente and the Nixon Doctrine,* 50–75.

69. See Thompson, *Diplomacy and Values,* 284.

70. Earl C. Ravenal, *Large-Scale Foreign Policy Change: The Nixon Doctrine as History and Portent* (Berkeley: Institute of International Studies, University of California, 1989).

71. See Henry Kissinger, *Diplomacy* (New York: Simon and Schuster, 1994), 705.

72. Finding a moderate middle path that can weave together both the aggressive and the peaceful elements within a society is the task of a statesman, according to Plato. See Plato, *The Statesman,* trans. J. B. Skemp (London: Routledge and Kegan Paul, 1952), 306a–311c. See also Stanley Rosen, *Plato's Statesman: The Web of Politics* (New Haven: Yale University Press, 1995), 179–90; and Joseph Cropsey, *Plato's World: Man's Place in the Cosmos* (Chicago: University of Chicago Press, 1995), 141–44.

73. See Coral Bell, *The Diplomacy of Détente: The Kissinger Era* (London: Martin Robertson, 1977).

74. See *DOSB,* 14 October 1974; see also Gaddis, *Strategies,* 282–83.

75. *DOSB,* 14 October 1974, 516.

76. For critics, see, for example, G. Warren Nutter, *Kissinger's Grand Design* (Washington, D.C.: American Enterprise Institute for Public Policy Research, 1975), 15–25; and Raymond Garthoff, *Détente and Confrontation: American-Soviet Relations from Nixon to Reagan* (Washington, D.C.: Brookings Institution, 1994). See Kissinger's three volumes of memoirs for a defense.

77. For a fuller treatment of détente, see Garthoff, *Détente and Confrontation.*

78. See Kissinger, *World Restored,* 329.

79. See, for example, Richard C. Thornton, *The Nixon-Kissinger Years: Reshaping of America's Foreign Policy* (New York: Paragon House, 1989).

80. Bundy makes this argument for the wrong reasons. He is correct to point out that Nixon did not build a lasting structure, but he makes the point in contrast to Truman. The argument is effective, but the comparison is inaccurate. Truman led a powerful country that was united in support behind an internationalist outlook, and he enjoyed a psychological and material preponderance of power. Nixon, on the other hand, inherited a nearly bankrupt economy, and a psychologically divided country. See Bundy, *Tangled Web,* 517–22.

81. See Dickson, *Meaning of History,* 160–62; and J.G.A. Pocock, *The Machiavellian Moment: Florentine Political Thought and the Atlantic Republican Tradition* (Princeton: Princeton University Press 1975), 531–52.

82. See Bundy, *Tangled Web,* 503–9, on covert operations; on the Middle East Crisis, see 440–42. See also Kissinger, *Years of Upheaval,* 575–611, on the Middle East crisis; on Chile, see 374–406.

83. *DOSB,* 27 January 1975, 101.

84. Kissinger, *World Restored,* 326.

85. See Bundy, *Tangled Web.*

86. Two incidents highlight Kissinger's loss of status. The first is when Ford, in an effort to deflect criticism about the state of the nation's foreign policy and status in the world, stripped him of the position of national security advisor; the second was the banning of the word *détente* from press releases during the election. Kissinger became the focus of Carter's attacks on the Nixon administration's foreign policy style during the election year. See Kissinger, *Years of Renewal,* 834–44.

87. See Sloan, *Geopolitics,* 181–89.

88. See, for example, *DOSB,* 5 May 1975, 557.

89. *DOSB,* 6 October 1975.

90. See, for example, the interview with "L'Express," *DOSB,* 12 May 1975, 608.

91. *DOSB,* 15 December 1975, 848. "America's challenge today is to demonstrate a new kind of leadership—guiding by our vision, our example, and our energy, not by our predominance."

92. *DOSB,* 14 July 1975, 51.

93. See Richard Rosecrance, ed., *America as an Ordinary Country: U.S. Foreign Policy and the Future* (Ithaca: Cornell University Press, 1976), 66.

94. *DOSB,* 2 June 1975, 718–19.

95. See *DOSB,* 715.

96. *DOSB,* 25 November 1974, 743.

97. *DOSB,* 12 April 1976, 483.

98. *DOSB,* 16 September 1974, 375.

99. See, for example, Joseph Sisco in *DOSB,* 15 April 1974, 381. "Our interests, our strengths, our resources compel an active and responsible role in the world. This does not mean there is, or should be, a Washington blueprint for every international conflict—military or economic. It does mean a policy of selective engagement on the critical problems of our times."

100. *DOSB,* 14 October 1974, 505. Kissinger also reiterated the need for restraint in *DOSB,* 25 November 1974, 742.

101. *DOSB,* 11 November 1974, 645.

102. On Kissinger's lack of familiarity with the "heartland," see Walter LaFeber, "Kissinger and Acheson: The Secretary of State and the Cold War," *Political Science Quarterly* 92, no. 2 (Summer 1977): 194.

103. Kissinger accepted that by focusing on power he was acting in an "un-American" way. By this he did not mean that he was ignorant about the American experience but, rather, that he was trying to educate Americans to the requirements of international power. See, for example, Kissinger, *White House Years,* 1089.

104. *DOSB,* 1 October 1973, 425.

105. See Kissinger, *Diplomacy,* 676.

106. See George F. Kennan, *American Diplomacy, 1900–1950* (London: Secker and Warburg, 1952). For a counterargument, see Louis Henkin, *How Nations Behave: Law and Foreign Policy* (London: Pall Mall, 1968).

107. See *DOSB*, 29 October 1973, 527. "This country has always had a sense of mission. Americans have always held the view that America stood for something above and beyond its material achievements."

108. See *DOSB*, 29 October 1973, 531. "If we are to shape a world community we must first restore community at home."

109. *DOSB*, 1 October 1973, 428; see also *DOSB*, 29 October 1973, 525.

110. The word *confidence* recurs often in Kissinger's speeches during his tenure as secretary of state.

111. Kissinger, "Central Issues in American Foreign Policy," cited in Brown, *Crises of Power*, 5.

112. Michael J. Smith, *Realist Thought from Weber to Kissinger* (Baton Rouge: Louisiana State University Press, 1986), 199.

113. See Richard Rosecrance, ed., *America as an Ordinary Country: U.S. Foreign Policy and the Future* (Ithaca: Cornell University Press, 1976).

114. See, for example, *DOSB*, 17 February 1975, 197, in which Kissinger says that America has acquired a sense of tragedy. Such a view, as we will see in the next chapter, suggests that Kissinger did not fully grasp the American experience because he failed to see that the American Civil War had taught the republic the same brutal lessons about the uses of power and embarking on military campaigns in pursuit of virtue.

115. *DOSB*, 16 September 1974, 373.

116. See, for example *DOSB*, 11 November 1974, 643, in which Kissinger suggests that the United States must overcome its loss of innocence and meet the new challenges it faces.

117. See *DOSB*, 15 November 1976, 597–605. On the general problems facing the American republic, see Hannah Arendt, *Crises of the Republic* (New York: Harcourt Brace Jovanovich, 1972).

4. RUSK AND KISSINGER

1. J.G.A. Pocock, "Between Gog and Magog: The Republican Thesis and the Ideologia Americana," *Journal of the History of Ideas* 48, no. 2 (April–June 1987): 346.

2. Warren I. Cohen, *Dean Rusk* (Totowa, N.J.: Cooper Square, 1980), 321.

3. Orrin Schwab, *Defending the Free World: John F. Kennedy, Lyndon Johnson, and the Vietnam War, 1961–1965* (London: Praeger Studies in Diplomacy and Strategic Thought Praeger, 1998); and Robert R. Tomes *Apocalypse Then: American Intellectuals and the Vietnam War, 1954–1975* (New York: New York University Press, 1998).

4. See, for example, Ole R. Holsti and James N. Rosenau, *American Leadership in World Affairs: Vietnam and the Breakdown of Consensus* (London: Allen and Unwin, 1984).

5. Sacvan Bercovitch, *The American Jeremiad* (Madison: University of Wisconsin Press, 1978), 4–29. Bercovitch, in modifying the work of Perry Miller, differentiates between an American jeremiad focusing on renewal within the promise and potential of America against the more pessimistic and anxious European jeremiad. In this typology Kissinger's jeremiad would be European because his anxiety over the United States' future

belies a belief in its power to renew itself and the world. Kissinger believed that the Soviet Union would remain a permanent problem and that the United States could only hope to adapt to its own diminished role. He did not see the possibility that the United States could achieve more than the modest goal of reducing tensions with the Soviet Union and stabilizing the international system. For a careful assessment of Miller and for Bercovitch's variations on Miller, see Francis T. Butt, "The Myth of Perry Miller," *American Historical Review* 87, no. 3. (June 1982): 665–94.

6. This is not to suggest that the United States has never practiced realpolitik. On the contrary, it has rarely shied away from this approach if it has suited its interests. What is being suggested here is that Nixon and Kissinger were trying to shift the foundation of U.S. foreign policy philosophy away from its inherent liberalism to one based upon realpolitik. They approached the United States' position in world affairs as if it had suffered a Machiavellian Moment. The United States had to retrench and reorder its priorities because it no longer had the will or the resources to continue to defend a decent world order, whose liberal vision, based upon a notion of exceptionalism, had vanished in the jungles of Vietnam. A new world order was emerging, and it required a new approach to foreign policy.

7. See *DOSB*, 27 January 1975, 96–102.

8. See Kissinger, *Years of Renewal*, 1061. In a telling passage Kissinger suggests that the United States must accept that its unique relationship with history is at an end.

9. See H. W. Brands, *What America Owes the World: The Struggle for the Soul of Foreign Policy* (Cambridge: Cambridge University Press, 1998).

10. See *DOSB*, 29 October 1973, 527. Kissinger stated: "This country has always had a sense of mission. Americans have always held the view that America stood for something above and beyond its material achievements . . . But when policy becomes excessively moralistic it may turn quixotic or dangerous. A presumed monopoly on truth obstructs negotiation and accommodation." Kissinger thus suggests that the United States might indeed have a mission, yet it is one that is not open-ended but limited and mindful of the constraints on U.S. power.

11. While the literature on republicanism is vast, it is suggestive that the major works within republicanism emerged in the 1960s. See Cecilia Kenyon, "Republicanism and Radicalism in the American Revolution: An Old Fashioned Interpretation," *William and Mary Quarterly*, 3d ser., 19 (1962): 153–82; Richard Buel, "Democracy and the American Revolution: A Frame of Reference," *William and Mary Quarterly*, 3d ser., 21 (1964): 165–90; Fredric C. Lane, "At the Roots of Republicanism," *American Historical Review* 71, no. 2 (January 1966): 403–20; Bernard Bailyn, *The Ideological Origins of the American Revolution* (Cambridge, Mass.: Belknap Press of Harvard University Press, 1967); Gordon S. Wood, *The Creation of the American Republic, 1776–1787* (Chapel Hill: University of North Carolina Press, 1969). Lance Gilbert Banning suggests that his dissertation, "The Quarrel with Federalism: A Study in the Origins and the Character of Republican Thought" (Ph.D. diss., Washington University, 1971), contributed to the renewed interest in republicanism ("Jeffersonian Ideology Revisited: Liberal and Classical Ideas in the New American Republic," *William and Mary Quarterly*, 3d ser., 43, no. 1 [January 1986]: 3–19). See also Robert E. Shalhope, "Toward a Republican Synthesis: The Emergence of an Understand-

ing of Republicanism in American Historiography," *William and Mary Quarterly*, 3d ser., 29, no. 1 (1972): 49–80; J.G.A. Pocock, *The Machiavellian Moment: Florentine Political Thought and the Atlantic Republican Tradition* (Princeton: Princeton University Press, 1975). See also Laurence Veysey, "The Autonomy of American History Reconsidered," *American Quarterly* 31, no. 4 (Fall 1979): 455–77, esp. 458; Joyce Appleby, "Republicanism and Ideology," *American Quarterly* 37, no. 4 (1985): 461–73; Jeffrey C. Isaac, "Republicanism vs. Liberalism? A Reconsideration," *History of Political Thought* 9, no. 2 (Summer 1988): 349–77; Daniel T. Rodgers, "Republicanism: The Career of a Concept," *Journal of American History* 79, no. 1 (June 1992): 11–38.

12. See Charles Gati, "Another Grand Debate? The Limitationist Critique of American Foreign Policy," *World Politics* 21, no. 1 (October 1968): 133–51. Gati explores how the foreign policy debate focused on finding an alternative to the globalist foreign policy that had failed in Vietnam. Whether there needs to be a complete reassessment or whether the current system could be modified to work more effectively fuels the debate between limitationists and globalist, which at heart is based upon realist premises (135).

13. Richard P. Nathan, "A Retrospective on Richard M. Nixon's Domestic Policies," *Presidential Studies Quarterly* 26 (Winter 1996): 155–64.

14. Charles A. Barker, "Another American Dilemma: Multilateral Authority versus Unilateral Power," in *Power and Law: American Dilemma in World Affairs*, papers of the Conference on Peace Research in History, ed. Charles A. Barker (Baltimore: Johns Hopkins Press, 1971), 3.

15. Kissinger's first book, *A World Restored*, discussed the importance of maintaining equilibrium within the Concert of Europe period that developed after the Napoleonic Wars. Paul Schroeder elaborates on the question of equilibrium and argues that a balance of power and of legitimacy create it. In other words, both power and legitimacy must work together to create equilibrium. See Paul Schroeder, "Did the Vienna Settlement Rest on a Balance of Power?" *American Historical Review* 97, no. 3 (June 1992): 695–97.

16. Cohen, *Dean Rusk*, 321–30.

17. Michael Joseph Smith, "Liberalism and International Reform," in *Traditions of International Ethics*, ed. Terry Nardin and David R. Mapel (Cambridge: Cambridge University Press, 1992), 201–24.

18. See transcript, Dean Rusk Papers, interview 2, tape 2, 26 September 1969, by Paige E. Mulhollan, Internet copy, LBJ Library, 17.

19. Transcript, Dean Rusk Papers.

20. Transcript, Dean Rusk Papers.

21. For Kennan's view of how the United States had to keep its capabilities and commitments in balance in the post–World War II period, see *FRUS, 1948*, 1:509–28.

22. Henry Kissinger, *White House Years* (Boston: Little, Brown, 1979), 192.

23. Kissinger, "Central Issues," 612.

24. Kissinger's first and last speeches as secretary of state were to the United Nations. See *DOSB*, 15 October 1973, 469–73; and 25 October 1976, 497–510.

25. *World order* here means achieving a stable pattern of behavior among the states. In other words, stability, as the absence of conflict, is the goal with peace as the ideal. Sta-

bility, as such, does not have the normative overtones of peace. The inherent challenge for each statesman is to make sure the external world matches up with his or her ideal of the world order and that any efforts to achieve that world order do not cause more disorder than stability.

26. For an interesting exploration of the legalist foundation to the United States' view of the world order, see Francis A. Boyle, *Foundations of World Order: The Legalist Approach to International Relations (1898–1922)* (Durham: Duke University Press, 1999).

27. See Coral Bell, *The Diplomacy of Detente: The Kissinger Era* (London: Martin Robertson 1977), 24–32. Bell suggests that détente was more a strategy than a goal and that what the Soviet Union, China, and the United States had in common was their strategies, not their objectives. Even though Kissinger rejected the possibility of a loose alliance among nations similar to the Concert of Europe, because the common interests that underpinned that agreement no longer existed and advances in technology made the world more unstable militarily, he did accept that a stable order had to be the result of the conscious and continual practice of statecraft. See also Seyom Brown, *The Crises of Power: An Interpretation of United States Foreign Policy during the Kissinger Years* (New York: Columbia University Press, 1979), 12. Brown suggests that Kissinger's critics have missed the point that Kissinger was in fact developing a concert of powers rather than a balance of powers because he was trying to develop a world order that rested on a military equilibrium and a principle of legitimacy.

28. For a good discussion of the balance of power at the heart of the United Nations, see Ruth B. Russell, "The Management of Power and Political Organization: Some Observations on Inis L. Claude's Conceptual Approach," *International Organization* 15, no. 4 (Fall 1961): 630–36. A further development on this theme can be seen in Earl C. Ravenal, "An Autopsy of Collective Security," *Political Science Quarterly* 90, no. 4 (Winter 1975–76): 697–714; and Inis L. Claude Jr., "Comment on 'An Autopsy of Collective Security,'" *Political Science Quarterly* 90, no. 4 (Winter 1975–76): 715–17.

29. Walter Lafeber, "Kissinger and Acheson: The Secretary of State and the Cold War," *Political Science Quarterly* 92, no. 2 (Summer 1977): 194–95.

30. Robert Osgood, in *Retreat from Empire*, used the term *Nixon Strategy* to show how the policy of détente and the Nixon Doctrine worked together.

31. See Bell, *Diplomacy of Detente*, 5.

32. Rusk raised his concerns about the relationship between the center and the periphery at a press conference. See *DOSB*, 22 May 1961, 763. On Kissinger's concern, see Sloan, *Geopolitics*, 175–81.

33. Sloan, *Geopolitics*, 181.

34. Rusk's concern with China's militancy reflects his reaction to the Korean War as assistant secretary of state for Far Eastern Affairs in 1950. See Schoenbaum, *Waging Peace*, 230–33. The point was reinforced by Rusk's belief in Lin Piao's statement in the *Peking Review* concerning the people's wars against U.S. imperialism. Lin Piao, "Long Live the Victory of People's War," *Peking Review* 8, no. 36, 3 September 1965.

35. Cohen, *Dean Rusk*, 283. Stanley Hoffmann argues that multilateral institutions such as the United Nations contribute to moderating behavior within the international

system ("International Organizations and the International System," *International Organization* 24, no. 3 [Summer 1970]: 389–413).

36. Charles de Gaulle was worried about such designs when he spoke with Rusk concerning South Vietnam. See Lloyd Gardner, *Pay Any Price: Lyndon Johnson and the Wars for Vietnam* (Chicago: Ivan R. Dee, 1995), 155.

37. Henry Kissinger, *A World Restored: Metternich, Castlereagh and the Problems of Peace, 1812–22* (Boston: Houghton Mifflin, 1957), 1.

38. Henry Kissinger, "Central Issues of American Foreign Policy," in *Agenda for the Nation,* ed. Kermit Gordon (Washington, D.C.: Brookings Institution, 1968), 588.

39. See Kissinger, *World Restored;* and Schroeder, "Vienna Settlement," 695–97.

40. Robert S. Litwak, *Détente and the Nixon Doctrine: American Foreign Policy and the Pursuit of Stability, 1969–1976* (London: Cambridge University Press, 1984), 116.

41. See Richard C. Thornton, *The Nixon-Kissinger Years: Reshaping of America's Foreign Policy* (New York: Paragon House, 1989).

42. See, for example, Dean Rusk, *The Winds of Freedom,* ed. Ernest K. Lindley (Boston: Beacon Press, 1963), 1–9.

43. Cohen, *Dean Rusk,* 133. See Ernest Lee Tuveson, *Redeemer Nation: The Idea of America's Millenial Role* (Chicago: University of Chicago Press: 1968); Anders Stephanson, *Manifest Destiny: American Expansionism and the Empire of Right* (New York: Hill and Wang, 1996); see also Albert K. Weinberg, *Manifest Destiny: A Study of Nationalist Expansionism in American History* (Chicago: Quadrangle Books, 1963).

44. Bercovitch, *American Jeremiad,* 25. "The American Puritan jeremiad seeks (in effect) to prevent these excesses [antinomianism and self-interest created by unfettered individualism] by turning liminality itself into a mode of socialization."

45. See *DOSB,* 9 March 1964, 361.

46. On Kissinger being out of touch with the "American heartland," see Walter Lafeber, "Kissinger and Acheson: The Secretary of State and the Cold War," *Political Science Quarterly* 92, no. 2 (Summer 1977): 194. This is not to suggest that travel throughout the United States is a necessary or sufficient requirement to become secretary of state, but it is to suggest that such travel can give one a deeper appreciation of the United States.

47. Kissinger accepted that by focusing on power he was acting in an "un-American" way. By this he did not mean that he was ignorant of the American experience but that the requirements of being an international power meant that the United States had to extend its traditional ways of thinking. See, for example, Kissinger, *White House Years,* 1089.

48. See Henry Brandon, *The Retreat of American Power* (London: Bodley Head, 1973). Brandon offers a good overview of the political, economic, and social situation faced by Nixon and Kissinger at the inauguration. On the matter of America's psyche, see Daniel Bell, "The End of American Exceptionalism," *Public Interest* 41 (1975–76): 193–224; and Veysey, "Autonomy," 458.

49. Kissinger's views resemble those of Hobbes on the dangers of domestic disunity and their possible effect on a state's ability to carry out foreign relations. See George Kateb, "Hobbes and the Irrationality of Politics," *Political Theory* 17, no. 3 (August 1989): 356, 380, 383, and 387.

50. *DOSB*, 1 October 1973, 425.

51. See Kissinger, *Diplomacy*, 676.

52. See George F. Kennan, *American Diplomacy, 1900–1950* (London: Secker and Warburg, 1952). For a counterargument, see Louis Henkin, *How Nations Behave: Law and Foreign Policy* (London: Pall Mall, 1968).

53. See *DOSB*, 29 October 1973, 527. "This country has always had a sense of mission. Americans have always held the view that America stood for something above and beyond its material achievements."

54. See *DOSB*, 29 October 1973, 531. "If we are to shape a world community we must first restore community at home."

55. *DOSB*, 1 October 1973, 428. See also *DOSB*, 29 October 1973, 525.

56. Henry Kissinger, *Years of Upheaval* (Boston: Little, Brown, 1982), 122–27. Even though Kissinger is speaking here of the effect of Watergate on foreign policy, he could easily be speaking of the United States in the post–Vietnam War phase. See *White House Years*, 54–72 and 195–311, for an assessment of the psychological needs of the United States as the Vietnam War wound down.

57. See, for example, Khong, *Analogies*, 45. See also Oswald Spengler, *The Decline of the West*, ed. Helmut Werner (1927–28; rpt., New York: Oxford University Press, 1991).

An interesting avenue for future research would be to compare Rusk's and Kissinger's views of time. Rusk's training in the China-Burma-India (CBI) theater of World War II gave him a view that efforts in a secondary, but necessary, theater could prove important in the long run to the central arena. From his experience in the CBI and the situation in Korea, when America appeared to be on the brink of losing the military conflict, Rusk could believe that time was on America's side and the situation would eventually improve. At its root Rusk's view of time reflected his optimism and belief in progress. In contrast, Kissinger appeared to act as if time were not on the side of the United States. Instead, his policies appear designed to buy time to prepare for a future with diminished capabilities.

58. See Khong, Yeun Foong, *Analogies at War: Korea, Munich, Dien Bien Phu, and the Vietnam Decisions of 1965* (Princeton: Princeton University Press, 1992), 45. See also *FRUS, January–February 1964–1968*, vol. 2: *Vietnam, January–June 1965*, 95–97.

59. Ernest Lee Tuveson, *Redeemer Nation: The Idea of America's Millenial Role* (Chicago: University of Chicago Press, 1968), 1.

60. See Cohen, *Dean Rusk*, 321–30.

61. See, for example, Graham Greene, *The Quiet American* (London: Bodley Head, 1973).

62. See Gardner, *Pay Any Price*, 155.

63. See, for example, *DOSB*, 17 February 1975, 197.

64. The theme of limits runs through Kissinger's speeches, although it occurs less in 1976, when his rhetoric turns more toward confidence building. See, for example, *DOSB*, 29 October 1973, 525; 11 November 1974, 643; 16 September 1974, 373; 4 August 1975, 167. On the issue of confidence as a theme in Kissinger's speeches and statements, see *DOSB*, 10 May 1976, 597–603; 1 March 1976, 253; 12 April 1976, 489. One can almost argue that focusing on confidence is an attempt to respond optimistically to the newly discovered

limits to American power: the United States would no longer try to undertake great things, but could still be confident of its remaining power.

65. See *DOSB*, 5 May 1976, 563.

66. Peter Dickson, *Kissinger and the Meaning of History* (London: Cambridge University Press, 1978), 8. Even though Kissinger challenged this view in the final pages of *Years of Renewal*, his focus there and as a policy maker was upon the distinction between what an individual might believe and pursue and what a statesman or policy maker, who is responsible for the survival of a state, might believe and pursue in the international arena.

67. See the conclusion of Strauss, *Thoughts on Machiavelli*.

68. Rusk had a limited view of progress and did not believe, for example, that it was necessarily the right or only path for all people of the world. Rather, he acknowledged that beneath modern humanity's relative success at achieving peace and prosperity is the possibility that humans could destroy those gains. See Schoenbaum, *Waging Peace*, 265.

69. See, for example, Rusk, *As I Saw It*, 532.

70. By identifying Kissinger as a conservative, I am making reference to his affinity for stability and the status quo over reform and revolution. The statement is not a comment on his standing in the American political landscape. For an interesting account of Kissinger's relationship to the neoconservatives in George W. Bush's administration, see James Mann, *Rise of the Vulcans: The History of Bush's War Cabinet* (London: Penguin Books, 2004).

71. Kissinger, "Central Issues in American Foreign Policy," cited in Brown, *Crises of Power*, 5.

72. Michael J. Smith, *Realist Thought from Weber to Kissinger* (Baton Rouge: Louisiana State University Press, 1986), 199.

73. See, for example, Rusk, *As I Saw It*, 532.

74. Rusk, *DOSB*, 9 March 1964, 361.

75. See Kissinger, *Years of Renewal*, 1061.

76. See, for example, *DOSB*, 17 February 1975, 197, in which Kissinger spoke about the United States never having experienced tragedy. Kissinger reiterated this theme but noted that, except for the Civil War, the United States had escaped tragedy. See *DOSB*, 12 April 1976, 482.

77. As Thucydides had pointed out, prestige or honor can be a motive for war, but in this case critics dismissed Rusk's claims concerning the threats to the United States' credibility or honor.

78. Kissinger disavows such a stark dichotomy in the last volume of his memoirs, *Years of Renewal*, when he says that justice and order have to work together. This reflects his views on equilibrium, but Kissinger would be the first to admit that the promises of justice and morality can never be fulfilled unless the boundaries of power are clearly set. Kissinger understood that legitimacy and power had to be balanced, but his writings emphasize the fundamental importance of power. He saw the relationship through the prism of power even as he sought to promote legitimacy. See Kissinger, *Years of Renewal*, 1078–79.

79. See Gowa, *Closing the Gold Window.*

80. See, for example, *DOSB*, 11 November 1974, 630.

81. Wolfgang Friedman, "United States Policy and the Crisis of International Law: Some Reflections on the State of International Law in 'International Co-Operation Year,'" *American Journal of International Law* 59, no. 4 (October 1965): 866.

82. *DOSB*, 12 April 1976, 483.

5. RUSK OR KISSINGER

1. I say unavoidable because the regime did not change into an empire. By remaining a republic, the underlying philosophy remained intact, even though it had been challenged.

2. Using an analytical framework of unilateralism versus multilateralism avoids addressing the underlying question of why the United States acts in a given way and focuses, instead, on how it acts. Moreover, one must define *multilateralism* (see article by John Van Oudenaren, "Unipolar versus Unilateral," *Policy Review*, no. 124 [2004], http://www .questia.com/PM.qst?a=o&d=5006642198 [accessed 28 August 2005]; and John Van Oudenaren, "What Is 'Multilateral'?" *Policy Review* [2003], http://www.questia.com/ PM.qst?a=o&d=5000604508 [accessed 28 August 2005].

3. For a good overview of the relationship between the United States and the United Nations, see Gary B. Ostrower, *The United Nations and the United States* (New York: Twayne, 1998).

4. I have purposefully not mentioned Johnson's domestic policy and its relationship to the problems of executive dominance. A fuller analysis of the interrelationship of Johnson's foreign and domestic policy and the role of his statesmanship is beyond the scope of this book.

5. Uday Mehta, *Liberalism and Empire: A Study in Nineteenth-Century British Liberal Thought* (Chicago: University of Chicago Press, 1999).

6. APPLYING THE MACHIAVELLIAN MOMENT TO THE PRESIDENCY OF GEORGE W. BUSH

I relied upon a number of works to help me understand the Bush Doctrine: Michael Cox, "Empire, Imperialism, and the Bush Doctrine," *Review of International Studies* (2004): 30, 585–608; Ivo H. Daalder, "The Use of Force in a Changing World—US and European Perspectives," *Leiden Journal of International Law* 16 (2003): 171–80; Christian Henderson, "The Bush Doctrine: From Theory to Practice," *Journal of Conflict and Security Law* 9, no. 1 (2004): 3–24; Jackson Nyamuya Maogoto, "New Frontiers, Old Problems: The War on Terror and the Notion of Anticipating the Enemy," *Netherlands International Law Review* 51 (2004): 1–39; Joshua Muravchik, "The Bush Manifesto," *Commentary* 114 (December 2002): 23–30; Stephen Skowronek, "Leadership by Definition: First Term Reflections on George W. Bush's Political Stance," *Perspectives on Politics* 3, no. 4 (December 2005): 817–31, http://www.apsanet.org/imgtest/PerspectivesDec05Skowronek.pdf.

1. Lloyd Gardner, *Pay Any Price: Lyndon Johnson and the Wars for Vietnam* (London: Ivan Dees, 1995), 253. I have modified the original passage to remove references to indi-

viduals within the Johnson administration. The passage, as modified or in the original, points out an enduring challenge for any president who seeks to develop and sustain a domestic consensus for policies in the external realm.

2. See James Mann, *Rise of the Vulcans: The History of Bush's War Cabinet* (London: Penguin Books, 2004), 311–58.

3. For a very interesting analysis of virtue and *virtu* within Machiavelli's writings, see Harvey C. Mansfield Jr., *Machiavelli's Virtue* (Chicago: University of Chicago Press, 1996), 6–52. One could argue that Johnson displayed Machiavellian virtue throughout his political career, but the extent of it was insufficient to meet the crisis it had created. Johnson lacked the *virtu* to overcome Fortuna.

4. See Douglass Adair, "Fame and the Founding Fathers," in *Fame and the Founding Fathers: Essays by Douglass Adair*, ed. Trevor Colbourn (Indianapolis: Liberty Fund, 1998).

5. Paul C. Light, "Fact Sheet on the President's Domestic Agenda," Brookings Institution, 12 October 2004, http://www.brook.edu/views/papers/light/20041012.htm (accessed 21 August 2005). See also Garance Franke-Ruta, "Hidden Agenda," *American Prospect* online, 2 September 2004, http://www.prospect.org/web/page.ww?section=root &name=ViewWeb&articleId=8449 (accessed 21 August 2005).

6. "Therefore, the United States has adopted a new policy, a forward strategy of freedom in the Middle East." "President Bush Discusses Freedom in Iraq and Middle East," 6 November 2003, http://www.whitehouse.gov/news/releases/2003/11/20031106-2.html (accessed 30 August 2005).

7. In the fall of 2002, twenty months after taking office Bush acknowledged that his administration was moving in this direction: "Today, the distinction between domestic and foreign affairs is diminishing." "The National Security Strategy of the United States of America," September 2002, http://www.whitehouse.gov/nsc/nss.html (accessed 21 March 2005). The problem emerges from the type of "war" that the Bush administration is waging. Without a declared war—but, rather, than an authorization to use force, which clouds the distinction between peacetime and wartime—legal due process is weakened. Kenneth Roth, "The Law of War in the War on Terror," *Foreign Affairs* (January–February 2004): 2–7.

8. Although the 1964 Gulf of Tonkin incident was used to justify Johnson's expanded war powers and the underlying principle used to justify an escalation of military force may be similar, the attacks of 11 September 2001 presented a different magnitude of threat. Even if the comparison could reasonably be made, it would reinforce my point concerning Johnson's use of statesmanship. His war effort, though carried out within the existing legal framework, was based on an ambiguous event because it appears the attacks did not occur in the way the White House claimed at the time. The Gulf of Tonkin incident displays more of his Machiavellian virtue, however, than his ability to present a clear vision for his statesmanship.

9. The Kosovo conflict and the apparent violation of sovereignty by the United States and its allies led Chinese president Jiang Zemin and Russian president Boris Yeltsin to issue a joint communiqué arguing against intervention and stressing the primacy of state

sovereignty. See, for example, Gwyn Prins, "The Politics of Intervention," Pugwash Occasional Papers, Pugwash Study Group on Intervention, Sovereignty, and International Security, Papers from the Venice Workshop, vol. 1, no. 1, February 2000, http://www .pugwash.org/reports/rc/prins.htm (accessed 23 August 2005).

10. "Address to a Joint Session of Congress and the American People," 20 September 2001, http://www.whitehouse.gov/news/releases/2001/09/20010920-8.html (accessed 21 March 2005).

11. The State of the Union Address 2002, 29 January 2002, http://www.whitehouse .gov/news/releases/2002/01/20020129-11.html (accessed 30 August 2005).

12. "National Security Strategy," September 2002.

13. Second Inaugural Address 2005, 20 January 2005, http://www.whitehouse.gov/ news/releases/2005/01/20050120-1.html (accessed 30 August 2005).

14. "President Bush Delivers Graduation Speech at West Point" 1 June 2002, http:// www.whitehouse.gov/news/releases/2002/06/20020601-3.html (accessed 21 March 2005).

15. "National Security Strategy," 17 September 2002, introductory letter.

16. "The survival of liberty in our land increasingly depends on the success of liberty in other lands. The best hope for peace in our world is the expansion of freedom in all the world." Second Inaugural Address 2005.

17. On the Athenian thesis, see Clifford Orwin, *The Humanity of Thucydides* (Princeton: Princeton University Press, 1994), Chap. 8 focuses on the domestic consequences of the Athenian thesis. Leo Strauss, *City and Man* (Chicago: University of Chicago Press, 1977); Emil A. Kleinhaus, "Piety, Universality, and History: Leo Strauss on Thucydides," *Humanitas* 14, no. 1 (2001): 68–95.

18. Discussions of *empire* as it is used in the current debates over American foreign policy tends to confuse and cloud the issue. The term is rarely defined with consistency or analytical rigor. *Empire* is usually employed as shorthand to advocate a political position rather than as an analytical device that sheds light on the alternatives expressed through Bush's foreign policy. The question that needs to be answered by those who use the term *empire* to describe the United States is: Has the nation stopped being a republic? If America has been an empire from its inception, its founding principles and institutions make it an empire unlike any other ever seen. The Anti-Federalists had raised similar issues at the founding, and although they offered important criticism, their arguments did not carry the day, then or now. On that issue, see Jonathan Marshall, "Empire or Liberty: The Anti-federalists and Foreign Policy, 1787–1788," *Journal of Libertarian Studies* 4, no. 3 (Summer 1980): 233–54, http://www.mises.org/journals/jls/4_3/4_3_1.pdf (accessed 23 August 2005). If the United States were to become a traditional empire, the Rubicon would be the moment the truths of the Declaration of Independence were defeated on the intellectual or military battlefield. For a fuller appreciation of these issues, see Harry V. Jaffa, *Crisis of the House Divided: An Interpretation of the Issues in the Lincoln-Douglas Debates* (Chicago: University of Chicago Press, 1982); and *A New Birth of Freedom: Abraham Lincoln and the Coming of the Civil War* (Lanham, Md.: Rowman & Littlefield, 2000).

19. "The United States and Great Britain have labored hard to help make the United Nations what it is supposed to be—an effective instrument of our collective security." "President Bush Discusses Iraq Policy at Whitehall Palace in London," 19 November 2003, http://www.whitehouse.gov/news/releases/2003/11/20031119-1.html (accessed 30 April 2005).

20. "President Bush Discusses Iraq Policy."

21. One might argue that Bush's reelection signaled the basis for a new consensus, which would, broadly speaking, support the international agenda spelled out in the president's 2005 Inaugural Address (see n. 16). Bush's language is similar to that used by Johnson to justify U.S. involvement in South Vietnam: "We are in South Vietnam not only for [t]he South Vietnamese but for ourselves, not only to preserve the freedom of the South Vietnamese but to preserve the freedom of others and ultimately of our own." Qtd. in Tucker, *Nation or Empire*, 14.

22. Recent ongoing debates over reforming the United Nations highlight efforts by the Bush administration and others to reassess the UN role in dealing with issues of national sovereignty See Jeffrey Boutwell, ed., Pugwash Occasional Papers, Pugwash Study Group on Intervention, Sovereignty, and International Security, Papers from the Como Workshop, vol. 2, no. 1, January 2001, http://www.pugwash.org/publication/op/opv2n1 .htm (accessed 23 August 2005); Alain Pellet, "State Sovereignty and the Protection of Fundamental Human Rights: An International Law Perspective," Pugwash Occasional Papers, Papers from the Venice Workshop, vol. 1, no. 1, February 2000, http://www.pug wash.org/reports/rc/pellet.htm (accessed 23 August 2005); Hugo Beach, "Secessions, Interventions and Just War Theory: The Case of Kosovo," Pugwash Occasional Papers, Papers from the Venice Workshop, vol. 1, no. 1, February 2000, http://www.pugwash. org/reports/rc/beach.htm (accessed 23 August 2005). For more on the emergence of the principle of "responsibility to protect" and the reforms in the United Nations, see "The Responsibility to Protect," Report of the International Commission on Intervention and State Sovereignty, December 2001, http://www.iciss.ca/pdf/Commission-Report .pdf (accessed 30 August 2005); Kofi Annan, "Secretary-General Reflects on 'Intervention,'" in Thirty-fifth Annual Ditchley Foundation Lecture, 26 June 1998, http://www .un.org/News/Press/docs/1998/19980626.sgsm6613.html (accessed 30 August 2005); Annan, "Two Concepts of Sovereignty," *Economist*, 18 September 1999, http://www.un.org/ News/ossg/sg/stories/kaecon.html (accessed 1 September 2005);
John T. Correll, "The Doctrine of Intervention," *Air Force Magazine Online: Journal of the Air Force Association* 83, no. 2 (February 2000), http://www.afa.org/magazine/feb2000/ 0200edit.asp (accessed 1 September 2005); "A More Secure World: Our Shared Responsibility," Report of the High-Level Panel on Threats, Challenges, and Change, United Nations, 2004, http://www.un.org/secureworld/report2.pdf (accessed 1 September 2005).

23. Colin S. Gray, *The Sheriff: America's Defense of the New World Order* (Lexington: University Press of Kentucky, 2004).

24. John Lewis Gaddis, *Surprise, Security, and the American Experience* (Cambridge, Mass.: Harvard University Press, 2004).

NOTES TO PAGES 164–166

25. "Our country has accepted obligations that are difficult to fulfill and would be dishonorable to abandon." Second Inaugural Address 2005. The phrasing and the underlying issue at stake remind one of Pericles' warning about empire as being dangerous to undertake and still more dangerous to give up. See Thucydides, *The History of the Peloponnesian War*, 2.63.2.

26. The State of the Union Address 2002.

27. Bush touched upon the need for the nation to renew itself in his Second Inaugural Address: "In America's ideal of freedom, the public interest depends on private character—on integrity, and tolerance toward others, and the rule of conscience in our own lives. Self-government relies, in the end, on the governing of the self."

BIBLIOGRAPHY

PRIMARY SOURCES

Manuscripts and Archives

University of Texas at Austin, Lyndon B. Johnson Library, Austin, Tex.
Dean Rusk Papers, University of Georgia, Richard Russell Library, Athens, Ga.

Unpublished Essays

Banning, Lance Gilbert. "The Quarrel with Federalism: A Study in the Origins and the Character or Republican Thought." Ph.D. diss., Washington University, 1971.

Gutierrez, G. G. "Dean Rusk and Southeast Asia: An Operational Code Analysis." Paper presented at the Annual Meeting of the American Political Science Association, New Orleans, 1973.

Nelson, Wayne. "Two Machiavellian Moments in Twentieth-Century American Political Culture." Ph.D. diss., University of Minnesota, 1986.

Oral Histories

University of Texas at Austin, Lyndon B. Johnson Library, Austin, Tex. Dean Rusk, 28 July 1969; 2 January and 8 March 1970.

Dean Rusk Papers, University of Georgia, Richard Russell Library, Athens, Ga. Dean Rusk tapes.

Government Publications

Bush, George W. "President Bush Discusses Freedom in Iraq and Middle East," 6 November 2003, http://www.whitehouse.gov/news/releases/2003/11/20031106-2 .html (accessed 30 August 2005).

———. "The National Security Strategy," September 2002, http://www.whitehouse .gov/nsc/nss.html (accessed 21 March 2005).

———. "Address to a Joint Session of Congress and the American People," 20 September 2001, http://www.whitehouse.gov/news/releases/2001/09/20010920-8.html (accessed 21 March 2005).

———. The State of the Union Address 2002, 29 January 2002, http://www.white house.gov/news/releases/2002/01/20020129-11.html (accessed 30 August 2005).

———. Second Inaugural Address 2005, 20 January 2005, http://www.whitehouse .gov/news/releases/2005/01/20050120-1.html (accessed 30 August 2005).

———. "President Bush Delivers Graduation Speech at West Point," 1 June 2002, http://www.whitehouse.gov/news/releases/2002/06/20020601-3.html (accessed 21 March 2005).

———. "President Bush Discusses Iraq Policy at Whitehall Palace in London," 19 November 2003, http://www.whitehouse.gov/news/releases/2003/11/20031119-1.html (accessed 30 April 2005).

International Commission on Intervention and State Sovereignty. "The Responsibility to Protect." Report of the International Commission on Intervention and State Sovereignty, December 2001, http://www.iciss.ca/pdf/Commission-Report.pdf (accessed 30 August 2005).

Nixon, Richard M. "U.S. Foreign Policy for the 1970's: A New Strategy for Peace." Report to the Congress. Vol. 1. Washington, D.C.: Government Printing Office, 1971.

———. "U.S. Foreign Policy for the 1970's: Building for Peace." Report to the Congress. Vol. 2. Washington, D.C.: Government Printing Office, 1972.

———. "U.S. Foreign Policy for the 1970's: The Emerging Structure of Peace." Report to the Congress. Vol. 3. Washington, D.C.: Government Printing Office, 1972.

———. "U.S. Foreign Policy for the 1970's: Shaping a Durable Peace." Report to the Congress. Vol. 1. Washington, D.C.: Government Printing Office, 1971.

Public Papers of the Presidents of the United States: Lyndon B. Johnson. 10 vols. Washington, D.C.: Government Printing Office, 1965–70.

United States Department of State. *Department of State Bulletin.* Washington, D.C.: Office of Public Communication, Bureau of Public Affairs, 1939–89.

———. *Foreign Relations of the United States, 1964–1968.* Vol. 2: *Vietnam: January–June 1965.* Washington, D.C.: Government Printing Office, 1996.

United Nations. "A More Secure World: Our Shared Responsibility." Report of the High-Level Panel on Threats, Challenges, and Change, United Nations 2004, http://www.un.org/secureworld/report2.pdf (accessed 1 September 2005).

SECONDARY SOURCES

Books

Adair, Douglass. "Fame and the Founding Fathers." In *Fame and the Founding Fathers: Essays by Douglass Adair,* ed. Trevor Colbourn. Indianapolis: Liberty Fund, 1998.

Ambrose, Stephen E. *Rise to Globalism: American Foreign Policy since 1938.* 4th rev. ed. New York: Penguin Books, 1985.

Arendt, Hannah. *Crises of the Republic.* New York: Harcourt Brace Jovanovich, 1972.

Arkes, Hadley. *Bureaucracy, the Marshall Plan, and the National Interest.* Princeton: Princeton University Press, 1972.

———. *First Things: An Inquiry into the First Principles of Morals and Justice.* Princeton: Princeton University Press, 1986.

———. *The Return of George Sutherland: Restoring a Jurisprudence of Natural Rights.* Princeton: Princeton University Press, 1994.

Aron, Raymond. *The Imperial Republic: The United States and the World, 1945–1973.* Trans. Frank Jellinek. Englewood Cliffs, N.J.: Prentice-Hall, 1974.

Bailyn, Bernard. *The Ideological Origins of the American Revolution.* Cambridge, Mass.: Belknap Press of Harvard University Press, 1967.

Barker, Charles A. "Another American Dilemma: Multilateral Authority versus Unilateral Power." In *Power and Law: American Dilemma in World Affairs: Papers of the Conference on Peace Research in History,* ed. Charles A. Barker. Baltimore: Johns Hopkins Press, 1971.

Barnett, David M. *Uncertain Warriors: Lyndon Johnson and His Vietnam Advisors.* Lawrence: University Press of Kansas, 1993.

Bell, Coral. *The Diplomacy of Détente: The Kissinger Era.* London: Martin Robertson, 1977.

Bercovitch, Sacvan. *The American Jeremiad.* Madison: University of Wisconsin Press, 1978.

Berman, Larry. *Planning a Tragedy: The Americanization of the War in Vietnam.* New York: Norton, 1982.

Boyle, Francis A. *Foundations of World Order: The Legalist Approach to International Relations (1898–1922).* Durham: Duke University Press, 1999.

Brandon, Henry. *The Retreat of American Power.* London: Bodley Head, 1973.

Brands, Henry W. *The Wages of Globalism: Lyndon Johnson and the Limits of American Power.* Oxford: Oxford University Press, 1995.

———. *What America Owes the World: The Struggle for the Soul of Foreign Policy.* Cambridge: Cambridge University Press, 1998.

Baybrooke, David, and Charles E. Lindblom. *A Strategy of Decision.* New York: Free Press, 1963.

Brown, Seyom. *The Crises of Power: An Interpretation of United States Foreign Policy during the Kissinger Years.* New York: Columbia University Press, 1979.

Bundy, William. *A Tangled Web: The Making of Foreign Policy in the Nixon Presidency.* New York: Hill and Wang, 1998.

Califano, Joseph A., Jr. *The Triumph and the Tragedy of Lyndon Johnson: The White House Years.* New York: Simon and Schuster, 1991.

Cohen, Benjamin J. *Organizing the World's Money: The Political Economy of International Monetary Relations.* London: Macmillan, 1977.

Cohen, Warren I. *Dean Rusk: The American Secretaries of State and Their Diplomacy.* Ed. Samuel Flag Bemis. Totowa, N.J.: Cooper Square, 1980.

Conkin, Paul K. *Big Daddy from the Pedernales: Lyndon Baines Johnson.* Boston Twayne, 1986.

Corwin, Edward S. *The President: Office and Powers, 1787–1984: History and Analysis of Practice and Opinion,* 5th rev. ed., ed. Randall W. Bland, Theodore T. Hindson, and Jack W. Peltson. New York: New York University Press, 1984.

Crabb, Cecil V., and Pat M. Holt. *Invitation to Struggle: Congress, the President, and Foreign Policy.* Washington D.C.: Congressional Quarterly Press, 1980.

Cropsey, Joseph. *Plato's World: Man's Place in the Cosmos.* Chicago: University of Chicago Press, 1995.

Dallek, Robert. *Flawed Giant: Lyndon Johnson and His Times, 1961–1973.* New York: Oxford University Press, 1998.

Debenedetti, Charles, and Charles Chatfield. *An American Ordeal: The Antiwar Movement of the Vietnam War.* Syracuse Studies on Peace and Conflict Resolution. Syracuse: Syracuse University Press, 1990.

Dickson, Peter. *Kissinger and the Meaning of History.* Cambridge: Cambridge University Press, 1978.

Doyle, Michael W. *Empires.* Ithaca: Cornell University Press, 1986.

Eckstein, Otto. *The Great Recession: With a Postscript on Stagflation.* Amsterdam: North-Holland, 1978.

Evans, Rowland, and Robert Novak. *Lyndon B. Johnson: The Exercise of Power: A Political Biography.* New York: New American Library, 1966.

Forde, Steven. *The Ambition to Rule: Alcibiades and the Politics of Imperialism in Thucydides.* Ithaca: Cornell University Press, 1989.

Gaddis, Johns Lewis. *Strategies of Containment: A Critical Appraisal of Postwar American National Security Policy.* New York: Oxford University Press, 1982.

———. *Surprise, Security, and the American Experience.* Cambridge, Mass.: Harvard University Press, 2004.

Gardner, Lloyd. *Pay Any Price: Lyndon Johnson and the Wars for Vietnam.* London: Ivan Dees, 1995.

Garthoff, Raymond. *Détente and Confrontation: American-Soviet Relations from Nixon to Reagan.* Washington, D.C.: Brookings Institution, 1994.

Geyelin, Philip L. *Lyndon B. Johnson and the World.* New York: Praeger, 1966.

Gibbons, William C. *The U.S. Government and the Vietnam War,* pt. 3: *January–July 1965.* Princeton: Princeton University Press, 1989.

Gowa, Joanne. *Closing the Gold Window: Domestic Politics and the End of Breton Woods.* Ithaca: Cornell University Press, 1983.

Gray, Colin S. *The Sheriff: America's Defense of the New World Order.* Lexington: University Press of Kentucky, 2004.

Greene, Graham. *The Quiet American.* London: Bodley Head, 1973.

Halberstam, David. *The Best and the Brightest.* New York: Random House, 1972.

Hamilton, Alexander, James Madison, and John Jay. *The Federalist; or, The New Constitution*. Ed. and intro. Max Beloff. Oxford: Blackwell, 1948.

Hartley, Anthony. *American Foreign Policy in the Nixon Era*. Adelphi Paper 110. London: International Institute for Strategic Studies, 1990.

Hatcher, Patrick L. *The Suicide of an Elite: American Internationalism and Vietnam*. Stanford: Stanford University Press, 1990.

Head, Richard G., Frisco W. Short, and Robert C. McFarlane. *Crisis Resolution: Presidential Decision Making in the Mayageuz and Korean Confrontations*. Boulder: Westview Press, 1978.

Henkin, Louis. *How Nations Behave: Law and Foreign Policy*. London: Pall Mall, 1968.

Herring, George C. *America's Longest War: The United States and Vietnam, 1950–1975*. New York: Wiley, 1979.

———. *LBJ and Vietnam: A Different Kind of War*. Austin: University of Texas Press, 1995.

Hersh, Seymour M. *The Price of Power: Kissinger in the Nixon White House*. New York: Summit Books, 1983.

Hobsbawm, E. J. *The Age of Empire, 1875–1914*. New York: Pantheon, 1987.

Hoffman, Elizabeth C. *All You Need Is Love: The Peace Corps and the Spirit of the 1960s*. Cambridge, Mass.: Harvard University Press, 1998.

Hoffmann, Stanley. *Gulliver's Troubles; or, The Setting of American Foreign Policy*. New York: McGraw-Hill, for the Council on Foreign Relations, 1968.

———. *Primacy or World Order: American Foreign since the Cold War*. New York: McGraw-Hill, 1978.

Holsti, Ole R., and James N. Rosenau. *American Leadership in World Affairs: Vietnam and the Breakdown of Consensus*. London: Allen and Unwin, 1984.

Hunt, Michael H. *Lyndon Johnson's War: America's Cold War Crusade in Vietnam, 1945–1965*. New York: Hill and Wang, 1996.

Iriye, Akira. *The Globalizing of America, 1913–1945*. Cambridge: Cambridge University Press, 1993.

Jaffa, Harry V. *Crisis of the House Divided: An Interpretation of the Issues in the Lincoln-Douglas Debates*. Seattle: University of Washington Press, 1973.

———. *A New Birth of Freedom: Abraham Lincoln and the Coming of the Civil War*. Lanham, Md.: Rowman and Littlefield, 2000.

Johnson, Lyndon B. *My Hope for America*. New York: Random House, 1964.

———. *The Vantage Point: Perspectives of the Presidency, 1963–1969*. New York: Holt, Rinehart and Winston, 1971.

Kahin, George McT. *Intervention: How America Became Involved in Vietnam*. New York: Knopf, 1986.

Kattenberg, Paul M. *The Vietnam Trauma in American Foreign Policy, 1945–1975*. New Brunswick: Transaction Books, 1980.

Kearns, Doris. *Lyndon Johnson and the American Dream*. New York: Harper and Row, 1976.

Kennan, George F. *American Diplomacy, 1900–1950.* London: Secker and Warburg, 1952.

Kettl, Donald F. "The Economic Education of Lyndon Johnson: Guns, Butter, and Taxes." In *The Johnson Years,* vol. 2: *Vietnam the Environment, and Science,* ed. Robert A. Divine. Lawrence: University Press of Kansas, 1987.

Kissinger, Henry A. "Central Issues in American Foreign Policy." In *Agenda for the Nation,* ed. Kermit Gordon. Washington, D.C.: Brookings Institution, 1968.

———. *White House Years.* Boston: Little, Brown, 1979.

———. *A World Restored: Metternich, Castlereagh and the Problems of Peace, 1812–22.* Boston: Houghton Mifflin, 1957.

———. *Years of Upheaval.* Boston: Little, Brown, 1982.

———. *Diplomacy.* New York: Simon and Schuster, 1994.

———. *Years of Renewal.* New York: Simon and Schuster, 1999.

Kunz, Diane, ed. *The Diplomacy of the Crucial Decade: American Foreign Relations during the 1960s.* New York: Columbia University Press, 1994.

Lafeber, Walter. "American Empire, American Raj." In *America Unbound: World War II and the Making of a Superpower,* ed. Warren F. Kimball. New York: St. Martin's, 1992.

Lasch, Christopher. *True and Only Heaven: Progress and Its Critics.* New York: Norton, 1991.

Lee, Steven H. *Outposts of Empire: Korea, Vietnam, and the Origins of the Cold War in Asia, 1949–1954.* Liverpool: Liverpool University Press, 1995.

Liska, George. *War and Order: Reflections on Vietnam and History.* Baltimore: Johns Hopkins Press, 1968.

Litwak, Robert S. *Détente and the Nixon Doctrine: American Foreign Policy and the Pursuit of Stability, 1969–1976.* London: Cambridge University Press, 1984.

Logevall, Fredrik. *Choosing War: The Lost Chance for Peace and the Escalation of War in Vietnam.* Berkeley: University of California Press, 1999.

Lundestad, Geir. *The American "Empire": And Other Studies in U.S. Foreign Policy in a Comparative Perspective.* Oxford: Oxford University Press, 1990.

Macdonald, Douglas J. "The Truman Administration and Global Responsibilities: The Birth of the Falling Domino." In *Dominoes and Bandwagons: Strategic Beliefs and Great Power Competition in the Eurasian Rimland,* ed. Robert Jervis and Jack Snyder. Oxford: Oxford University Press, 1991.

Machiavelli, Niccolò. *Discourses on Livy.* Trans. Harvey C. Mansfield and Nathan Tarcov. Chicago: University of Chicago Press, 1998.

———. *The Prince.* Trans. and ed. Angelo M. Codevilla. Rethinking the Western Tradition. New Haven: Yale University Press, 1997.

Mann, James *Rise of the Vulcans: The History of Bush's War Cabinet.* London: Penguin, 2004.

Mansfield, Harvey C., Jr. *Machiavelli's Virtue.* Chicago: University of Chicago Press, 1996.

———. *Taming the Prince: The Ambivalence of Modern Executive Power.* London: Free Press, 1989.

Matusow, Alan. *The Unraveling of America: A History of Liberalism in the 1960s.* New York: Harper and Row, 1984.

Mazlish, Bruce. *Kissinger: The European Mind in American Policy.* New York: Basic Books, 1976.

McNamara, Robert, with Brian VanDeMark. *In Retrospect: The Tragedy and Lessons of Vietnam.* New York: Vintage, 1996.

Mehta, Uday. *Liberalism and Empire: A Study in Nineteenth-Century British Liberal Thought.* Chicago: University of Chicago Press, 1999.

Melanson, Richard A. *American Foreign Policy since the Vietnam War: The Search for Consensus from Nixon to Clinton.* Armonk, N.Y.: M. E. Sharpe, 1996.

Morgenthau, Hans J. *Vietnam and the United States.* Washington, D.C.: Public Affairs Press, 1966.

Morris, Roger. *Uncertain Greatness: Henry Kissinger and American Foreign Policy.* New York: Harper and Row, 1977.

Mueller, John F. *War, Presidents, and Public Opinion.* New York: Wiley, 1973.

Muslin, Hyman L., and Thomas H. Jobe. *Lyndon Johnson: The Tragic Self: A Psychohistorical Portrait.* New York: Plenum Press, 1991.

Nisbet, Robert A. *History of the Idea of Progress.* London: Heinemann, 1980.

Nixon, Richard M. *RN: The Memoirs of Richard Nixon.* New York: Grosset and Dunlap, 1978.

Noble, David. *The End of American History: Democracy, Capitalism, and the Metaphor of Two Worlds in Anglo-American Historical Writings, 1880–1980.* Minneapolis: University of Minnesota Press, 1985.

Nutter, G. Warren. *Kissinger's Grand Design.* Washington, D.C.: American Enterprise Institute for Public Policy Research, 1975.

Orwin, Clifford, *The Humanity of Thucydides.* Princeton: Princeton University Press, 1994.

Osgood, Robert E., ed. *Retreat from Empire? The First Nixon Administration.* Baltimore: Johnson Hopkins University Press, 1973.

Ostrower, Gary B. *The United Nations and the United States.* Twayne's International History Series. London: Twayne, 1998.

Plato. *The Statesman.* Trans. J. B. Skemp. London: Routledge and Kegan Paul, 1952.

Pocock, J.G.A. *The Machiavellian Moment: Florentine Political Thought and the Atlantic Republican Tradition.* Princeton: Princeton University Press, 1975.

Ravenal, Earl C. *Large-Scale Foreign Policy Change: The Nixon Doctrine as History and Portent.* Berkeley: Institute of International Studies, University of California, 1989.

Riddell, Tom. "The Vietnam War and Inflation Revisited." In *Lyndon Baines Johnson and the Uses of Power,* ed. Bernard J. Firestone and Robert C. Vogt. Contributions in Political Science 221. New York: Greenwood Press, 1988.

Rodman, Peter. *More Precious than Peace: Fighting and Winning the Cold War in the Third World.* New York: Scribner's, 1994.

Rosencrance, Richard, ed. *America as an Ordinary Country: U.S. Foreign Policy and the Future.* Ithaca: Cornell University Press, 1976.

Rosen, Stanley. *Plato's Statesman: The Web of Politics.* New Haven: Yale University Press, 1995.

Rostow, W. W. *The Stages of Economic Growth: A Non-Communist Manifesto.* Cambridge: Cambridge University Press, 1960.

————. *The Diffusion of Power: An Essay in Recent History.* New York: Macmillan, 1972.

————. *View from the Seventh Floor.* New York: Harper and Row, 1964.

Rotter, Andrew. *The Path to Vietnam: Origins of the American Commitment to Southeast Asia.* Ithaca: Cornell University Press, 1987.

Rusk, Dean. As told to Richard Rusk. *As I Saw It.* New York: Norton, 1990.

————. *The Winds of Freedom.* Ed. Ernest K. Lindley. Boston: Beacon Press, 1963.

Safire, William, *Before the Fall: An Inside View of the Pre-Watergate White House.* New York: Doubleday, 1975.

Schlesinger, Arthur M., Jr. *The Bitter Heritage: Vietnam and American Democracy, 1941–1966.* Greenwich, Conn.: Fawcett, 1967.

————. *The Imperial Presidency: With a New Epilogue.* Boston: Houghton Mifflin, 1989.

Schoenbaum, Thomas J. *Waging Peace and War: Dean Rusk in the Truman, Kennedy, and Johnson Years.* New York: Simon and Shuster, 1988.

Schumpeter, Joseph A. *Imperialism and Social Class.* Trans. Heinz Norden, ed. Paul M. Sweezy. Oxford: Blackwell, 1951.

Schwab, Orrin. *Defending the Free World: John F. Kennedy, Lyndon Johnson, and the Vietnam War, 1961–1965.* Studies in Diplomacy and Political Thought. Westport, Conn.: Praeger, 1998.

Shapley, Deborah. *The Promise and the Power: The Life and Times of Robert McNamara.* Boston: Little, Brown, 1993.

Silverstein, Gordon. *Imbalance of Powers: Constitutional Interpretation and the Making of American Foreign Policy.* Oxford: Oxford University Press, 1976.

Sloan, Geoffrey R. *Geopolitics in United States Strategic Policy, 1890–1987.* London: Wheatsheaf Books, 1988.

Small, Melvin. *Johnson, Nixon, and the Doves.* New Brunswick: Rutgers University Press, 1988.

Smith, Michael J. "Liberalism and International Reform." In *Traditions of International Ethics,* ed. Terry Nardin and David R. Mapel. Cambridge: Cambridge University Press, 1992.

————. *Realist Thought from Weber to Kissinger.* Baton Rouge: Louisiana State University Press, 1996.

Smith, Tony. *America's Mission: The United States and the Worldwide Struggle for Democracy in the Twentieth Century.* Princeton: Princeton University Press, 1994.

Steel, Ronald. *Temptations of a Superpower*. Cambridge, Mass.: Harvard University Press, 1995.

———. *Walter Lippmann and the American Century*. Boston: Little, Brown, 1980.

———. Stephanson, Anders. *Manifest Destiny: American Expansionism and the Empire of Right*. New York: Hill and Wang, 1996.

Strauss, Leo. *City and Man*. Chicago: University of Chicago Press, 1977.

———. *Thoughts on Machiavelli*. Glencoe, Ill.: Free Press, 1959.

———. *What Is Political Philosophy? and Other Studies*. Glencoe, Ill. Free Press, 1959.

Strong, Robert J. [*sic*]. *Bureaucracy and Statesmanship: Henry Kissinger and the Making of American Foreign Policy*. The Credibility Institute, Policies and Leadership series vol. 9, series ed. Kenneth W. Thompson. Lanham, Md.: University Press of America, 1986.

Thompson, Kenneth W. *Traditions and Values in Politics and Diplomacy: Theory and Practice*. Baton Rouge: Louisiana State University Press, 1992.

Thornton, Richard C. *The Nixon-Kissinger Years: Reshaping of America's Foreign Policy*. New York: Paragon House, 1989.

Thucydides. *History of the Peloponnesian War*. Trans. Rex Warner; intro. M. I. Finley. Rev. ed. Harmondsworth, UK: Penguin, 1972.

Tomes, Robert R. *Apocalypse Then: American Intellectuals and the Vietnam War, 1964–1975*. New York: New York University Press, 1998.

Tucker, Robert W. *Nation or Empire? The Debate over American Foreign Policy*. Baltimore: Johns Hopkins Press, 1968.

Tuveson, Ernest Lee. *Redeemer Nations: The Idea of America's Millennial Role*. Chicago: University of Chicago Press, 1968.

Van Alstyne, Richard W. *The Rising American Empire*. New York: Norton, 1974.

VanDeMark, Brian. *Into the Quagmire: Lyndon Johnson and the Escalation of the Vietnam War*. New York: Oxford University Press, 1991.

Weinberg, Albert K. *Manifest Destiny: A Study of Nationalist Expansionism in American History*. Chicago: Quadrangle Books, 1963.

Wicker, Tom. *LBJ and JFK: The Influence of Personality upon Politics*. New York: Morrow, 1968.

Williams, William Appleman. *Empire as a Way of Life: An Essay on the Causes and Character of America's Present Predicament Along with a few Thoughts about an Alternative*. Oxford: Oxford University Press, 1982.

———. *The Roots of American Empire*. London: Blond. 1970.

———. *The Tragedy of American Diplomacy*. New York: Norton, 1988.

Wood, Gordon S. *The Creation of the American Republic, 1776–1789*. Chapel Hill: University of North Carolina Press, 1969.

Xenophon. *The Education of Cyrus*. Trans. H. G. Dakyns Everyman's Library, ed. Ernest Rhyrs. London: J. M. Dent and Sons, 1914.

Yeung Fong Khong. *Analogies at War: Korea, Munich, Dien Bien Phu, and the Vietnam Decisions of 1965*. Princeton: Princeton University Press, 1992.

Zuckert, Michael P. "Hobbes, Locke, and the Problems of the Rule of Law." In NO-
MOS 36: Yearbook of the American Society of Political and Legal Philosophy.
The Rule of Law, ed. Ian Shapiro. New York: New York University Press, 1994.

Articles

Annan, Kofi. "Secretary-General Reflects on 'Intervention' in Thirty-fifth Annual
Ditchley Foundation Lecture," 26 June1998, http://wwww.un.org/News/Press/
docs/1998/19980626.sgsm6613.html (accessed 30 August 2005).
———. "Two Concepts of Sovereignty." *Economist*, 18 September 1999, http://www
.un.org/News/ossg/sg/stor ies/kaecon.html (accessed 1 September 2005).
Appleby, Joyce. "Republicanism and Ideology." *American Quarterly* 37 (Fall 1985):
461–73.
Ball, Moya Ann. "The Phantom of the Oval Office: The John F. Kennedy Assassina-
tion's Symbolic Impact on Lyndon B. Johnson, His Key Advisers, and the Vietnam Decision-Making Process." *Presidential Studies Quarterly* 24 (Winter 1994):
105–19.
Barratt, David M. "Doing Tuesday Lunch at Lyndon Johnson's White House: New
Archival Evidence." *PS: Political Science and Politics* 24 (1991): 575–679.
Beach, Hugo. "Secessions, Interventions and Just War Theory: The Case of Kosovo."
Pugwash Occasional Papers, Pugwash Study Group on Intervention, Sovereignty,
and International Security. Papers from the Venice Workshop. Vol. 1, no. 1, February 2000, http://www.pugwash.org/reports/rc/beach.htm (accessed 23 August
2005).
Beisner, Robert L. "1898 and 1968: The Anti-Imperialists and the Doves." *Political Sci-
ence Quarterly* 85 (June 1970): 187–216.
Bell, Daniel. "The End of American Exceptionalism." *Public Interest* 41 (1975–76):
193–224.
Boutwell, Jeffrey, ed. Pugwash Occasional Papers, Pugwash Study Group on Intervention, Sovereignty, and International Security. Papers from the Como Workshop.
Vol. 2, no. 1, January 2001, http://www.pugwash.org/publication/op/opv2n1.htm
(accessed 23 August 2005).
Bostdorff, Denis M., and Steven R. Goldzwig. "Idealism and Pragmatism in American
Foreign Policy Rhetoric: The Case of John F. Kennedy and Vietnam." *Presidential
Studies Quarterly* 24 (Summer 1994): 515–601.
Brands, Henry W. "Johnson and Eisenhower: The President and the Former President
and the War in Vietnam." *Presidential Studies Quarterly* 15 (1985): 589–601.
Buel, Richard. "Democracy and the American Revolution: A Frame of Reference."
William and Mary Quarterly, 3rd ser., 21 (1964): 165–90.
Bundy, McGeorge. "The End of Either/Or." *Foreign Affairs* 45 (January 1967): 159–201.
Butt, Francis T. "The Myth of Perry Miller." *American Historical Review* 87 (June 1982):
665–94.

Chang, Gordon H. "China, JFK, and the Bomb." *Journal of American History* 74 (March 1988): 1287–1310.

Chen Jian. "China's Involvement in the Vietnam War, 1964–1969." *China Quarterly* 132 (June 1995): 356–87.

Claude, Inis L., Jr. "Comment on 'An Autopsy of Collective Security.'" *Political Science Quarterly* 90 (Winter 1975–Winter 1976): 715–17.

Collins, Robert M. "The Economic Crisis of 1968 and the Waning of the American Century." *American Historical Review* 101 (April 1996): 396–422.

Correll, John T. "The Doctrine of Intervention." *Air Force Magazine Online: Journal of the Air Force Association* 83, no. 2 (February 2000), http://www.afa.org/magazine/feb2000/0200edit.asp (accessed 1 September 2005).

Dobel, J. Patrick. "The Corruption of a State." *American Political Science Review* 72 (September 1978): 958–73.

Eckstein, Otto. "The Economics of the 1960s: A Backward Look." *Public Interest* 18 (1970): 86–97.

Fand, David. "Keynesian Monetary Theories, Stabilization Policy, and the Recent Inflation." *Journal of Money, Credit and Banking* (Conference of University Professors) 1 (August 1969): 556–87.

Forsythe, David P., and Ryan C. Hendrickson. "The Use of Force Abroad: What Law for the President?" *Presidential Studies Quarterly* 26 (Fall 1996): 950–61.

Franke-Ruta, Garance. "Hidden Agenda." *American Prospect Online*, 2 September 2004, http://www.prospect.org/web/printfriendly-view.ww?id=8449 (accessed 21 August 2005).

Friedman, Wolfgang. "United States Policy and the Crisis of International Law: Some Reflections on the State of International Law in 'International Co-operation Year.'" *American Journal of International Law* 59 (October 1965): 857–971.

Gaddis, John Lewis. "The Emerging Post-Revisionist Synthesis on the Origins of the Cold War." *Diplomatic History* 7, no. 3 (Summer 1983): 171–90.

Gati, Charles. "Another Grand Debate? The Limitationist Critique of American Foreign Policy." Review of *The Arrogance of Power*, J. William Fulbright; *The Limits of Power: America's Role in the World*, Eugene J. McCarthy; *The Bitter Heritage: Vietnam and American Democracy, 1941–1966*; Arthur M. Schlesinger; *Pax Americana*, Ronald Steel, in *World Politics* 21 (October 1968): 133–51.

Greenstein, Fred I., and Richard H. Immerman. "What Did Eisenhower Tell Kennedy about Indochina? The Politics of Misperception." *Journal of American History* 79 (September 1992): 568–87.

Hilsman, Roger. "Must We Invade the North?" *Foreign Affairs* 46 (April 1968): 425–41.

Hoffmann, Stanley. "International Organizations and the International System." *International Organization* 24 (Summer 1970): 389–413.

Humphrey, David C. "Tuesday Lunch at the Johnson White House." *Diplomatic History* (Winter 1984): 81–101.

Huntington, Samuel. "Coping with the Lippmann Gap." *Foreign Affairs* 66 (Winter 1987–88): 453–77.

Hutcheson, Ron, and James Kuhnhenn. "Bush Using a Little-Noticed Strategy to Alter the Balance of Power." *Knight Ridder Newspapers* (6 January 2006), http://www .realcities.com/mld/krwashington/13568438.htm.

Isaac, Jeffrey C. "Republicanism vs. Liberalism? A Reconsideration." *History of Political Thought* 9 (Summer 1988): 349–77.

Javits, Jacob K. "Congressional Presence in Foreign Relations." *Foreign Affairs* 48 (January 1970): 221–34.

Kateb, George. "Hobbes and the Irrationality of Politics." *Political Theory* 17 (August 1989): 355–91.

Kenyon, Cecilia. "Republicanism and Radicalism in the American Revolution: An Old-Fashioned Interpretation." *William and Mary Quarterly*, 3rd ser., 19 (April 1962): 153–82.

Kissinger, Henry A. "The White Revolutionary: Reflections on Bismarck." *Daedulus* 97 (Summer 1968): 888–937.

Kleinhaus, Emil A. "Piety, Universality, and History: Leo Strauss on Thucydides." *Humanitas* 14, no. 1 (2001): 68–95.

Lafeber, Walter. "Kissinger and Acheson: The Secretary of State and the Cold War." *Political Science Quarterly* 92 (Summer 1977): 189–97.

Lane, Fredric C. "At the Roots of Republicanism." *American Historical Review* 71 (January 1966): 403–20.

Light, Paul C. "Fact Sheet on the President's Domestic Agenda." Brookings Institution, 12 October 2004, http://www.brook.edu/views/papers/light/20041012.htm (accessed 21 August 2005).

Lin Piao. "Long Live the Victory of People's War." *Peking Review* 8 (September 1965): 9–30.

Lindblom, Charles. "The Science of Muddling Through." *Public Administration Review* 19 (1959): 79–88.

Marshall, Jonathan. "Empire or Liberty: The Antifederalists and Foreign Policy, 1787–1788." *Journal of Libertarian Studies* 4, no. 3 (Summer 1980): 233–54, http://www .mises.org/journals/jls/4_3/4_3_1.pdf (accessed 23 August 2005).

Montgomery, John D. "The Education of Henry Kissinger." *Journal of International Affairs* 29 (1975): 49–62.

Morgenbesser, Sidney. "Imperialism: Some Preliminary Distinctions." *Philosophy and Public Affairs* 3 (Fall 1973): 3–44.

Nadon, Christopher. "From Republic to Empire: Political Revolution and the Common Good in Xenophon's Education of Cyrus." *American Political Science Review* 90 (June 1996): 361–74.

Pellet, Alain. "State Sovereignty and the Protection of Fundamental Human Rights: An International Law Perspective." Pugwash Occasional Papers, Pugwash Study Group on Intervention, Sovereignty, and International Security. Papers from the

Venice Workshop. Vol. 1, no. 1, February 2000, http://www.pugwash.org/reports/ rc/pellet.htm (accessed 23 August 2005).

Perkins, Bradford. "The Tragedy of American Diplomacy: Twenty-Five Years After." *Reviews in American History* 12 (March 1984): 1–18.

Pocock, J.G.A. "Between Gog and Magog: The Republican Thesis and the Ideologia Americana." *Journal of the History of Ideas* 48 (April–June 1987): 49–72.

———. "The Machiavellian Moment Revisited: A Study in History and Ideology." *Journal of Modern History* 53 (March 1981): 49–72.

Prins, Gwyn. "The Politics of Intervention." Pugwash Occasional Papers, Pugwash Study Group on Intervention, Sovereignty, and International Security. Papers from the Venice Workshop. Vol. 1, no. 1, February 2000, http://www.pugwash .org/reports/rc/prins.htm (accessed 23 August 2005).

Ravenal, Earl C. "An Autopsy of Collective Security." *Political Science Quarterly* 90 (Winter 1975–Winter 1976): 697–714.

Richardson, J. S. "Imperium Romanum: Empire and the Language of Power." *Journal of Roman Studies* 81 (1991):1–9.

Rodgers, Daniel T. "Republicanism: The Career of a Concept." *Journal of American History* 79 (June 1992): 11–38.

Roth, Kenneth. "The Law of War in the War on Terror." *Foreign Affairs* (January– February 2004): 2–7.

Rusk, Dean. "The President." *Foreign Affairs* 38 (April 1960): 353–69.

Russell, Ruth B. "The Management of Power and Political Organisation: Some Observations on Inis L. Claude's Conceptual Approach." *International Organisation* 15 (Fall 1961): 630–36.

Schroeder, Paul. "Did the Vienna Settlement Rest on a Balance of Power?" *American Historical Review* 97 (June 1992): 695–97.

Shallope, Robert E. "Toward a Republican Synthesis: The Emergence of an Understanding of Republicanism in American Historiography." *William and Mary Quarterly*, 3rd ser., 29 (1972): 49–80.

Skowronek, Stephen. "Leadership by Definition: First Term Reflections on George W. Bush's Political Stance." *Perspectives on Politics* 3, no. 4 (December 2005): 817–31, http://www.apsanet.org/imgtest/PerspectivesDec05Skowronek.pdf.

Slater, Jerome. "Is United States Foreign Policy 'Imperialist' or 'Imperial'?" *Political Science Quarterly* 91 (Spring 1976): 63–87.

Stupak, Ronald J. "Dean Rusk on International Relations: An Analysis of His Philosophical Perceptions." *Australian Outlook: Journal of the Australian Institute for International Affairs* 25 (April 1971): 13–28.

Veysey, Laurence. "The Autonomy of American History Reconsidered." *American Quarterly* 31, no. 4 (Fall 1979): 455–77.

Viorst, Martin. "Incidentally, Who Is Dean Rusk?" *Esquire* (April 1968): 98.

Weatherford, M. Stephen. "The International Economy as a Constraint on U.S. Macroeconomic Policymaking." *International Organisation* 42 (Fall 1988): 611–25.

Williams, T. Harry. "Huey, Lyndon, and Southern Radicalism." *Journal of American History* 60 (September 1973): 267–93.

Xioming Zhang. "The Vietnam War, 1964–1969: A Chinese Perspective." *Journal of Military History* 60 (October 1996): 731–62.

INDEX

Acheson, Dean, 14, 173n35

Adair, Douglas, 67

Afghanistan war, 154

Algeria, 75

Alliance for Progress, 33

alliances: and economics, 106, 107; and freedom, 38; and Kissinger's foreign policy philosophy, 88, 107,·139-40; military alliances, 30, 32; and Nixon Strategy, 84, 85, 139, 140; and statesmanship, 171n10

American Civil War, 197n114, 203n76

American dream, 13, 15–16, 34–36, 152

American foreign policy: and American identity, 108, 117, 142, 148; and bipolar geopolitical framework, 11, 93, 107; and Bush, 151, 157, 162; and crisis of authority, 87, 147; and decent world order, 22, 38, 40, 68, 82, 87, 90, 91; and executive/legislative branch tensions, 3, 11–12, 47, 49, 68–70, 182n11; geopolitical shift in, 39, 40, 41; and idealism, 91; and international system, 2, 78, 84, 105, 108; Kissinger's reordering of, 18, 87–88, 112, 115, 122, 130; and Machiavellian Moment, 8, 10, 41; and multilateralism versus unilateralism, 143, 204n2; and Nixon, 83–86, 88–89, 101–4, 115, 117, 123, 147, 192n27; ongoing crisis in, 6; origins of, 4; political principles reflected in, 35; post–Vietnam era of, 90–91; in post–World War II era, 13, 24–26, 28, 33, 60, 83, 86, 113, 127, 128; and regime goals, 34; role of ideology in, 86, 93, 104; shift from Rusk to Kissinger, 142, 144, 147; and Truman Doctrine, 4; and undeclared war, 43; and Vietnam War, 17, 112, 113, 143. *See also* domestic/foreign policy interrelationship; foreign policy crisis of Vietnam War; Kissinger, Henry; Rusk, Dean

American founding: and consent of governed, 37, 128, 133, 134; and freedom, 36–37; and idealism, 37, 135; and republicanism, 117; and Rusk, 35, 118, 127–29, 134, 135; and U.S. as revolutionary country, 110

American identity: and American foreign policy, 108, 117, 142, 148; and American regime, 2–3; and America's exceptionalism, 91, 116; and limited government, 43, 45, 78; and republicanism, 117, 145; and Vietnam War, 118; within international system, 1, 10, 11, 18, 79, 110, 133, 152

American regime: and American foreign policy, 4, 25, 34, 78, 80-81, 117, 145, 163; and American identity, 2–3; Bush's changes to, 165, 167; and Civil Rights protests, 67; and domestic/foreign policy interrelationship, 46, 64, 67–68, 78, 81–82, 114; and fear of corruption, 66; and foreign policy crisis

223